LOCAL ECONOMIC POLICY

edited by

Mike Campbell

**PROFESSOR AND HEAD OF THE POLICY RESEARCH UNIT,
LEEDS POLYTECHNIC**

CASSELL

First published 1990 by
Cassell Educational Limited
Artillery House, Artillery Row, London SW1P 1RT, England

© Cassell Educational Limited 1990

ISBN 0-304-31731-4

Printed and bound in Great Britain by
Biddles Ltd., Guildford and King's Lynn

Contents

Contributors

Mike Campbell is Professor and Head of the Policy Research Unit at Leeds Polytechnic.

Allan Cochrane is Senior Lecturer in Urban Studies, Faculty of Social Sciences, at the Open University.

Phil Cooke is Reader in Planning, Department of Town Planning, at the University of Wales, Cardiff.

Andrew Coulson is Lecturer in Economics, Institute of Local Government Studies, at the University of Birmingham.

Richard Evans is Research Associate, Centre for Urban Studies, at the University of Liverpool.

Alan Harding is Research Associate, Centre for Urban Studies, at the University of Liverpool.

Graham Haughton is Senior Lecturer in Urban Development, Department of Urban Planning, at Leeds Polytechnic.

John Gunnell is the Chairman of Yorkshire Enterprise Limited.

Stephen Martin is Lecturer in Public Sector Management in the Public Sector Management Research Centre, Aston Business School, at Aston University.

David Miller is Director of Economic Development at Lancashire Enterprises Limited.

Michael Parkinson is Director, Centre for Urban Studies, at the University of Liverpool.

Peter Roberts is Professor and Head of Department, Department of Urban Planning, at Leeds Polytechnic.

Introduction

Mike Campbell

Local economic policy has become highly significant in recent years. As an area both of academic study and of policy practice it has grown enormously in importance (see, for example, Campbell, 1988). This is largely due to five factors. Firstly, while there have always been significant variations between localities in levels of economic activity, employment and social well-being, which tend to become even more pronounced in periods of rapid economic change and in recessions, the transformations in the British and international economies that have occurred in recent years have impacted in a highly differentiated fashion across the United Kingdom. Both in recession *and* recovery, patterns of economic activity, employment and social well-being have been produced which are characterized by sharp contrasts in different areas' economic fortunes. This provides an objective, or technical, case for policies designed at least to assist those areas experiencing economic decline and/or to affect the overall distribution of economic activity.

Secondly, many local authorities have responded to the problems posed by local economic change and unemployment by developing a range of policies to tackle these problems, and sometimes in the process to pursue their own political objectives. Thirdly, and again for both economic and political reasons, central government has increasingly pursued a wide range of policies targeted especially on what Mrs Thatcher has called 'those inner cities'. Fourthly, increasing numbers of people look to local economic policy initiatives, whether emanating from local government, central government or the private sector, for lessons that can be learnt for regenerating the *national* economy. Finally, the field of local economic policy is replete with controversy over the effectiveness of different policy initiatives and the appropriate agencies for initiating and implementing them. It might be added, too, that our understanding of the processes of local economic development and the amount of intellectual effort expended in the study of them, has grown enormously in recent years (see, for example, Massey and Allen, 1988).

This book aims to provide an examination of local economic policy which will be useful both to students of economics, policy studies, planning, geography and urban development, and to the increasing numbers of practitioners in the field who require a concise overview of current issues. It draws upon a distinguished range of contributors to provide a systematic and coherent study of contemporary local economic policy and provides through extensive references a guide to further reading for those who wish to pursue their study. The book is divided into four sections. Section 1 consists of two chapters which provide the empirical and theoretical context for the study of local economic policy, by examining the changes taking place in local economies; Section 2 consists of three chapters which examine central government policy; Section 3 provides four chapters on local government policy; and Section 4 examines the prospects for local economic policy. The remainder of this introduction identifies some of the key themes addressed in the volume and summarizes the central arguments.

Chapter 1, by Mike Campbell, charts and examines the major economic changes that have occurred in the 1980s, focusing particularly on employment. It shows the depth of the recession and the extent of the economic recovery post-1983, as well as the shifts that have taken place in the structure of output and employment from manufacturing to services. It also charts the deeply uneven pattern of employment change within sectors in both the recession and the subsequent recovery. Parallel to these changes in the structure of employment have been profound changes in the composition of employment, with a shift away from male, full-time and employee-based employment towards female, part-time and self-employment. These changes are likely to continue into the 1990s and are experienced unevenly in different parts of the United Kingdom as the outcome of deepening geographical divides.

Chapter 2, by Phil Cooke, argues that the conjunction of the concentration of capital, the changing spatial division of labour and the nature of state policies has ushered in the demise of the 'local' in local economies. However, the transformation of local economies associated with the transition from 'Fordism' to 'Post-Fordism' does offer increased scope for local authority involvement, especially in a small-firm-led development if it is linked to developments in the organisation of large firms and/or the state. The chapter examines three areas on the continent (the north-central districts of Italy, the Basque Country and southern France) which have all pursued local economic initiatives that are more successful than those currently pursued in the United Kingdom. The lessons drawn for the UK include a shift from a property/finance focus for central government towards manufacturing; the recognition of the deep change in production methods in manufacturing; the importance of developing local strategies to stimulate co-operation between small local firms and large ones; and the vital role of local authorities in supplying business and economic information and know-how. The chapter provides a salutory reminder that there are lessons to be learnt from the rest of Europe as well as from the USA.

Chapter 3, by Stephen Martin, provides an evaluation of central government's grant schemes designed to lever in private sector investment. The Urban Development Grant system, modelled on US experience, was introduced in 1982 and was designed as a partnership between central and local government and the private sector. The chapter evaluates its effectiveness with reference to the four objectives of take-up, additionality, leverage, and jobs based on a sample of UDG projects. It finds that on take-up the budget was underspent. On additionality, over 80 percent of schemes would not have proceeded without the UDG. With regard to leverage, estimates vary from 2.5 private sector £s to each public sector £, to 4.4 to 1. On employment, jobs created may be as few as 700. The chapter considers the reasons for these results and provides some pointers as to how the new City Grant, which replaced the UDG (and its sister private Urban Regeneration and Derelict Land grants) in 1988, is likely to fare.

In Chapter 4, Michael Parkinson and Richard Evans provide an assessment of Urban Development Corporations – the 'jewel in the crown' of central government's urban regeneration strategy. While recognizing that assessment is difficult (not least because most UDCs have been in operation for a very short period), the performance of UDCs is examined primarily through the work of the London Docklands Development Corporation (LDDC) and the Merseyside Development Corporation (MDC) and in terms of three criteria: efficiency, accountability and equity. It is important to note that the experiences of LDDC and MDC have been different in many ways. For example, while both have generated major physical transformations, the leverage ration is considerably higher in LDDC than in MDC. Although UDCs are not required to provide training or to target jobs on local people, both are making strides in this direction after serious deficiencies in the early stages. Accountability to local people is limited by the organizations' financing and reporting as well as by the composition and operation of their boards, though it appears that the actual relationships between Development Corporations, local authorities and communities does vary. The chapter concludes by arguing that while UDCs have an impressive record of physical regeneration their record on social regeneration, employment, accountability and the distribution of benefits is more uneven. In order to obtain a more 'balanced' regeneration, their goals need to be broadened and the policy instruments at their disposal widened.

Graham Haughton and Peter Roberts, in Chapter 5, examine national urban policy since 1979, focusing less on problems of policy co-ordination than on an assessment of perceived urban problems and potentials and the Government's political objectives. It is argued that it is important to examine the relationship between the causes of urban economic problems and the policies actually pursued because of the link between causal mechanisms and the mechanisms for releasing urban potential. The political agenda of policy is also subjected to examination: its private sector bias (both in strategy and implementation); its lack of concern over equity issues; its targeting; and its creation of conditions for enterprise activity. In its own terms, the chapter argues, policy has to an extent been successful, though there remain gaps and overlaps despite both innovatory and incremental policy changes since 1979. In terms of the future it is argued that policy needs to be reviewed in an integrated manner and that a local city-wide perspective must be taken where all key actors are written into the script. Otherwise development *in* rather than *of* cities will continue.

In Chapter 6, Alan Harding examines what is a major recurring theme of the book, the development of partnerships between public and private sectors which have become a key element of central government policy since 1979. The increasing involvement of the private sector relates to funding, the policy process (problem definition and solution) and the programmes themselves, and represents a major shift in the policy environment. The chapter argues that it is now the case that, while private sector participation is seen as vital to urban regeneration, local authority involvement (in contrast to the 1970s) is seen by central government as, at best, optional. As a result, local authorities themselves are changing the nature of their relations with the private sector. The main forms of partnership are outlined and their characteristics (membership, resources, scale, location, mode of operation and impact) examined. The chapter concludes by comparing the policy environments in the USA and the UK relevant to a consideration of their relative likelihood of success and makes a strong plea for greater empirical research before we can be sure of their contribution to local economic policy and the factors that maximize their likely success.

John Gunnell, in Chapter 7, provides an analysis of the experience of Enterprise Boards, as well as seven 'profiles' of investments they have undertaken. The chapter begins by showing how their creation was in many ways an unintended consequence of the early years of the first Thatcher Government and that as institutions they have key advantages over the traditional city council department as an agent of economic change. There are different models of intervention behind each of the Enterprise Boards – including the relative weight of commercial and social(-ist?) objectives – and the scope of their operations also varies. However, their similarity is that their focus is on the provision of corporate investment, even if their approach to it varies between Boards. The case study of West Yorkshire Enterprise Board (now Yorkshire Enterprise) provides an insight into their investment behaviour and the extent of their operations. The Boards between them have now invested well over £50 million in more than 250 companies which employ more than 20,000 people. They are also involved in property, training, co-operatives and technology development. The chapter concludes by suggesting that the high hopes for a wider socializing role for the Boards that was suggested by some in the early 1980s were in practice unrealistic, but that the Boards do have an important role to play in the provision of venture capital providing central government legislation and increasing competition from the private sector do not crowd them out.

In Chapter 8, Allan Cochrane provides an analysis of the ways in which local authority economic policies have developed in recent years. By the mid-1980s local authorities were spending at least £400 million a year on economic development, while the form of their policies had evolved from one of land/premises provision and promotion/attraction in the 1970s, through more 'radical' policy initiatives in the early 1980s, to what seems now to be a generally 'modified market' model of intervention. There are two major changes that have occurred in recent years. The first is towards partnership approaches, though the form of these, and the key role of the local authority within them, is at variance to a degree with central government notions of the nature of partnership between private and public sectors. The second is the wider range of policy initiatives pursued and hence the shift from what was really an *industrial* policy towards a wider *economic* policy, and even an economic strategy in some cases. Overall there has been a growth of *political* confidence (and consensus?) at local level in the roles that local authorities can play in local economic development, in part reflected in the growth of agencies bringing local actors together (like the Centre for Local Economic Strategies and the Local Economy Policy Unit) and increasing research into local economic development issues. A wider definition of local economic policy is also helping to integrate policy and to see the role of the local authority as a whole in the local economy. In particular, it is hoped that local authorities will increasingly attempt to influence the whole range of local economic change, including the operation of the local labour market. The recent interest in the development of 'local-authority-related employment programmes', linking economic, social and employment policies, is particularly relevant (Campbell *et al.*, 1988; Campbell and Sutherland, 1989), and illustrates the 'dynamism' and innovation of local authorities' role in the development of local economic policy.

Andrew Coulson, in Chapter 9, provides an evaluation of local economic policy. The chapter begins by arguing that *ex post* policy evaluation is neglected and that what little there is tends to be simplistic. The reasons for this are identified and there then follows a discussion of six key issues in local economic policy evaluation: the degree of displacement; deadweight effects; indirect effects; leverage; job substitution; and identifying the counterfactual position. It is also noted that an understanding of the specifically *local* characteristics of local labour markets is necessary if projects are to be effectively assessed, particularly for their applicability in other localities. The chapter then goes on to review three types of evaluation: local authority support to small businesses; central government assistance; and action research. It concludes by attempting to explain why there are so few evaluations of local authority initiatives. Nearly two-thirds of local authorities have no arrangements (even in-house ones) for assessing the performance of their economic development programmes. It is suggested that there are gaps to be filled (for example, in terms of examining the effectiveness of policy to attract inward investment); that some comparative policy evaluation across different localities would be useful (and inexpensive); and that more policy reviews and qualitative evaluations are required in order to go beyond simple cost per job assessments (see also Coulson, 1988).

David Miller, in the final chapter, assesses the prospects for local economic policies. While the 1989 legislation finally provides a statutory basis for local authority economic development activities, it does so in a policy context where local initiatives are seen as significant by central government but the role of local authorities within them is seen as relatively minor compared to those of the private sector and central government. Historically, local authorities have played an important role in local economic development, though its extent and form have varied geographically, politically and across economic cycles. Nevertheless the 1980s witnessed major economic and policy changes, most notably in the latter context a move from attempting to influence the *distribution* of industry and employment to the *generation* of industry and employment. These policy changes focused on the development of indigenous industrial investment strategies; improved training provision, particularly for disadvantaged groups; and attempts to meet some of the needs of the unemployed. However, because of the uneven economic recovery of the mid/late 1980s and changes in central government policy, local authorities need to change policy direction again, recognising the limits and opportunities provided both by legislation and by wider engagement with the private sector. In terms of central government local economic policy, the proliferation of policies and agencies has led to potential problems of co-ordination, overlap, duplication and direction at the same time as there has been a withdrawal by central government from a strategic view of local and regional economic development. The increasing reliance on enterprise-related policies is questioned, as is what is seen as a shift from partnership towards the 'privatisation' of local economic policy, currently exemplified by the development of private-sector-led Training and Enterprise Councils.

Whether such policies would survive a deterioration in economic conditions, or a change of government, however, is another matter. Under these conditions both the agencies and policies felt most relevant to effective local economic policies may well change once again. The search for successful and agreed local economic policies continues in a period when they are more necessary than ever before.

REFERENCES

Campbell, M. (ed.) (1988) *Local Economy, Special Issue: Urban Problems and Policies in Mrs Thatcher's Third Term*, Vol. 3, No. 2.

Campbell, M., Healey, N., Stead, R. and Sutherland, J. with Leach, R. and Percy-Smith, J. (1988) *Meeting Real Needs – Creating Real Jobs*, Manchester, Centre for Local Economic Strategies.

Campbell, M. and Sutherland, J. (1989) 'Long-term unemployment and local government: towards a local authority related employment programme (LAREP)', Paper to Campaign for Work Local Labour Market Conference, Policy Studies Institute, London.

Coulson, A. (ed.) (1988) *Local Economy, Special Issue: Evaluation and Monitoring*, Vol. 2, No. 4.

Massey, D. and Allen, M. (1988) *Uneven Re-Development: Cities and Regions in Transition*, London, Hodder and Stoughton.

·PART 1·

Local and National Economies in Transition

Employment and the Economy in the 1980s and Beyond

Manufacturing Miracles: The Changing Nature of the Local Economy

CHAPTER 1

Employment and the Economy in the 1980s and Beyond

Mike Campbell

INTRODUCTION

This chapter provides the broad economic and employment context for the chapters which follow. It charts the major changes in the economy and patterns of employment in the 1980s so that the study of local economic policy can be informed by an understanding of the behaviour of the aggregates that it seeks to influence, the economy and employment, at a local level. This is particularly important for, as we shall see, economic and employment patterns have been, and still are being, fundamentally transformed. Moreover one key aspect of this transformation is its *uneven* nature, bearing witness to the importance of pursuing *local* economic and employment policies, whether through central government, local government or other agencies, which therefore recognize these variations in existing spatial patterns; the way in which they are being transformed; and their importance for the effective pursuit of economic and employment objectives at local, regional *and* national levels.

This unevenness results from the major restructuring of the economy, and hence of employment, that has taken place in recent years and it is with these major structural changes that we begin our discussion. The first section charts the phases of recession and recovery in the *economy* and in particular examines the behaviour of the manufacturing and service sectors outlining the sectoral shifts that have occurred. The second section examines the same phenomena but in relation to *employment* – we shall see that the pattern of employment change differs somewhat from that of output change.

The third section demonstrates the major transformations that are occurring in the *composition* of employment, largely reflective of the economic and employment changes previously outlined. Whilst previous sections document the changes that have occurred in recent years, the fourth briefly considers the *future* pattern of the economy and employment into the 1990s The fifth section considers the spatial patterns that have developed, and that are developing, as a result of the foregoing changes. Finally we conclude by briefly outlining why the transformations of the 1980s make local economic policy an even more important area of study and policy development for the 1990s.

FROM RECESSION TO RECOVERY

The total output of the UK economy fell between 1979 and 1981 and indeed it was 1983 before total output, as measured by gross domestic product (GDP), regained its 1979 level. However, as Figure 1.1 shows, since 1982, when it regained its 1980 level, GDP has grown by 20 per cent and indeed the annual *rate* of growth has been increasing in more recent years. This is the much heralded 'supply side

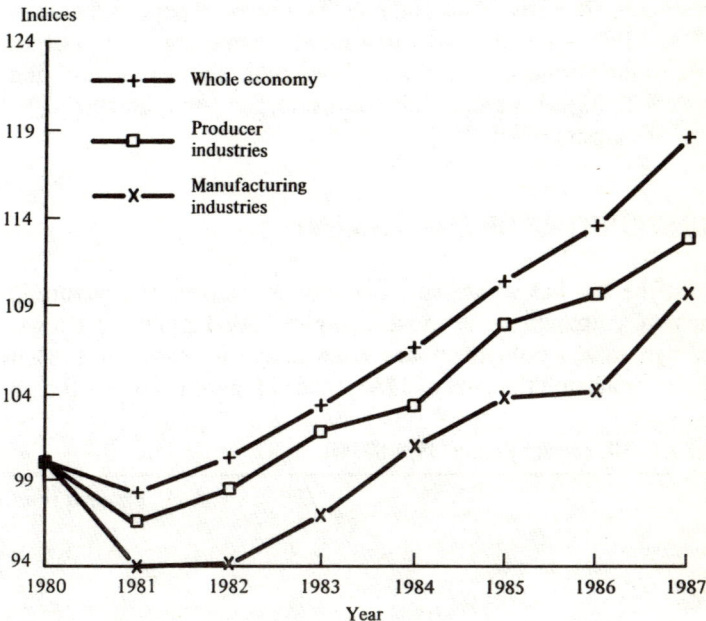

Figure 1.1 UK output indices, 1980–87 (Source: Campbell *et al.*, 1988)

[11]

boom' of the British economy and clearly demonstrates the sustained and considerable recovery in output following the deep recession in the early 1980s.

However, just as importantly there has been a considerable shift in the *pattern* of this output from manufacturing to services over the period. One might suspect this from inspecting Figure 1.1, which clearly shows the output of the whole economy growing much faster than the output of the manufacturing sector. Table 1.1 demonstrates the extent of the shift. Whilst it is the case that manufacturing's share of output has been declining since 1969 (when it was 31 per cent) if measured in constant prices and since 1951 (when it was 39 per cent) if measured in current prices, it has never declined so quickly as in the 1979–87 period. This declining share of output is sometimes referred to as 'deindustrialization' or the relative decline of manufacturing. In 1987 the service sector accounted for virtually 2½ times the contribution to national output of manufacturing. Though it is true that manufacturing output has grown since 1982/3 (at constant prices) it has done so much more slowly than service output. Such was the decline in manufacturing output from 1979 to 1982 that it regained its 1979 level only in 1987 (itself below the peak output of 1973), while service sector output held up better in the recession of the early 1980s and grew by nearly 30 per cent between 1982 and 1988 – this compares to a growth in manufacturing output in the same period of less than 25 per cent. So in recession and recovery the service sector has 'outperformed' manufacturing in terms of output growth.

THE STRUCTURE OF EMPLOYMENT

Whilst the UK has witnessed an *economic* recovery the picture in terms of employment is more complex. As Figure 1.2 shows, although total employment has risen above its nadir of 1983 it remains at around the level of 1980. Indeed Figure 1.3 shows that in

Table 1.1 UK output by sector, 1979–87 (%)

	1979	1987	Change in share
Manufacturing	27	24	– 3
Services	56	59	+ 3

Source: *Economic Trends* (CSO) various issues.

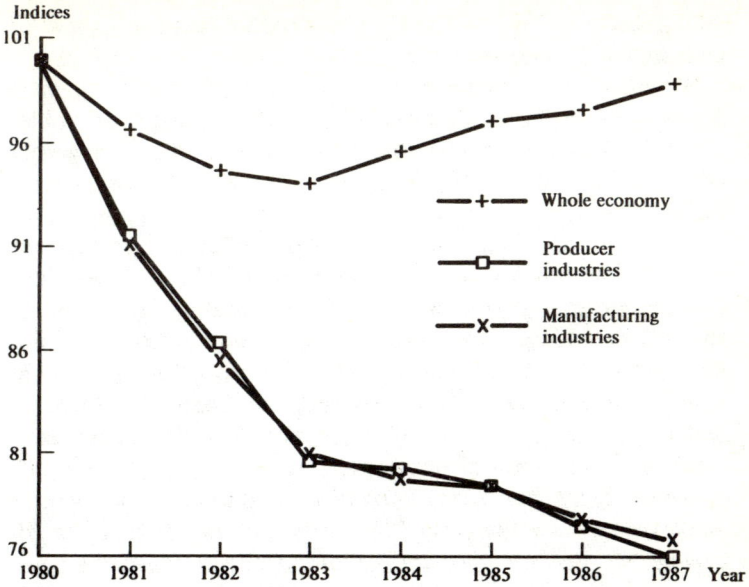

Figure 1.2   UK employment indices, 1980–87 (Source: Campbell *et al.*, 1988)

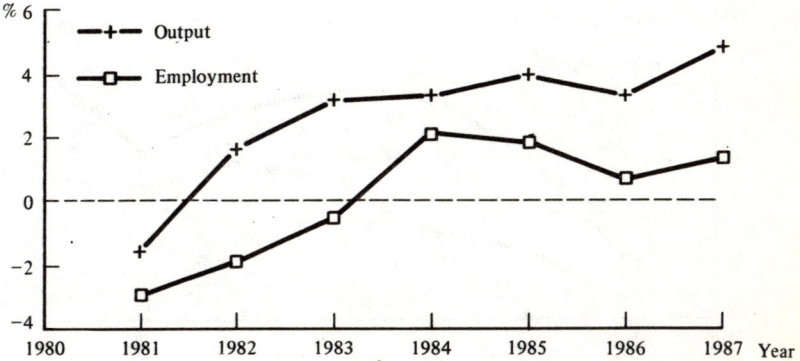

Figure 1.3   UK output and employment change: whole economy, year on year, 1980–87
(%) (Source: Campbell *et al.*, 1988)

every year the rate of change of output growth in the economy as a
whole exceeds that of employment growth. In no year does employment growth exceed 2 per cent per annum whilst in each of the last
five years output growth has exceeded 3 per cent. None the less
employment has grown in the *latter* part of the period. Whilst
employment fell by 2 million between 1979 and 1983, it grew by 1.5

[13]

million between 1983 and 1987. The composition of this growth is discussed in the next section.

When one examines the relation between output and employment at the *sectoral* level, the possibility of the existence of 'jobless growth' – that is, economic expansion without employment generation – is observed. As can be seen from Figure 1.4, whilst manufacturing output has *risen* in every year since 1982 manufacturing employment has *fallen* in every year. Indeed, manufacturing employment in 1987 was 24 per cent below its 1980 level (see Figure 1.2) despite the growth of manufacturing output. As Table 1.2 shows, manufacturing's share of total employment has now declined to only 22 per cent whilst nearly 7 out of every 10 people work in the service sector. As can be seen from comparing Tables 1.1 and 1.2, the extent of the shift from manufacturing to services is twice as great in terms of employment as it is in relation to output.

Whilst there has been a *relative* decline in manufacturing employment since the early 1960s it is only rather later that the decline has become *absolute*. Total manufacturing employment increased from 6.6 million in 1946 to a peak of 8.8 million in 1966, since when it has fallen to 5.4 million in 1987. The decline has been

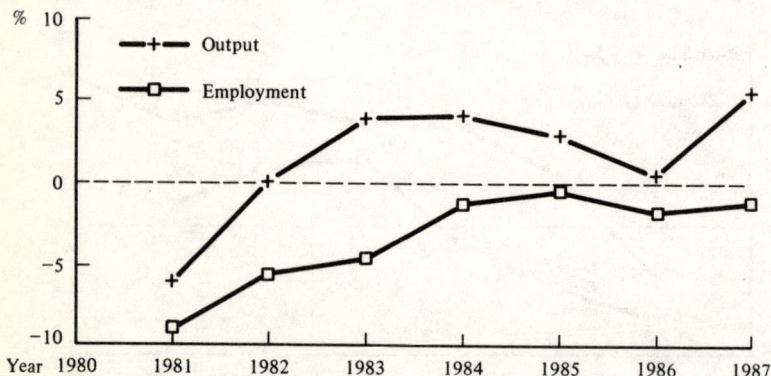

Figure 1.4 UK output and employment change: manufacturing industries, year on year, 1980–87 (%) (Source: Campbell *et al.*, 1988)

Table 1.2 UK employment by sector, 1979–87 (%)

	1979	1987	Change in share
Manufacturing	30	22	– 8
Services	59	67	+ 8

Source: *Economic Trends* (CSO) various issues.

[14]

particularly steep since 1980 with 1.7 million jobs disappearing – a fall of nearly 25 per cent in just seven years. Service sector employment by contrast has grown steadily from less than 10 million in 1946 to 16 million in 1987, with particularly rapid growth since 1983. Over the period 1980–87 service employment grew by over 10 per cent.

Of course *within* the manufacturing and services sectors there are differences in the rate of decline or growth of particular industries and Table 1.3 indicates those which have declined or grown most over recent years.

Table 1.3 UK national employment by sector (% change)

	1981–84	1984–86
Manufacturing		
Sectors of rapid decline		
Metals	− 28	− 10
Clothing/footwear	− 23	+ 2
Motor vehicles/parts	− 21	− 8
Mechanical engineering	− 17	− 5
Food, drink and tobacco	− 12	− 5
Electrical and electronic engineering	− 10	− 9
Sectors of slow decline/positive growth		
Office machinery	+ 10	+ 7
Rubber/plastics	0	+ 7
Timber and furniture	− 5	+ 5
Paper, printing and publishing	− 5	− 1
Services		
Sectors of rapid growth		
Business services	+ 22	+ 13
Real estate	+ 16	+ 9
Repairs	+ 12	+ 3
Banking and finance	+ 9	+ 3
Hotels and catering	+ 7	+ 5
Personal services	+ 6	+ 2
Recreation and culture	+ 3	+ 13
Sectors of slow growth/decline		
Railways	− 12	− 6
Wholesale distributors	+ 2	− 2
Retailing	− 1	+ 2
Posts/telecoms	− 1	+ 1
Other		
Coal	− 18	− 23
Electricity/gas	− 10	− 5
Average of all	− 2	+ 2

[15]

It can be clearly seen from this section that in both recession and recovery the pattern of employment change is deeply uneven across sectors and industries.

THE COMPOSITION OF EMPLOYMENT

In parallel to the deep shifts in the above *structure* of employment there have been profound changes in the *composition* of employment. The workforce is being *recomposed* partly as a result of the *restructuring* of industry outlined in the previous section. Table 1.4 and Figure 1.5 below summarize the key changes.

The first major change is the shift from employment by others to self-employment. As can be seen from Table 1.4, total employment fell by nearly 3 per cent or over 700,000 between 1980 and 1987 whilst the numbers of employees in employment (those working for others) fell by nearly 1.5 million or 6.5 per cent. The difference is largely accounted for by the dramatic increase in self-employment of over 800,000 or 43 per cent. It is worth noting in passing that the decline in employees is a manufacturing sector phenomenon – here it fell by 25 per cent or 1.7 million whereas in the service sector the number of employees increased by around 1 million. The second major change is the growth of part-time employment, by 15 per cent overall and by over 20 per cent in the service sector. Over 90 per cent of those

Table 1.4 The changing composition of UK employment, 1981–87

	1980 (000s)	1987 (000s)	Change in employment	
			(000s)	(%)
Total employment	25,143	24,435	− 708,000	− 2.8
Employees in employment	22,788	21,316	− 1,472,000	− 6.5
Self-employment	1,963	2,801	+ 838,000	+ 42.7
Part-time employees	4,499[1]	5,163	+ 664,000	+ 14.8
of which service sector	3,890[1]	4,678	+ 778,000	+ 20.3
Female employment	9,084[1]	9,697	+ 613,000	+ 6.7
of which service sector	7,043[1]	7,919	+ 876,000	+ 12.4

Note: [1]1981.
Source: *Employment Gazette* (various issues).

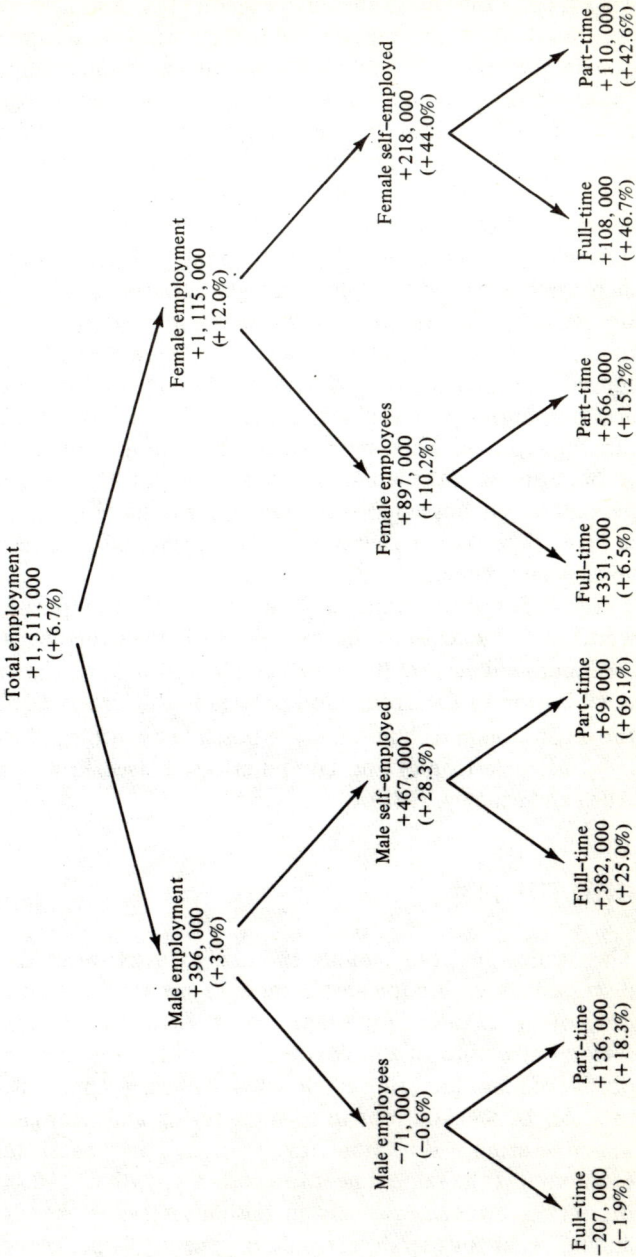

Figure 1.5 Components of UK national employment growth, 1983–87

working part time are in the service sector. The third major change is the growth of female employment by 8 per cent overall and by 12 per cent in the service sector. A decline of nearly 300,000 in female employment in manufacturing was compensated for by the growth of nearly 900,000 jobs for women in the service sector. Women now account for 46 per cent of all employees in employment.

When we examine the components of the employment growth generated in the recovery post-1983 (see Figure 1.5) we can see that the main growth has been in part-time jobs (58 per cent of the total increase in jobs), self-employment (45 per cent) and jobs filled by women (74 per cent). As a result nearly 1 in 5 workers are now part time, 1 in 8 are self-employed and more than 4 in 10 are women. Indeed, the number of male full-time employees in employment actually continues to decline in the recovery – a loss of over 200,000 jobs in a period when more than 1.5 million were created. This recomposition of the workforce means that less than two-thirds (64 per cent) of all those in jobs are now full-time employees, 22 per cent are part time, 12 per cent are self-employed and 2 per cent are on government schemes.

It is important to note, however, that this recomposition of the workforce is not entirely due to the shifts in the structure of employment outlined earlier. It is also a result of profound changes in the organization of the production process itself, largely as a result of the revolution in techniques made possible by information technology, microelectronics and computerization (see Rowthorn, 1988; Allen and Massey, 1988).

INTO THE 1990s

This section briefly examines the likely trajectory of the changes discussed above into the next decade. Figure 1.6 represents the forecasts of the Institute for Employment Research in relation to the sectoral structure of employment by 1995. The IER forecasts a decline of manufacturing employment by nearly 9 per cent, resulting in a loss of 460,000 jobs in manufacturing and a situation where manufacturing will account for less than 1 in 5 of all jobs in the economy. At the same time it forecasts a growth of 500,000 jobs in the service sector, especially in business services, hotels/catering and miscellaneous services, resulting in nearly 71 per cent of all jobs in the economy being in the service sector.

With regard to the composition of employment, the IER expects that existing trends will continue so that, while numbers employed will rise by 1.4 million by 1995, this will mostly be accounted for by: a growth of female employees of nearly 1 million; a growth of self-employment of over ½ million; and, most dramatic of all, a growth in part-time employment of over 1.25 million. In terms of occupational structure (see Table 1.5) it is expected that the rapid growth of employment amongst managers and especially professionals *will* continue, with reasonable growth in clerical/secretarial employment and slower rates of growth amongst sales/personal service occupations. The slowest growth is amongst craft/skilled

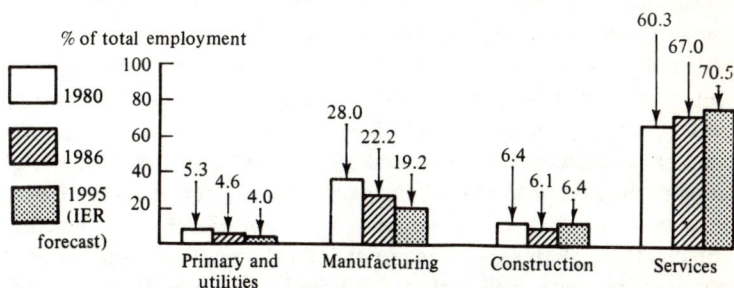

Figure 1.6 The sectoral structure of UK employment, 1980, 1986, 1995 (%)

Table 1.5 UK occupational structure, 1971–95

	Change in employment (000s)				Change in employment (%)
	1971	*1986*	*1995*	*1986–95*	*1986–95*
Managers	2,746	3,339	3,747	+ 408	12.2
Professionals	3,423	4,919	5,786	+ 867	17.6
Clerical/ secretarial	3,550	3,728	3,958	+ 350	9.4
Sales/ personal	3,707	4,333	4,627	+ 294	6.8
Craft/skilled	3,792	3,196	3,357	+ 161	5.0
Operatives/ labourers	6,924	4,758	4,204	− 555	− 11.7

Source: Institute for Employment Research (1988).

manual workers, with a continued very rapid decline in semi-skilled occupations.

THE SPATIAL PATTERN OF EMPLOYMENT CHANGE

It is to be expected that the considerable changes in the structure of the economy, as well as in the structure and composition of employment, will be experienced *unevenly* in different parts of the UK. This is so for several reasons. Firstly, both the structure of industry and the composition of employment vary between different geographical areas, and consequently changes in structure and composition will produce a changed 'geography' of the economy and employment. Secondly, the relative attractiveness of different locations for employers in general changes over time together with their relative attractiveness for particular sectors, whether due to shifts in the structure of transport costs, economies of geographical concentration, labour costs, material costs or whatever. So as the restructuring of economic activity proceeds it also restructures the spatial organization of the economy and employment. Thirdly, of course, in addition to the changes wrought by market forces, government policy shifts the spatial pattern of activities, whether directly through its explicit regional and urban policies (and through changes in such policies) or indirectly through its transport, industry, housing and other explicitly 'non-spatial' policies, which clearly have a spatial impact whether intended or unintended. Finally, as we noted earlier, the changes in the organization of production in manufacturing and service sectors that accompany economic change also alter the spatial pattern of both the organization of production and the structure and composition of employment. This is because geographical areas exhibit different characteristics of relatively greater or less attractiveness for different *forms* of production *irrespective* of the sector of industry concerned. Thus spatial change arises out of the changing form as well as the changing structure of production. The rest of this section outlines the major changes in the spatial pattern of employment that have occurred in the 1980s.

At the level of the so-called 'North–South divide', the changes in employment patterns are considerable. Whilst total employment in Great Britain fell by 745,000 between 1979 and 1986, it grew by 345,000 in the 'South' and declined by 1,100,000 in the 'North' (Martin and Townroe, 1988). Nor is this a feature solely of the effects of the recessionary phase: during the recovery between 1983 and 1987 the 'South' increased employment by 8.7 per cent, while services employment (Massey and Allen, 1988). This last category is particularly important as it constitutes the most dynamic sector of the 'North' gained only 1.9 per cent, thus dramatically widening the divide (MacInnes and Townroe, 1988).

At a regional level there is also a wide variation in employment experience as Table 1.6 indicates. In the recession, employment fell by more than the national average in the North, the North-West, Wales, the West Midlands, Yorkshire and Humberside, Scotland and Northern Ireland, while it declined by less than the average in the South-East and East Anglia. In the South-West it did not fall at all. In the recovery, employment still fell against the trend in the North-West, Wales and Scotland, while significantly above average growth was recorded in East Anglia, the East Midlands and the West Midlands.

With regard to sectoral shifts in employment it can be seen from Figure 1.7 that the geographies of both manufacturing growth and decline *and* service sector growth and decline are almost mirror images of each other. This illustrates well the enormous mismatch in the resulting geography of labour supply and demand that has occurred. By 1987 41 per cent of employment in the 'growing' manufacturing sectors was in the South-East, as was 55 per cent of research and development employment and 49 per cent of producer

Table 1.6 UK employment change by region, 1979–87 (%)

	1979–83	1983–87		1979–83	1983–87
North	− 17	+ 4	West Midlands	− 15	+ 7
Yorkshire and Humberside	− 13	+ 2	North-West	− 16	− 10
			Wales	− 16	− 4
East Midlands	− 9	+ 9	Scotland	− 11	− 2
East Anglia	− 2	+ 17	Northern Ireland	− 11	+ 5
South-East	− 5	+ 5	UK	− 9	+ 4
South-West	0	+ 5			

Source: *Regional Trends*, various issues; *Employment Gazette*, various issues.

the economy (banking, finance, insurance and business services) and now accounts for a larger number of jobs in the economy than does manufacturing industry. The occupational structure also has a marked regional skewness: the proportion of employment accounted for by unskilled and semi-skilled manual workers varies

[21]

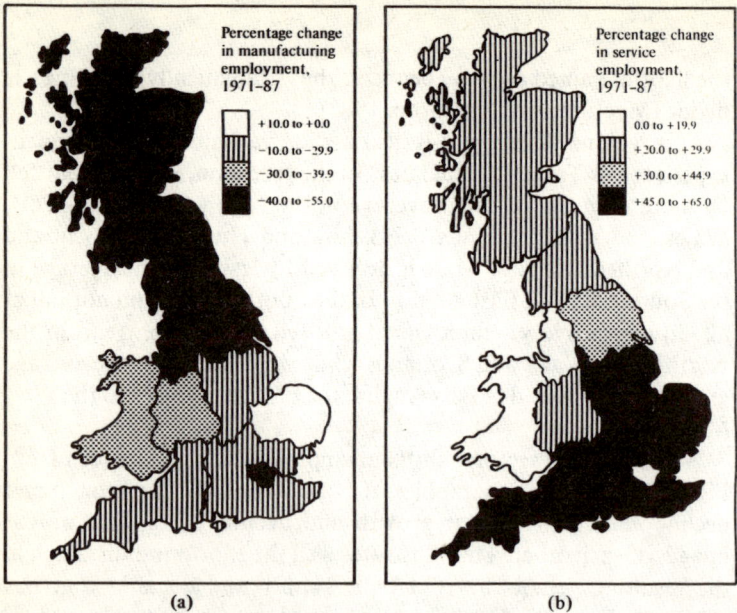

Figure 1.7 The geography of UK manufacturing and services (Source: Massey and Allen, 1988)

from 16 per cent above the national average in the North to 20 per cent below average in the South-East, whilst the proportion of employment accounted for by managerial and professional workers varies from 10 per cent below the national average in Scotland, the North and Yorkshire and Humberside to 25 per cent above the average in the South-East (Martin and Townroe, 1988).

Because of the limited and late availability of employment data at local level (the 1984 census of employment data has only recently become available and little work has yet been done on it at a nationally comparable level), we know less empirically about how these patterns are working out locally, as for example between urban and rural areas. However, it would appear that manufacturing employment is decentralizing from large urban centres and that service employment, except for relatively 'low-level' forms of activity, is concentrating in urban centres. For example, evidence for the 1960s and 1970s clearly shows a marked shift of manufacturing to 'rural areas' from urban centres (Fothergill *et al.*, 1986), while on a number of indicators, including total employment change and employment change in producer services, the 'gap' between medium-sized towns and rural areas, particularly in the 'South', and the large cities and industrial towns of the 'North', is widening beyond its already considerable level (Champion and Green, 1988).

Projections of regional changes in employment in the 1990s appear to demonstrate that major changes in the pattern of employment will continue. Table 1.7 shows the projected regional distribution of the expected 1.5 million jobs to be created by the end of the 1990s. As can be seen, they are likely to be deeply unevenly distributed with, for example, East Anglia, the South-West and the East Midlands securing increases in employment of nearly one-quarter (more than three times the national average growth) whilst employment actually falls in Northern Ireland, the North and the North-West.

Table 1.7   Projected regional changes in employment, 1986–2000

	Change in total employment (as % of 1986 level)		Change in total employment (as % of 1986 level)
East Anglia	+ 24.2	Scotland	+ 2.6
South-West	+ 24.2	Wales	+ 0.7
East Midlands	+ 23.5	Northern Ireland	− 5.4
South-East	+ 8.1	North	− 5.8
Yorkshire and Humberside	+ 7.2	North-West	− 7.2
West Midlands	+ 3.6	United Kingdom average	+ 7.2

Source: Cambridge Econometrics (1987), Table 3.

CONCLUSIONS

This chapter has charted the profound and deeply significant changes that are occurring both in the economy and in the consequent patterns in the structure, composition and location of employment. However it is not just the case that such an understanding of the national and spatial context within which local economic and employment policy operates is necessary to provide a framework within which it can be studied. It is also hoped that the chapter has demonstrated that local economic and employment policy needs to be sensitive to the dramatic changes in the structure and composition of the economy and of employment that have occurred in recent years. Moreover it should also have shown, at an empirical level, the necessity for specifically local economic policies in order to reduce the evident spatial divisions; the feasibility of securing more effective national employment policies and of making both supply-side economic policies and macroeconomic management more successful.

ACKNOWLEDGEMENTS

Thanks to the Centre for Local Economic Strategies for commissioning the report in the course of which much of the information presented here was gathered, and to my colleagues, John Sutherland, Nige Healey, Richard Stead, Bob Leach and Janie Percy-Smith, who co-operated in the writing of it. Thanks also to Chris Tebbutt of Leeds City Council.

REFERENCES

Allen, J. and Massey, D. (eds) (1988) *The Economy in Question*, London, Sage.

Cambridge Econometrics (1987) *Regional Economic Prospects, 1986–2000*, Cambridge.

Campbell, M., Healey, N., Stead, R. and Sutherland, J. with Leach, R. and Percy-Smith, J. (1988) *Meeting Real Needs – Creating Real Jobs*, Manchester, Centre for Local Economic Strategies.

Champion, A. and Green, A. (1988) *Economic Prosperity and the North–South Divide*, Warwick, Institute for Employment Research.

Fothergill, S. and Monk, S. (1986) in Martin, R. and Rowthorn, R. (eds) *The Geography of Deindustrialisation*, London, Macmillan.

Institute for Employment Research (1988) *Review of the Economy and Employment 1987/88*, Warwick.

MacInnes, J. and Townroe, P. (1988) 'Regional employment change in Britain, 1975–1987', Centre for Urban and Regional Research, Discussion Paper No. 34, University of Glasgow.

Martin, R. and Townroe, P. (1988) 'Regional development in the UK in the 1990s', Regional Studies Association Theme Paper, London.

Massey, D. and Allen, J. (eds) (1988) *Uneven Re-Development: Cities and Regions in Transition*, London, Hodder and Stoughton.

Rowthorn, R. (1988) 'Life after Henry (Ford)', *Marxism Today*, October.

CHAPTER 2

Manufacturing Miracles: The Changing Nature of the Local Economy

Phil Cooke

INTRODUCTION

It has always been difficult to justify the concept of 'the local economy'. The defining characteristic of advanced economies, especially those which are very open to world trade in both imports and exports, could be said to be their very lack of local economies. Indeed the experience of advanced capitalism has been precisely the breaking down of formerly strong local and regional economic identities. Three main elements have accounted for this process. The first of these is the continuing drive towards the concentration of capital and the centralization of its control. The process of capital concentration has resulted in both a significant amount of economic activity being accounted for by large corporations and a growing proportion of trade being under the control of foreign-based companies. Thus even in 1976, Murray (1985) has estimated, multinationals were responsible for 70 per cent of British exports. Furthermore, Dunning (1981) has shown showed that in the 30 years up to 1976 ownership of capital by foreign firms in Britain grew from £3 billion to £19 billion.

The second factor bringing about the demise of local and regional economic control has been the development of what Massey (1984) has called a 'spatial division of labour'. As capital concentrated in functional terms, ownership also became centralized in spatial terms. Ownership has increasingly been centralized in London. It has been shown that in the highly localized, high-job-density areas of central London, where there are few factories, employment in manufacturing industry grew by over 10,000 in the relatively short period between 1978 and 1981. This shift can only be explained in terms of the growth in employment of employers, managers and support staff in manufacturing firms headquartered in London (Simmie, 1985). To this must be added the growth and increasing internationalization of London as a base for commercial capital. For example, in 1970 only some 12,000 people were employed in London's foreign banks whereas by 1986, after 'Big Bang', the deregulation of City institutions, the equivalent employment figure was 54,000. The number of foreign banks in the City rose from 163 to 400 during the period (Thrift, 1987). Commercial office floor-space in central London increased by 1.6 million square metres between 1974 and 1982, and will probably have tripled that growth rate by 1992.

The third factor accounting for these changes is the state. The state regulates capital growth and influences the nature and form of markets. When Britain traded mostly with its empire, competition with other advanced economies was minimized by tariff barriers. The decision to enter the EEC in 1973 changed that relationship significantly. British trade switched rapidly towards Europe. Government policy in the 1960s and 1970s encouraged capital concentration through, for example, Labour's Industrial Reorganization Corporation. Even though the Monopolies Commission nominally 'regulates' the process of capital concentration, it has become clear in the 1980s that little has been done to limit the continuing ownership internationalization of hitherto locally controlled companies such as Rowntree Mackintosh. Moreover, the abolition of exchange controls in the early 1980s has meant that an increasing amount of Britain's financial wealth actually gets invested in the national and local economies of other countries.

All of these factors have contributed significantly to the changing fate of local economies. They are unquestionably becoming more and more internationalized as locally owned companies merge with foreign ones, and as inward investors decide to locate in places which are attractive from wage-cost or state-subsidy viewpoints. This, of course, presents local policy makers with a dilemma. Can they afford not to become equally international in their outlook and should they aim to compete with each other in the process of seeking to convince inward investors that they have the best location? Everyone knows that they are involved in a zero-sum game: that is, another area's gain will be their loss, and vice versa.

Recognizing this, many localities, while perhaps continuing to

[26]

play that game, have realized that it is not the only game in town. Two strategies have been developed in order to supplement, even to transcend, the painful competition for scarce international capital. Under a general heading of 'place-marketing', part of which is devoted to attracting inward investors of the kind noted above, many local authorities have been seeking to sell an image of place which will, for example, attract tourists either for pleasure or for business. So, for many, the production of a range of marketing booklets, videos and the like is a first step towards establishing a place-marketing office, staffed by people who will inform the tourist or the conference organizer of the facilities available. Hence, conference centres, international quality hotels, even a 'world trade centre', are becoming local economic necessities. Either way, leisure facilities to entertain such visitors also have to be provided. So local museums, often of industrial history or archaeology, or theme parks which allow the tourist also to become a time traveller, are proliferating at the rate, according to Hewison (1987), of one a week in the Britain of the late 1980s.

The other strategy has, of course, been to try to encourage specifically local employment initiatives. Most localities now boast a local authority economic development department, enterprise agency, or business information unit. Local authorities have always played some role in local economic development through the provision of infrastructure and the building of small industrial estates. But with the onset in the 1980s of large-scale deindustrialization and the consequence of high local unemployment, many have sought to intervene more actively in aspects of business organization and finance. Stimulated partly by the examples of the new municipal socialism in the Greater London Council and elsewhere, this kind of activity has become widespread, though, in general, local initiatives are far more entrepreneurial than socialist in their objectives. There are problems with such a strategy, most palpably regarding the very limited resources, especially finance, that can be mobilized towards local economic development ends. Moreover, central government policies, under right-wing political hegemony, actively seek to undermine such initiatives, professing an attachment to the virtues of the market-place as a resolver of local economic problems as well as displaying what often seems to be a phobia towards collective, municipal activity in all its forms.

This chapter seeks to provide an overview of the economic conditions responsible for the tensions outlined above between structural forces of internationalization and strong central state control, and of local efforts to help revive local economies weakened by such forces. In doing so it will discuss some tendencies in corporate organization which point to the necessity for local economic development initiatives to become stronger rather than weaker. A section on local economic development in Italy, Spain and France suggests some of the more effective ways in which public–private links are being forged. Finally, these points will be related back to the prospects for revived local economic development in the present British context of apparently weakening local policy capacity.

THE LOCAL CONSEQUENCES OF 'FORDISM' AND ITS AFTERMATH

By the beginning of the post-war period the regional and local distinctiveness which had been so much a characteristic of the UK economy had begun to break down. The effects of, amongst other things, the inter-war return to the gold standard which made the export cost of traditional products prohibitively expensive, the closures and rationalizations which followed the loss of markets, and the ensuing Depression years had contributed to the erosion of local textile, shipbuilding, coal and steel economies. There had been the growth of important new spatial clusterings but these were to be found in the South and Midlands of England where consumer goods such as motor vehicles and domestic appliances were manufactured. Some of these newer industries were either modelled on or directly imported from overseas, notably the USA where advances in production technology pioneered by the Ford Motor Corporation had resulted in vast increases in economies of scale through mass production.

Such was the impact of the more modern production methods, incorporating scientific management, detailed task specification for and supervision of workers, and flowline assembly that producers in countries other than the USA began to adopt the rhetoric and sometimes the practices of Fordism (as it has subsequently been called – see Lipietz, 1985). In their full-blooded form, Fordist production methods involved considerable changes in the organization of manufacturing processes. In particular, companies became vertically integrated such that the production of, for example, a car would be carried out from the raw material stage to the final product within the same production complex. The best example of this was Ford's River Rouge plant near Detroit, where coal and iron ore entered the factory at one end and Model Ts emerged at the other, all painted black! Standardization was necessary because of the rigidity of the machine tooling and transfer machinery then in operation.

The American scale could not easily be emulated in the smaller, European economies, although the Fiat complex in Turin was an exception. Rather, European firms sometimes adopted parts of the new production technology and organizational methods, especially where they had entered mass markets, but retained older structurers where these were more appropriate. Thus, in the British car industry, production developed either in established industrial localities such as Coventry and Birmingham or in completely new ones such as Dagenham, where some of the country's first mass public housing was also built to house the workers at the new Ford plant there. In the more established localities old forms of production organization involving wide-ranging subcontracting relationships between assembly companies such as Austin and component suppliers such as Lucas helped recreate the sense of the local economy as a more modern version of the 'industrial district' which Marshall (1919) had earlier identified in cities such as Sheffield or Bradford.

It was during the post-war era, especially in the 1950s and 1960s that Fordism developed to its fullest extent in Britain. In the process local economic distinctiveness, though never totally obliterated, became increasingly diluted. By that time many of the requirements of a fully Fordist political economy had been put in place. For Fordism was not just a production methodology but a form of social and political organization too. Mass production needs mass consumption if it is to survive and expand. In the early days this expansion was stimulated by paying high wages, especially in the USA, so that workers could become, through saving or borrowing, the consumers of their own products. In Britain, of course, many consumer products such as washing machines or cars were luxury products until the late 1950s and early 1960s when Macmillan could claim that the British people had 'never had it so good'. Consumption norms were established by a Keynesian 'mode of regulation' of the economy which enabled a Fordist 'regime of accumulation' to be sustained. Advertising, hire-purchase, collective bargaining and demand management combined to reinforce economic growth.

Local economies suffering from the latter stages of failure to compete, failure to invest and failure to innovate sufficiently in traditional markets were now to be the recipients of the branch plants of Fordist industry as the Keynesian mode of spatial regulation through regional policy aided their partial reconversion. In the process, localities became not the centres but the peripheral recipients of economic decisions made increasingly in London or abroad. Other government policies such as that which encouraged concentration of capital ownership often resulted in the rationalization or closure of long-established factories. Meanwhile service industries, especially in the public sector where there was employment growth, were expanding nearly everywhere as the welfare state, another key element in the Fordist regime of accumulation, became more fully established. As a consequence, local economies began to look more like each other, except that London increasingly dominated the new 'spatial division of labour' (Massey, 1984).

POST-FORDISM

But Fordism contained its own internal contradictions. When, as happened in the 1970s, markets became saturated it began to enter crisis. Simultaneously, new competitors from Japan and South-East Asia began to eat into the markets for replacement goods. The rigidities of Fordist technology and business management became a severe drain on its effectiveness, as a result of which there has been a great deal of experimentation with new, more flexible methods of production and management (Cooke, 1988)

Successful Japanese methods have been perceived as a model that must be emulated and improved upon in what is now seen as the post-Fordist period. Amongst these methods are some which have possibly profound implications for the revival of local economies as modern versions of Marshall's 'industrial districts'. At the extreme, one Japanese car producer, Toyota, exists in a locality (Toyota City) surrounded by hundreds of local components suppliers. The main factory is thus essentially an assembly plant, fabricating components bought in, often in small batches and at short notice, 'just-in-time' to arrive at the appropriate point on the assembly line. 'Just-in-time' methods are capital saving in that stocks do not have to be held. Moreover, quality can be assured by joint design between client and supplier and by the strict adherence to standards which is a condition of the contract. Though not a universal spatially clustered model of local development, even in Japan, the Toyota City idea has been adopted in some American localities (for example, Buick City in Michigan and the Saturn project in Tennessee), and in Britain Nissan has established four local suppliers on-site in the North-East of England (Morris, 1988).

Thus, post-Fordism implies vertical disintegration of production to small firms, flexible purchasing arrangements with local suppliers, and the possibility of local economies becoming more integrated around a main production centre, rather as was the typical pre-Fordist industrial district of Britain and other European countries. As the mode of regulation by the state changes from Keynesian intervention to monetarism, more has to be achieved by the operation of market forces regarding the question of local economic development. But the market is never in fact a pure operator; even supposedly deregulated markets are simply regulated in different ways. However, one element which, in the present context, seems likely to be an important aid to the local spatial development process is the ability of local authorities to meet the new requirements of restructuring or inward-investing companies by providing facilities or encouraging the conditions for the development of new or rejuvenated local linkages. In theory, this chimes perfectly with the ideology of small-firm development as part of a revived 'enterprise culture'.

POST-FORDISM AND LOCAL ECONOMIC DEVELOPMENT: SOME EXAMPLES

The Japanese model of local economic development is by no means the only one that can be characterized as post-Fordist: there are others, most of which are much closer to home. This section discusses three examples of local economic development, each of which represents a major small-firm-led growth process but each of which is linked either to developments occurring within the practices of large firms, or to the state.

Industrial Districts in Italy

The first example is the by now rather well-known one of what has come to be called the 'Third Italy' model. There are, in reality, two models or perhaps more in operation in north-central Italy where, as Sabel (1988, p. 8) notes, there now exists:

> a string of industrial districts stretching from the Venetian provinces in the North through Bologna and Florence to Ancona in the South, producing everything from knitted

goods (Carpi), to special machines (Parma, Bologna), to ceramic tiles (Sassuolo), to textiles (Como, Prato), to agricultural implements (Reggio Emilia), to hydraulic devices (Modena), to shoes, white goods, plastic tableware, and electronic musical instruments (Ancona).

To illustrate by polarization, two models can be described. The first, which is found in the 'white' or Catholic and Christian Democrat regions such as Veneto or Marche, is highly entrepreneurial in the sense that business initiative receives very little interference from the local or regional state. Rather, a virtually non-existent development control process allows business investment to take place more or less wherever the entrepreneur wishes it to occur. The landscape is thus one of mixed, unplanned growth of both housing and small firms in and around towns and villages, particularly along transportation routes. Moreover, pollution controls have been relaxed in these regions while public services and the taxation to provide them have been comparatively low. Accordingly, dynamic growth on first the national and then the international scale has been registered by textile firms such as Benetton and its more recent emulator, Stefanel.

Brusco (1985) argues that this model, though placing fewer obstacles in small-firm growth paths, is less efficient and less advanced than that operating in 'red' or Communist- and Socialist-controlled regions such as Tuscany or Emilia-Romagna. In the latter case it seems likely that the more socially progressive local authorities have accelerated development while preserving a better local quality of life. As in Veneto, this region has a long history of artisan, small-firm activity but this experienced a revival in the post-war years. Whereas the Veneto small-firm growth in some cases meshes into very large international production and retailing networks, it has often been independent in origin. However, Emilia Romagna's extensive small-firm network was boosted by the placing of orders by large firms outside the region seeking subcontracting links. Industrial strife in Turin led Fiat, for example, to restructure its production processes in two ways. First, in the 1970s it embarked upon a massive programme of investment in flexible manufacturing systems, automation and robotization. Second, it began sourcing an increasing amount of componentry from the small metal-manufacturing companies in and around Bologna.

Of interest in Emilia-Romagna is the often close relationship between small-firm owners and the Communist Party. A large percentage are members of an artisan association affiliated to the party. Thus information on small-firm problems and opportunities filters back and forth readily. Accordingly the Communist Party, in concert with the Socialist Party at local and regional level, has been able to implement policies which aid local industry, influence labour and wage relations and keep up the quality of life in the region. Emilia-Romagna has moved from a relatively low regional income and productivity position to one of the highest in Italy in the 1980s. Amongst the policies pursued have been: assistance in traditional industries such as food (Parma ham, Parmesan cheese) to avoid the middleman in marketing produce through the establishment of co-operative agencies; provision of infrastructure and industrial parks; employer advice through specialist agencies on market strategy, technology and business information; increased placing of local orders; collective provision of accountancy services; identification of new market opportunities; workforce training; and technology assessment. Partly in consequence, many small Emilian firms have become producers of advanced manufacturing systems which link firms together in complex subcontracting systems, as well as simply users of them. Such technologies as computerized laser machines for cutting cloth and customized computer numerically controlled machine tools are now exported, as increasingly are the software and system engineering services which drive them (Martinelli, 1986).

The key to this impressive economic development process is 'local knowledge' (Geertz, 1983). Brusco (1985) makes clear that, whether in the white or red regions, the industrial districts tend to be found in the historic 'putting-out' areas. Putting out favoured the development of skills in management, accounting and payroll calculating within the family and, more importantly, within the social texture. Moreover, the industrial districts focus upon towns where trade, finance and commerce as well as markets are to be found. Two other crucial features are also worth mentioning. The first is the frequency with which small firms develop in an industry locally dominated by a large firm, or by a failed large firm. Spin-off, or the replacement of a company ceasing trading with a co-operative composed of former workers, is a common dynamic element in the development of Italian industrial districts. Where the market increasingly demands customized products, small firms can out-compete their more Fordist parents. Finally, the widespread existence of local technical schools is seen as the backbone of small-scale business competence in the industrial districts. These factors link together and generalize opportunities for local enterprise.

[33]

The Machine-Tool Industry in the Basque Country

In 1981 the Autonomous Government of the Basque Country was established to meet the political demands for regional self-government. The Basque Government, unlike the other regional authorities in Spain, has the power to receive income taxes, a proportion of which are transferred to Madrid and the remainder of which are spent on regionally and locally determined projects. Reflecting the seriousness of the unemployment situation, which was on average running at a rate of 25 per cent in the early 1980s as heavy industry entered severe crisis, the Government established three economic ministries: the Ministry of Economic Planning and Studies; the Ministry of Industry and Commerce; and the Ministry of the Budget. For purposes of this discussion, it is the second, the Ministry of Industry and Commerce, that warrants most attention.

The Basque economy has been dominated by declining Fordist industry: metal manufacture, steel production and shipbuilding. Traditionally, most companies have employed more than 200 people and some, such as the Altos Hornos steelworks at Barakaldo, Bilbao, more than 8,000. The region thus has much in common with declining heavy industry regions in Britain. The Government strategy is not to promote inward investment to find replacement jobs but to promote indigenous development. The Ministry of Industry and Commerce has a budget of £15 million per annum with which it pursues three main programmes. The first is the Programme for Industry in Fixed Capital. This is aimed at increasing the level of investment in existing small firms by providing subsidies on investment of 10 per cent upwards depending on sector, type of employment and number of employees. It also makes grants available which reduce interest rates on capital borrowed by up to 3.5 percentage points. The second form of intervention is the Technology Transfer Programme, which gives aids to innovation in product and process technology, mostly the latter (50–80 per cent of expenditure). Most of this aid has gone to the machine-tool and electronics industries. Regional Technology Centres and a Programme of Technological Diffusion have been set up to improve equipment, knowledge and information. The third intervention is what is called High Risk Projects. These can vary from establishing technology parks to funding postgraduate students to go abroad and learn about advanced technology in countries such as West Germany and the USA.

This effort is further supported, particularly for new enterprises, by SPRI, a specialist technology transfer agency. Its budget, also £15 million per year, is funded 70 per cent by the Ministry, 30 per cent by six banks. It also has financial programmes providing credits, loans and grants, and special programmes involving promotional, infrastructural, training and services activities (marketing, administration, consultancy).

The Basque machine-tool industry has benefited massively from these reconversion and new development programmes. Most of it is situated in the industrial district of Elgoibar-Eibar in Guipuzcoa province. The area produces 80 per cent of total Spanish machine-tool output, of which 60 per cent is exported. Output is divided between advanced computer numerically controlled (55 per cent) and traditional (45 per cent) machine tools. The companies consist of some small co-operatives belonging to the Debako group of the Mondragon organization, numerous private firms and one worker-owned company making a total of 140 in all (Bruce, 1988). The Debako group works as a flexible production system with continuous production passing from stage to stage between the co-ops. They have their own R. & D. centre and joint marketing, employee transfer and training arrangements. Industrial restructuring has involved employment rationalization such that between 1979 and 1986 there was a decline from 10,000 to 8,000, but retraining meant that there was effectively no resulting unemployment. The industry is in a healthy position and remains locally controlled, a fact testified by the location of the Spanish Machine Tools Association headquarters in San Sebastian, a few miles away, rather than in Madrid. The association has over 100 members, of which approximately 20 per cent are located outside the Basque Country.

Thus we see in this instance a successful small-firm modernization partnership between local and regional organizations and between public, private and co-operative interests. Finance, information and training have been linked imaginatively to enable a locality with long-established traditional skills (it dates back to the fifteenth century and originally produced armaments for the Spanish Armada) to restructure in post-Fordist vein using advanced technology and flexible production systems to cater for niche markets in the advanced economies and to discover new markets in Latin America and North Africa.

Software and Systems Engineering in Southern France

As capital restructures and information becomes a key commodity, the technologies which transfer and process information become increasingly central to the economic development process. Two technologies, in particular, are at the core of the information transfer and processing industries: computers and telecommunications. As well as constituting diverse product ranges in their own right, these technologies have already become key processes in industry and commerce. It is clear that in banking and finance, immediate information about variations in currency exchange rates is both available to and necessary for the functioning of the globalized financial system. But such technologies are also increasingly at the heart of the post-Fordist flexible manufacturing systems. These systems embody computer-aided design, engineering and management, and can produce a wholly linked computer integrated manufacturing system. Some older industries such as steel making and coal mining have, in effect, pioneered these systems but they are now becoming more widespread in industry.

However, there are problems in integrating computer and telecommunications technologies which derive from their very different technologies, languages, architectures and employment cultures. Many large producers of these technologies have been forming 'strategic alliances' (Cooke, 1988) to integrate them, nowhere more so than in France. But the problems of doing so have given rise to small-firm high-technology consultancies capable of engineering the new systems linkages through developing customized software programmes.

In France, where state intervention concerning industrial development has always been pronounced, high-technology industry was partly decentralized to the south of the country, especially to the Rhône-Alpes region where Grenoble is a leading 'technopole' and Provence where Montpellier, Marseilles, Nice and Sophia Antipolis play a similar role. Recent research (Moulaert, Chikhaoui and Djellal, 1988) shows that there has been significant recent establishment and employment growth in three industry subsectors covering software and systems engineering in southern France. Much of this growth is of smaller local firms and establishments of larger firms with a base in Paris.

It can be seen from Table 2.1 that establishment sizes in these activities are small, mostly with fewer than ten employees, and that the rate of growth has generally been greater both for establishments

Table 2.1 Establishment and employment growth in high-technology services, 1976-84

	Technical studies				Informatics studies				Data processing			
	Establishments		Employment		Establishments		Employment		Establishments		Employment	
	1984	Index (1976=100)	1984	Index (1976=100)	1984	Index (1976=100)	1984	Index (1976=100)	1984	Index (1976=100)	1984	Index (1976=100)
Paris	814	133	3,062	151	1,366	355	19,441	286	443	292	8,747	241
Rhône-Alpes	417	154	3,851	153	307	401	3,333	413	151	289	851	129
Provence	412	183	3,637	177	275	685	1,554	407	128	456	936	244

Source: Moulaert, Chikhaoui and Djellal (1988).

[37]

and for employment in the southern regions than in Paris. This is consistent with the thesis that previous decentralization of high-technology industry as part of first the growth pole, later the 'technopole', regional strategy has given rise to new small-firm subcontracting opportunities as technological change and development occur. Both Provence and Rhône-Alpes had traditionally been rather backward regions, and the combination of state indicative planning and large-firm requirements for advanced producer services expertise seems from the data to be producing something of a 'services spectacular' in addition to the manufacturing miracle of regional reconversion in an earlier period.

Clearly, the presence of some 14,000 specialist, advanced producer services jobs, their associated spending power and their cultural contribution to the two southern regions and their specific localities is a considerable boost to the local economy. Moreover, the sometimes dramatic employment growth rates, especially the quadrupling in informatics studies, are testimony to the developmental impact that judicious state intervention can have upon regional and local economic problems. However, it should not be assumed that this outcome is traceable solely to central state intervention. The more recent 'technopole' policy has left much to local discretion. Those localities, such as Montpellier, that have benefited most have often taken advantage of opportunities rather than simply waiting for them to arrive. And Sophia Antipolis, the large science park near Antibes, was the product of private local initiative and public support.

BACK TO BRITAIN: CENTRALISM AND BEYOND

It is plain that no local economic initiatives in Britain have matched the relative success of the cases discussed above. In Britain it has been traditional to leave questions of regional and local economic development to the central state. In good times, with expansion in the economic system, jobs have been created and shuffled around in the urban and regional system. In less good times, like the 1980s, such interventions have been far less pronounced, more has been left up to market forces, and local initiative has more often than not been threatened with the removal of funding sources (notably under Section 137 of the Local Government Act 1972) or has simply been closed down, as in the case of the Metropolitan Counties and the GLC.

That there is initiative in the local system is testified by recent findings on efforts by representative local authorities in different parts of England (Cooke, 1989). Swindon, for example, has been successful in mobilizing support for local development since the 1950s, enabling housing and local infrastructure to be provided and attracting new engineering, electronics and producer services jobs. Cheltenham too, with a more passive approach, displays an expanding manufacturing and producer services base. But these are located in the fortunate South. What about the North? There the picture is less sanguine. Lancaster has taken small, successful initiatives but remains more of a public-services-dominated economy vulnerable to central state cuts, while cities like Middlesbrough and Liverpool seem to have few chances to develop as local industrial districts.

Meanwhile, central state policies involve accruing increasing powers to Whitehall, then generalizing a model of local economic development which is largely private sector and consumption based. The spectacular housing, leisure and entertainments schemes now being mapped out for depressed inner cities everywhere reflect the strength of property and finance capital and the relative weakness of industrial capital in the country. It is, of course, partly a cultural question. Whereas in the European examples quoted there seems to be some cultural attachment to the idea of self-sustained, often collectively organized enterprise, that tradition may, especially in manufacturing industry, be impossible to revive in areas that were swamped long ago by capital concentration and Fordism. Nevertheless, there is little point in counselling despair, for there are lessons that can be learned from other countries, not the least of which is that successful regional reconversion can be achieved. The next section summarizes some of the key elements of those successes.

POST-FORDISM AND LOCALISM: IMPLICATIONS FOR POLICY

First of all, it is crucially important for local authorities to grasp the idea that production methods have changed and that a coherent strategy of stimulating and furthering co-operation between small, local firms and local or even non-local large ones will be swimming with rather than against the tide. This means another set of implications have to be grasped.

[39]

As well as marketing places as consumption centres to the outside world, local authorities should increase their general level of enterprise-related capacity. They are in a key position as suppliers of business information, databases, libraries of business plans and technological information. They may be able to integrate local economic information with training and retraining policies as well as undertaking normal infrastructural and land-use allocation policies. On a small scale they may be able to supply accountancy and marketing services to small firms and co-operatives struggling to fit into the new post-Fordist era of production.

Much has been written about the lack of resources available to local authorities to assist local economic development, and much greater local sources of capital will always be a help. But it is instructive to note Brusco's (1985) comments with regard to the question of capital in his discussion of the Third Italy phenomenon. He says that it is striking how little relevance the availability of capital or savings has had to the development of the Italian industrial districts. The capital invested was essentially human; work was treated as an alternative to rest or leisure. The key to this was the existence within the system of know-how. This enabled the transformation of vague ideas into practical projects.

Here, then, is the final lesson that British local authorities need to learn. The technical education process could be improved to the point where business know-how of local and more widespread relevance, of the kind discussed above, is made both available and attractive to the people whom it is their job to serve. Knowledge is, at the end of the day, power and too many people are presently powerless.

CONCLUSIONS

There is little point in reiterating the case that has been put for the development of the local economy. Perhaps it is more valuable to seek to underline two things that have been said. The first of these is that the mode of production has, in a sense, gone back to the future. Smaller firms are becoming more integral to the functioning of the economy. Small firms often cluster in local space for information exchange and economic transactions. Local economies are, in some countries, already on the march. The second point is that, for too long, Britain's economy has been run from a centre that is clearly inadequate to meet local needs, other than by generalizing a consumers' paradise of urban spectacle. Localities can, if they wish, develop along a different trajectory.

ACKNOWLEDGEMENTS

I wish to thank the University of Utrecht for providing me with the time to write this chapter through appointing me Belle Van Zuyl Visiting Professor in Geography. I am grateful also to Flavia Martinelli, Frank Moulaert and Erik Swyngedouw for discussing some of the issues mentioned and for allowing me to refer to their information on Italy and France. Finally, thanks are due to the British Council and the Spanish Ministry of Education for funding the research on which the information on the Basque Country was based, and to my research colleagues Arantxa Rodrigues and Goio Etxebarria of the University of Bilbao and Jon Morris of Cardiff Business School.

REFERENCES

Bruce, P. (1988) 'Spanish machine tool makers face new challenge,' *Financial Times*, 5 December, p. 5.

Brusco, S. (1985) *Small Firms and Industrial Districts: The Experience of Italy* (mimeo), University of Modena.

Cooke, P. (1988) 'Flexible integration, scope economies, and strategic alliances: social and spatial mediations', *Society and Space*, Vol. 6, pp. 281–300.

Cooke, P. (ed.) (1989) *Localities*, London, Unwin Hyman.

Dunning, J. (1981) *International Production and the Multinational Enterprise*, London, Allen and Unwin.

Geertz, C. (1983) *Local Knowledge*, New York, Basic Books.

Hewison, R. (1987) *The Heritage Industry*, London, Methuen.

Lipietz, A. (1985) 'The world crisis: the globalization of the general crisis of Fordism', *IDS Bulletin*, Vol. 16, pp. 6–11.

Marshall, A. (1919) *Industry and Trade*, London, Macmillan.

Martinelli, F. (1986) *Producer Services in a Dependent Economy: Their Role and Potential for Economic Development*, unpublished Ph.D. thesis, Berkeley, Calif., University of California.

Massey, D. (1984) *Spatial Divisions of Labour*, London, Macmillan.

Morris, J. (1988) 'New technologies, flexible work practices and regional sociospatial differentiation: some observations from the UK', *Society and Space*, Vol. 6, pp. 301–20.

Moulaert, F., Chikhaoui, Y. and Djellal, F. (1988) 'Locational behaviour of French high technology consultancy firms', Paper presented to the John Dyckman Memorial Sessions of the Regional Science Association Conference, Toronto, November.

Murray, R. (1985) 'London and the Greater London Council: restructuring the capital of capital', *IDS Bulletin*, Vol. 16, pp. 47–55.

Sabel, C. (1988) 'The re-emergence of regional economies', paper presented to a Colloquium on Logics of Enterprise and Forms of Legitimation, Paris, January.

Simmie, J. (1985) 'The spatial division of labour in London, 1978–81', *International Journal of Urban and Regional Research*, Vol. 9, pp. 557–70.

Thrift, N. (1987) 'The fixers: the urban geography of international commercial capital', in Henderson, J. and Castells, M. (eds) *Global Restructuring and Territorial Development*, London, Sage.

·PART 2·

Central Government Policy

City Grants, Urban Development Grants and Urban Regeneration Grants

---

Urban Development Corporations

Government Urban Economic Policy 1979–89: Problems and Potential

CHAPTER 3

City Grants, Urban Development Grants and Urban Regeneration Grants

Stephen Martin

INTRODUCTION

One of the most important developments in local economic policy in the late 1980s has been the increasing emphasis which central government has placed on the private sector's role in attempts to regenerate local economies. Nowhere has this theme been more evident than in the field of inner city policy, where it has become clear that increasing reliance is to be placed on the use of private finance rather than public sector funding (Campbell, 1988). In this context the Urban Development Grant programme, which was introduced in 1982, is of particular importance because it was one of the first schemes which was designed to draw the private sector into attempts to revitalize inner city areas. It therefore marked the departure from traditional Urban Programme activities based on the partnership of central and local government and provides valuable insights into the problems and the potential of local economic policies which are based on the concept of partnership between the public and private sectors.

This chapter first describes the evolution and management of the Urban Development Grant (UDG) programme, of its sister programme, the Urban Regeneration Grant (URG), and their successor, City Grant. It then examines the existing evidence about the effectiveness of these programmes, focusing on four particularly important performance indicators: the take-up of the available grants; the additionality of the assistance which they have provided; the amount of private sector investment that the programmes have levered into inner city areas; and the nature and scale of their employment impacts. The chapter concludes with a discussion of the prospects for City Grant in the light of past experience of the UDG and URG programmes.

THE HISTORY OF UDG, URG AND CITY GRANT

In the aftermath of the 1981 riots on Merseyside, Michael Heseltine, the then Secretary of State for the Environment, examined a number of strategies for inner city regeneration. As part of this process he established the Financial Institutions Group, a body made up of 26 senior managers seconded from banks, building societies, insurance companies and pension funds. This group made a number of recommendations, one of the most important of which was that the Department of the Environment (D.o.E.) should introduce a grant system modelled on the Urban Development Action Grant (UDAG) programme in the United States (D.o.E. 1982). As a result, in April 1982 the Government announced the launch of the Urban Development Grant programme. Like its American counterpart, the UDG scheme was designed to attract private sector investment into inner city areas. Its primary aim was 'to promote the economic and physical regeneration of inner urban areas by levering private sector investment into such areas' (D.o.E. 1984). It was expected to do this by providing money from the public purse to bridge the 'funding gap' which is associated with many inner city developments, in order to enable private sector developers to make a return on investments which would otherwise have been unprofitable. In addition to the UDG programme administered by the D.o.E. in England, a separate scheme also called Urban Development Grant was administered by the Welsh Office and an equivalent programme, named Local Enterprise Grants for Urban Projects (LEG-UP), was introduced in Scotland.

In 1987 a new grant programme, Urban Regeneration Grant, was introduced under the Housing and Planning Act 1986. This was intended to promote the redevelopment of large sites (usually more than 20 acres) and the refurbishment of buildings of comparable size. This, it was hoped, would involve the large developers and financial institutions, groups which had not generally been attracted by the UDG programme.

Although it was short-lived, being superseded by City Grant the following year (see below), URG marked an important change in the direction of inner city policy; namely that like subsequent programmes, but unlike UDG, there was no formal local authority involvement in the URG process. Part III of the Housing and Planning Act empowered central government to provide financial assistance direct to 'any person' to carry out a scheme which would lead to urban regeneration. As with Urban Development Corporations central government was therefore able to circumnavigate the traditional Urban Programme grant systems and make payments direct to the private sector. In addition, Section II of the Act enabled large areas eligible for URG to be designated as Simplified Planning Zones in which certain types of development could proceed without planning permission – thereby further reducing local authority involvement in the programme.

Following a review of inner city policy which was initiated by the Prime Minister after her return to power in 1987, a new programme, City Grant, was launched in May 1988. This was billed as 'A new simplified grant to support private sector developments in inner cities' (Action for Cities Press Release, 1988) and it replaced both UDG and URG, as well as a third programme – private sector Derelict Land Grant. City Grant was designed to simplify procedures for potential applicants, some of whom had in the past been confused by the wide variety of different grant regimes which were available to them and unsure about which they should apply for (D.o.E., 1988a). It was hoped that by combining several programmes it would be possible to overcome this difficulty.

The aims of City Grant are very similar to those of UDG and URG, namely 'to support private sector capital projects which benefit rundown urban areas and which cannot proceed without assistance' (D.o.E., 1988b). Projects can involve 'reclamation, new build or refurbishment projects in inner city areas which provide new jobs or private housing, bring derelict land and empty buildings back into use, improve the local environment and help build confidence in inner city areas' (D.o.E., 1988b). The programme is administered by the same inner cities directorate within the D.o.E. as was responsible for UDG and URG. Proposed projects are scrutinized by the same appraisal team are were UDG and URG applications and assistance is available for the same types of project as those at which its predecessors were targeted. Broadly the same areas are eligible for City Grant as was the case for UDG and URG, priority being given to projects from the 57 towns and cities shown on Table 3.1.

Table 3.1   City Grant priority areas

Barnsley	Islington	Preston
Birmingham	Kensington and Chelsea	Rochdale
Blackburn	Kingston on Hull	Rotherham
Bolton	Kirklees	St Helens
Bradford	Knowsley	Salford
Brent	Lambeth	Sandwell
Bristol	Langbaurgh	Sefton
Burnley	Leeds	Sheffield
Coventry	Leicester	South Tyneside
Derby	Lewisham	Southwark
Doncaster	Liverpool	Stockton
Dudley	Manchester	Sunderland
Gateshead	Middlesbrough	Tower Hamlets
Greenwich	Newcastle	Walsall
Hackney	Newham	Wandsworth
Halton	North Tyneside	Wigan
Hammersmith and Fulham	Nottingham	Wirral
Haringey	Oldham	Wolverhampton
Hartlepool	Plymouth	Wrekin

Source: D.o.E. (1988a).

A number of minor modifications were introduced. For example, projects which cost less than £200,000 which were eligible for UDG will not be given City Grant; instead they will be channelled into the Urban Programme. The most significant change, however, was that as with URG, but unlike UDG, local authorities do not provide any of the public sector contribution to projects which receive City Grant, and consequently they have very little formal role in the management of the programme. This move reflects the view of D.o.E. officials that local authority appraisals of UDG projects were often superficial and served only to lengthen the time which it took for the projects to be approved.

THE MANAGEMENT OF THE PROGRAMMES

In 1982 all of the county and district councils in England which were designated under the Inner Urban Areas Act of 1978 and those which contained Enterprise Zones were formally invited to make bids for UDG assistance. This amounted to a total of 47 local authorities. In 1983 a further 16 district councils were also invited to produce bids. Although not formally invited to do so, other authorities were entitled to make applications for UDG schemes. However in practice none has been successful in doing so.

[47]

Local authorities played a major role in the UDG process. They were responsible for working with the private sector to produce bids for UDG, and also for providing 25 per cent of the public sector contribution to projects which were subsequently approved. The remaining 75 per cent of the public sector contribution was provided by the D.o.E., and therefore once bids had been agreed on by the private sector participants and the local authorities they were forwarded to the D.o.E.'s headquarters in Marsham Street and scrutinized by an appraisal team consisting of civil servants and secondees from the private sector.

Some local authorities were very pro-active and worked with the private sector to initiate projects; others were largely responsive and waited for developers to approach them with proposals for bids. The D.o.E. guidelines for UDG required local authorities to satisfy themselves that each proposed project was suitable for UDG assistance, that the development budget seemed reasonable, and that the level of assistance sought was the minimum necessary in order for the project to go ahead. If the application for assistance fulfilled these requirements and local authority members approved the bid, a formal application was submitted by the local authority to the D.o.E. for detailed appraisal.

The appraiser's first task was to check that the project fell into one of the following categories and was therefore eligible for UDG assistance:

- the construction of industrial units, warehouses, shops and offices for letting, sale or owner-occupation;

- the refurbishment or conversion of existing buildings to provide industrial units, housing, shops, warehousing or offices;

- the provision of private sector housing either by new build or rehabilitation;

- the improvement of council housing which was difficult to let in order to sell it off;

- the provision of leisure, recreational and community facilities;

- the building or refurbishment of hotels.

Having checked the eligibility of a project, the appraiser then had to ensure that:

- the proposed project would be viable if UDG assistance was given;

- the project would not proceed in the form proposed in the absence of the assistance;

- the form and amount of assistance was the minimum required to enable the project to proceed;

- the project was practicable (i.e. all participants were capable of discharging their responsibilities);

- the project made a significant contribution towards improving the economic, social or environmental conditions of an inner city area.

Particular emphasis was placed on the requirement that the project would not proceed without finance from the public sector, and on ensuring that there were no alternative sources of public sector backing. The UDG programme was designed to provide 'finance of the last resort'. It is for this reason that it has been dubbed the 'Heineken Grant' – reaching the projects which other grants did not reach.

An additional requirement was that a substantial amount of the costs of a proposed project was met by the private sector. The 1984 Guidance Notes stated that 'The private sector contribution to an approved project will normally be several times the public sector contribution and overall, the ratio of private to public sector contributions in approved UDG projects has been about 4:1.' Assistance was given to projects with low leverage ratios only if it could be demonstrated that they were likely to provide particularly significant benefits.

The eligibility criteria for URG were slightly different from those for UDG. Projects which could be considered for URG assistance included:

- the acquisition of land and buildings;

- the development or redevelopment of land;

- the provision of equipment;

- the enhancing of access;

- the provision of services and environmental improvements.

The appraisal criteria for URG projects were the same as those applied to UDG.

The original intention was that the appraisal process would be completed within 90 days of an application having been received by

Marsham Street. However, in practice average decision times have been much longer. The length of time taken to appraise bids has been one of the main criticisms of the UDG programme (see below). Figure 3.1 shows the stages through which a project for which UDG or URG and now City Grant assistance is sought normally passes.

Since City Grant is funded 100 per cent by central government, the local authorities' role is now in theory restricted to passing on applications from the private sector to the regional offices of the D.o.E. In practice, however, many authorities seem to have continued to take a far more active interest in bids. The way in which City Grants are appraised by the D.o.E. is broadly the same as the procedures which existed for UDG and URG, and is summarized in Figure 3.2.

Each application for assistance which reaches Marsham Street is allocated to a member of the appraisal team, usually on a geographical basis. The appraiser studies the files relating to the application, visits the site of the proposed project, and may also enter into informal negotiations with the private sector about the details of the proposed project. He or she then compiles a case paper which outlines the nature of the proposed project (its objectives, likely impacts and time horizon) and summarizes the key appraisal issues. Case papers conclude with a recommendation about whether a grant should be given and, if so, what level of assistance is appropriate and what conditions (for example, clawback agreements) should be attached to it. The case paper and files are then examined by a secondary appraiser (usually the leader of the appraisal team), and if he or she agrees with the recommendation the application is sent to the Secretary of State for formal approval or rejection.

PROGRAMME EFFECTIVENESS

The effectiveness of programmes such as UDG, URG and City Grant can be evaluated in terms of the extent to which they have fulfilled their objectives. As explained above, the main aim of all three programmes is or was to encourage private sector investment in inner city areas in order to facilitate developments which would not otherwise proceed and which are or were likely to produce significant benefits when completed. Four types of performance indicator which relate to this objective will be discussed here: the level of take-up of the assistance offered under the programmes; the extent to which the programmes promoted activity which would not otherwise have

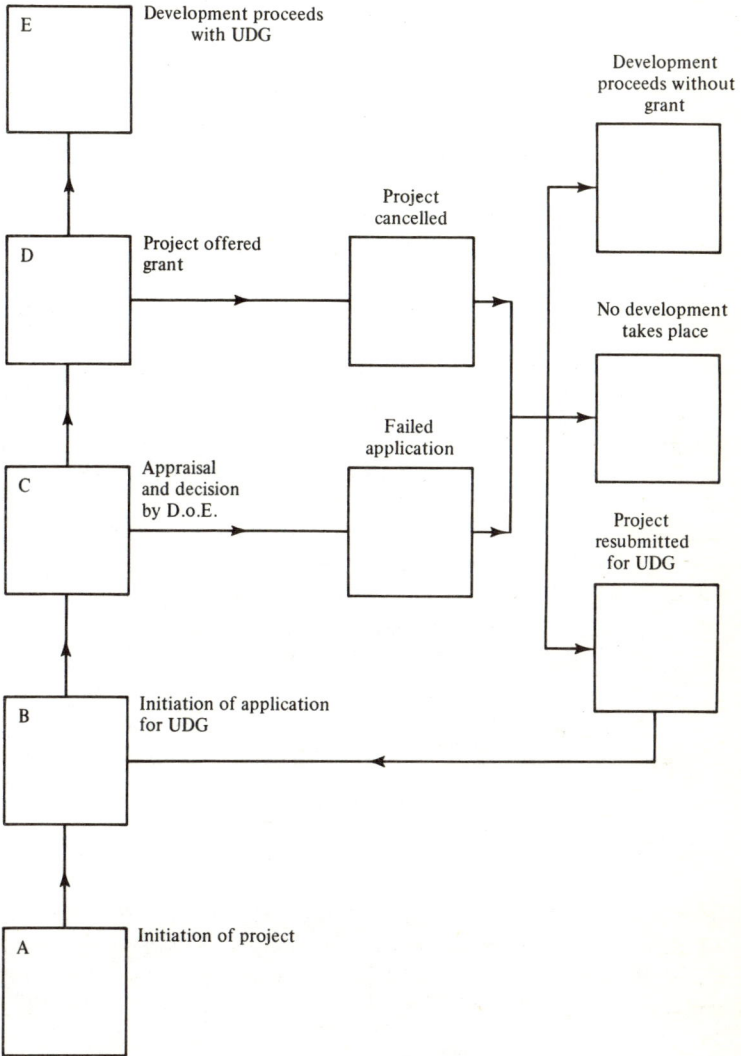

Figure 3.1 The Urban Development Grant process (Source: PSMRC, 1988)

Developer submits brief details
of scheme to regional office

↓

Regional office meets
developer to discuss scheme

↓

Developer submits formal
application to regional office

↓

Regional office checks that
application is complete

↓

Regional office passes
application to Marsham Street

↓

Within 4 weeks appraiser accepts
scheme for formal appraisal or
rejects it if lies outside
City Grant criteria

↓

Appraiser visits site and
discusses scheme with developer

↓

Formal decision made within 10 weeks
of acceptance for full appraisal

↓

Recommendation made to minister

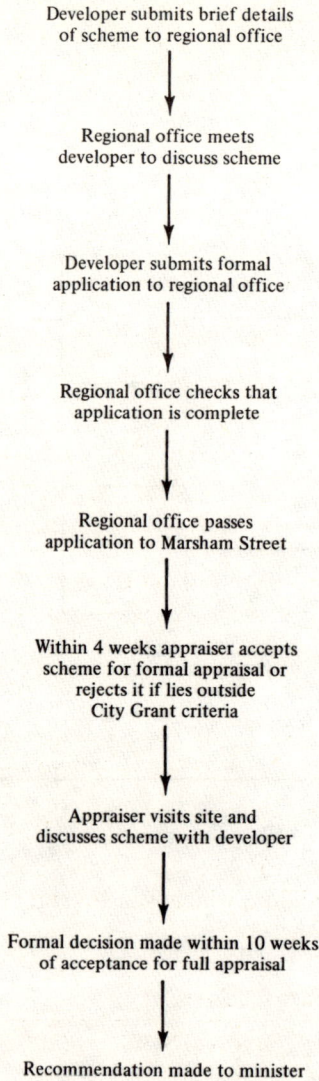

Figure 3.2 Stages in the D.o.E. appraisal of City Grant application

taken place; the amount of private sector investment which has been attracted into inner city areas; and the scale and significance of the employment benefits which have resulted from completed projects.

Since URG was a very short-lived programme and City Grant has at the time of writing been in existence for less than a year, there is as yet no independent evidence regarding their effectiveness. The following analysis is therefore primarily concerned with evidence regarding the effectiveness of the UDG programme, about which far more information is available.

The Take-up of Grants

The initial response to the invitation to bid for UDG assistance was encouraging. After just three years over 600 applications had been submitted to the D.o.E. However, a large proportion of these failed to gain approval. An analysis of the fate of the 604 bids which had been submitted by June 1986 showed that only a quarter had been given UDG backing (PSMRC, 1988). A fifth of all bids had been rejected by the D.o.E., and nearly 40 per cent had been withdrawn by the applicants (Figure 3.3).

As a result of the high drop-out rate of applications for assistance, the UDG budget was consistently underspent. The original budget for the first year of the programme (1983/4) was set at £70 million. Total expenditure in that year amounted to under £7 million (less than 10 per cent of the budget), and the following year expenditure reached just £13 million. As a result the budget for 1985/6 was reduced to £40 million. Even with this reduction, however, only just over half the budget was spent in 1985/6 (Cmnd 9143 and 9428) (Table 3.2). But the time City Grant replaced UDG, the programme had been in existence for five years, and total expenditure had amounted to £87.5 million, which was little more than the original budget for 1983/4 alone.

Table 3.2 UDG expenditure (£ millions)

	1983/4	1984/5	1985/6	1986/7	1987/8
UDG outturn expenditure	6.589	13.008	21.565	21.306	25.047
Administration costs	0.19*	0.21*	0.34*	0.35*	

Note: *Estimated.
Source: D.o.E. (1988a).

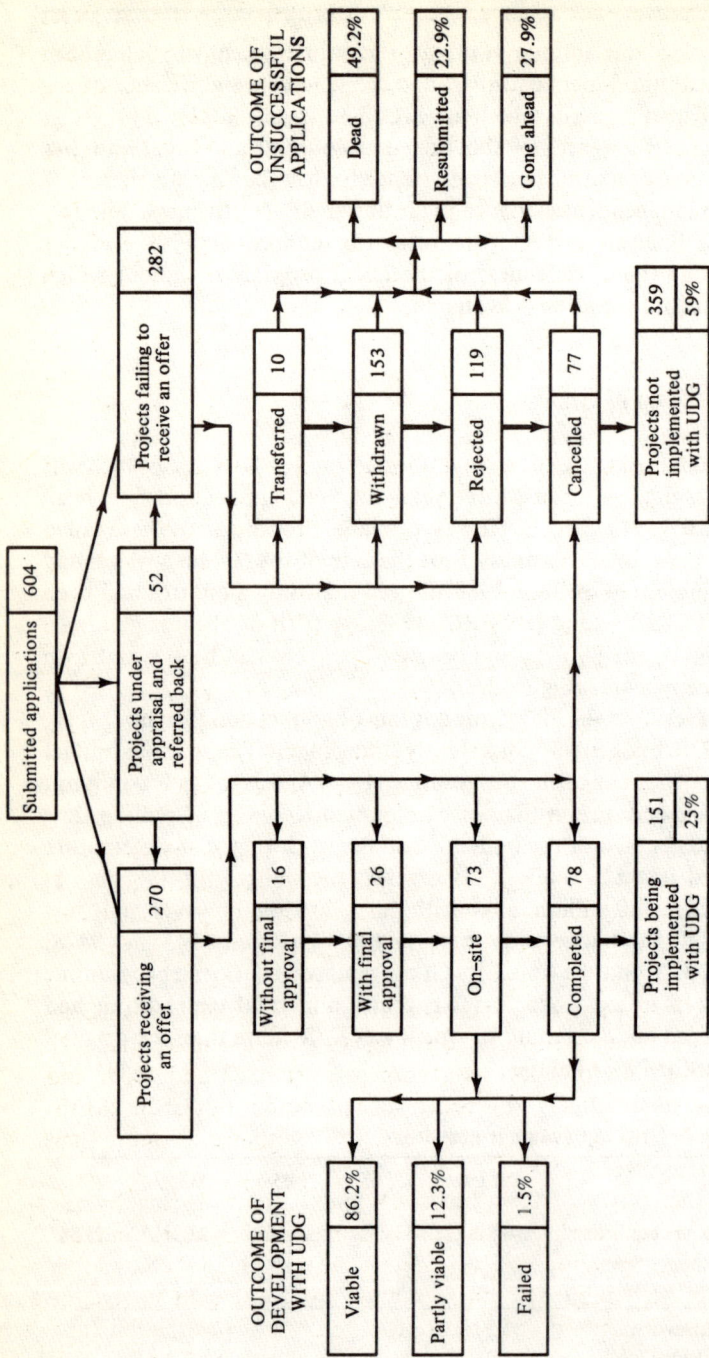

Figure 3.3 Status of applications for UDG (as of June 1986) (Source: PSMRC, 1988)

The continued underspend of the UDG budget has been a matter of considerable concern to the D.o.E., since the lack of successful projects clearly restricted the programme's potential to promote inner city regeneration. The low level of take-up of grant seems to have been related to a number of factors.

An analysis of the latest D.o.E. figures of UDG expenditure reveals marked variations between different regions and different local authority areas within the same region. In the West Midlands a total of 63 schemes received UDG assistance between 1983 and 1988, with expenditure totalling £20.6 million. In the South-East region expenditure between 1983 and 1988 amounted to £21 million on a total of 44 projects. By contrast total UDG expenditure in the Northern region totalled just £10.3 million. Although to some extent these differences reflect variations in development costs in different parts of the country, they are also undoubtedly the result of differences in the state of the market in different areas. Clearly, a grant regime such as UDG which aims to encourage partnership between the private and public sectors is unlikely to be as successful in areas where the market is relatively depressed (for example, the North-East of England) as it is in areas (such as the South-East) where the regional economy is relatively buoyant and the private sector is therefore more inclined to come forward with potential schemes.

It is also apparent that differences in the level of take-up of UDG assistance were partly due to the different approaches which local authorities had adopted to the programme. Some authorities were initially opposed to UDG for political reasons. Others decided early on to 'play the UDG game' and geared up their local economic development departments to take maximum advantage of any assistance that was on offer. Those authorities which were most successful in obtaining UDGs all set up well-staffed units specifically to deal with UDG projects. Some authorities were particularly successful in obtaining assistance. Birmingham, for example, made 22 successful bids for UDG assistance between 1983 and 1988, and Nottingham made 17. This contrasts with authorities in the Northern region, none of which received UDG assistance for more than seven projects.

Another reason for low level of take-up nationwide was that the private sector perceived the UDG scheme as being overly bureaucratic. Many private sector developers who sought grants found that their bids were subject to considerable delays and concluded that the amounts of money on offer were too small to justify the time and effort which was required to work up future bids. The D.o.E.'s original intention was that it would appraise each application for assistance within 90 days. In practice, however, most appraisals took considerably longer than this. Only 43 per cent of the projects which had received an offer by June 1986 had been appraised in less than six months, and the average appraisal time was nine months. In addition, many schemes were subject to even longer delays because of the time taken for bids to pass through the local authorities and regional offices prior to reaching the appraisal team in Marsham Street. Over a period of nine months market conditions can change considerably and projects may become unprofitable. As a result, the private sector may then lose interest in them, and it seems that this was one of the main reasons for large numbers of applications having been withdrawn from the UDG process by developers.

A final reason for the low level of take-up of grant seems to have been that many developers were either unaware of the programme or unsure whether it was applicable to the sorts of development with which they were involved. It has been suggested by developers that UDG was not effectively marketed to them and that the guidelines regarding which projects were eligible were confusing. It seems that one of the reasons for the relative success of the programme in areas like Birmingham and Nottingham was that the local authorities and/or D.o.E. regional offices made considerable efforts to work with the private sector in order to overcome the ignorance and confusion which surrounded the programme when it was first introduced.

The lack of take-up of UDG was one of the reasons for the introduction of URG in 1987. Since URG was designed to provide finance for larger projects than UDG, it was not expected that more than 10–15 projects would be approved each year, but the D.o.E. anticipated that these would consume a budget of comparable size to that devoted to UDG. In fact a total of nine projects were approved before URG was replaced by City Grant. The total anticipated cost of these amounted to £49.6 million to be spent over the six years from 1988/9 to 1994/5. The total budget for City Grants in the year 1988/9 is currently just over £50 million, but much of this is allocated to projects which have yet to be approved, and it remains to be seen whether take-up of City Grant will be significantly greater than that of its predecessors.

The Additionality of UDG Assistance

Since the main aim of the UDG programme was to facilitate developments in inner city locations which would not otherwise have taken place, the extent to which it has achieved this is a major indicator of its effectiveness. To measure programme performance in these terms it is necessary to assess the likelihood that schemes which received UDG financial backing would have proceeded if UDG assistance had not been available. The extent to which a grant was actually required in order for a project to proceed is usually referred to as the 'additionality' of a grant, and any portion of a grant which was not required in order for a project to go ahead is called 'deadweight' (Gregory and Martin, 1988).

The only available evidence regarding the additionality of UDG funding comes from the one comprehensive evaluation of the programme that has so far been undertaken (PSMRC, 1988). The researchers who undertook this evaluation based their findings on an in-depth analysis of a representative sample of 65 UDG-assisted projects which either had been completed or were under way by the summer of 1986. These projects included speculative industrial developments, business expansion schemes, office and shop developments, and housing schemes.

The additionality of the UDG given to these developments was assessed by detailed examination of the project files and case papers relating to each project and by interviewing the developers who had undertaken the projects. The researchers used these sources to make informed *ex post* judgements regarding the extent to which UDG assistance had been required for each of the 65 projects. They concluded that 53 (82 per cent) of the projects would probably not have proceeded without UDG assistance, but that the remaining twelve schemes probably would have done so. They then subdivided projects for which UDG assistance had probably been required into those for which the full amount of grant had been required (no deadweight) and those where a smaller grant than that which was given would probably have been sufficient to ensure that the schemes proceeded (low-level deadweight). Projects for which UDG funding did not seem to have been required were subdivided into those where the project would have gone ahead in a modified form in the absence of UDG assistance (medium-level deadweight) and those which would have proceeded unchanged in the absence of UDG assistance (full deadweight) (Table 3.3).

Table 3.3 The additionality of UDG and UDAG assistance

	Projects in categories of deadweight (%)			
	Full	*Medium*	*Low*	*No*
UDG	8	11	25	57
UDAG	8	13	15	64

Source: PSMRC (1988); HUD (1982).

The findings suggest that the level of deadweight in the UDG programme was approximately the same as that in the UDG programme's American counterpart UDAG. Research in the United States found that 79 per cent of projects assisted under UDAG were unlikely to have gone ahead in the absence of the funding provided by the UDAG programme (HUD, 1982) (Table 3.3). This compares with 82 per cent of the UDG projects in the sample for which assistance was thought to have been necessary.

An analysis of the sample of UDG schemes by project type showed that nearly half of the business expansion schemes had not in the researchers' view required UDG assistance in order to go ahead. This was a much higher level of deadweight than was found to be associated with any other type of project (industrial speculative building, commercial developments or housing schemes), and it seemed that, on these grounds at least, business expansion schemes had represented poor value for money.

Leverage Achieved by Grants

Since one of the major objectives of the UDG, URG and City Grant programmes is to lever private sector investment into inner city areas, leverage ratios are a key indicator of their effectiveness. The evaluation of a sample of UDG-assisted projects undertaken by PSMRC showed that the 65 sampled projects had cost a total of £83 million. £68 million of the total cost had been met by the private sector and £15 million had been provided by UDG assistance. This represents an impressively high private to public sector leverage ratio of 4.4:1 (Table 3.4).

However, as explained above, the researchers considered that several schemes would have gone ahead even if UDG assistance had not been provided. In these cases it was clear that the private sector investment in a scheme could not be attributed to the existence of the

Table 3.4 Leverage ratios in sampled projects

	Total investment (£m)		Private: public leverage ratio
	Public	Private	
All 65 projects	15.3	67.8	4.4:1
Excluding projects with medium/ high deadweight	15.3	37.7	2.5:1

Source: PSMRC (1988).

UDG programme. On the whole, the projects which the researchers considered had not required UDG assistance had much higher leverage ratios than those with little or no deadweight. As a result, when the private sector investment in projects with high levels of deadweight was excluded from the analysis the overall leverage ratio for the 65 sampled projects fell to just 2.5:1 (Table 3.4). This suggests that, if the projects in the sample were typical of those in the programme as a whole, the UDG programme was significantly less successful in attracting additional private sector into inner city areas than some figures published by central government have suggested (Johnson, 1988).

Employment Impacts

Projects funded by UDG, URG or City Grant can have a number of employment impacts. All schemes will provide temporary jobs in their construction phases, and most (with the exception of housing developments) are expected to create new permanent jobs or to safeguard existing permanent jobs once they are completed. It has been suggested that UDG and URG between them had provided nearly 30,000 jobs by 1988 (HMSO, 1988). However, this is a somewhat meaningless statistic because in order to identify the employment impacts of programmes such as UDG and URG it is necessary to define carefully what is meant by the term 'jobs provided by a development' (Bovaird, Gregory and Martin, 1988). In particular it is important to distinguish between jobs which are accommodated in completed developments but which would have existed in the absence of the programme, and jobs which would not have been created without the funding provided by the programme (Martin, 1988a).

The evaluation of the UDG programme undertaken by PSMRC

found that the 45 non-housing projects in the chosen sample accommodated a total of 3,383 permanent full-time equivalent (FTE) jobs (Martin, 1988b). This was just under 80 per cent of the total number of jobs which the D.o.E. appraisers had expected the projects to accommodate when they were completed (Figure 3.4). Since several of the projects were not fully operational at the time of the evaluation, there might have been a slight increase in the total number of jobs accommodated in the medium term. These findings might therefore be taken to indicate that the UDG-assisted projects in the sample had broadly met the employment targets set for them. However, the number of jobs *accommodated* in a completed project is not an accurate reflection of the number of jobs actually *created* by the UDG programme.

These are two reasons for this. Firstly, it is likely that some of the jobs accommodated in the completed projects would have been accommodated in alternative premises if the UDG-assisted developments had not taken place. Secondly, since several of the projects in the sample had not actually required UDG assistance in order to

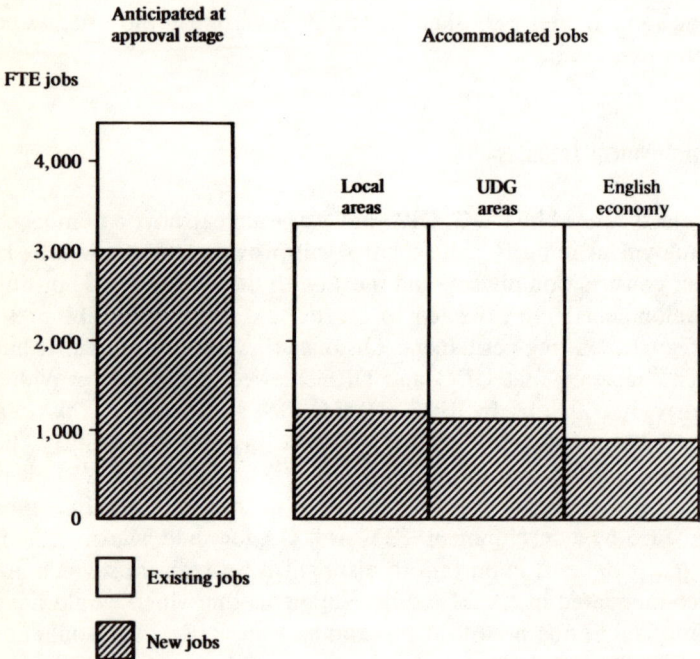

Figure 3.4 Anticipated and outturn jobs accommodated in sample UDG-assisted projects (Source: Martin, 1988b)

proceed, the jobs accommodated in these developments could not be attributed to the UDG programme. When allowance was made for these two factors, the number of new jobs which could be considered to have been created by UDG assistance fell to 687 FTEs (which was only a fifth of the total number of jobs accommodated in the developments) (Figure 3.5).

The D.o.E. appraisers had anticipated that the projects would create 3,000 new jobs. Since very few jobs had been safeguarded by the sampled projects, it was clear that the permanent employment impacts of these developments had been greatly overestimated at the appraisal stage. If the same is true of all UDG-assisted projects, it is clear that official estimates of the employment impacts of the programme considerably overstate their importance. However, this situation is unlikely to be unique to the UDG programme. It seems that the employment impacts of a number of similar grant regimes have been similarly overestimated, and this in turn points to the need for more accurate definitions of new jobs and more precise methods of measuring employment impacts (Martin, 1988a).

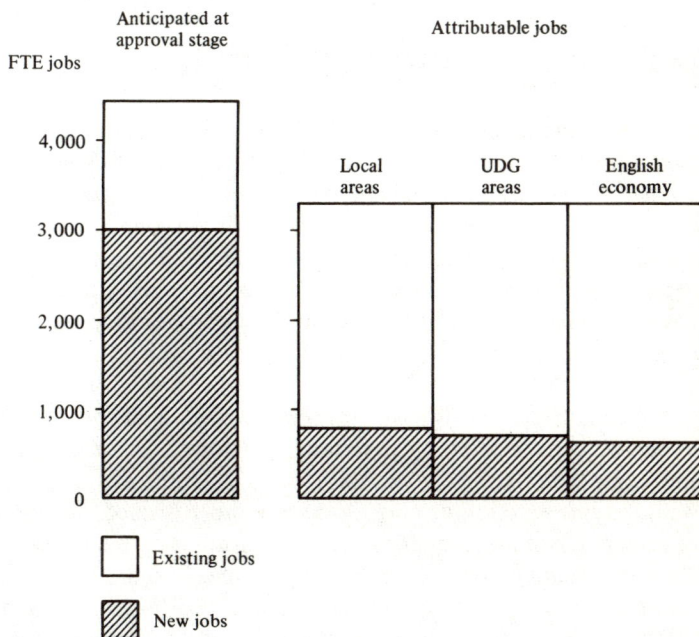

Figure 3.5 Anticipated and outturn jobs attributable to UDG assistance in sample projects (Source: Martin, 1988b)

When employment impacts were studied by project type, it became clear that business expansion schemes had created far fewer jobs than any other category of scheme. There were two reasons for this. Firstly, nearly half the business expansion schemes had failed to produce or safeguard any permanent jobs at all. Secondly, since two-thirds of business expansion projects were deemed to have not required UDG assistance in order to proceed, very few of the jobs which they had provided could be attributed to the UDG funding which they had received.

In addition to the permanent jobs provided by the sampled projects, 2,487 man/woman FTE temporary jobs had been associated with the construction phases of the developments. It was calculated that some 1,925 (77 per cent) would not have existed in the absence of the UDG programme. This represented a much smaller shortfall on the number of jobs which had been anticipated at the appraisal stage than was the case for permanent jobs, and reflects the fact that temporary employment impacts are usually much easier to predict . than are permanent impacts.

CONCLUSION: THE PROSPECTS FOR CITY GRANT

The evidence of the evaluation of the UDG programme discussed above suggested that relatively few projects (less than 20 per cent) which had been given grant had not in fact required UDG assistance. With the exception of business expansion schemes which involved much higher levels of deadweight than other projects, it did not therefore seem to be necessary to tighten up the existing appraisal procedures. The main problem with the UDG programme was not that public money was being wasted on schemes which the private sector would otherwise have funded, but that the level of take-up of the grants on offer was so low that far fewer projects had gone ahead than had been anticipated by government and the scale of benefits produced by the programme was therefore disappointing.

With the introduction of City Grant a number of modifications have been made in an attempt to increase the number of successful projects which are facilitated by the programme. In order to reduce the time taken to process applications, the D.o.E. has stated that decisions will now be reached within ten weeks of an application being accepted for formal appraisal. In addition, developers will now be able to submit brief details of a proposed scheme to D.o.E. regional offices to confirm that they are likely to meet with the objectives of the City Grant programme, before working up a detailed application. Developers who go on to submit schemes for full appraisal will be told within a month whether their proposed development does in fact fit the eligibility criteria laid down for City Grant. It is hoped that this will help to avoid a great deal of time and effort being put into a project by the developer before he has some indication of its likely chances of success. The D.o.E. also hopes that by excluding local authorities from any formal role in the process it will be possible to cut down on the time it takes for bids from the private sector to reach Marsham Street.

However, although these changes may speed up the appraisal process, they represent little more than a 'fine-tuning' of the system. Experience with the UDG programme suggests that far more radical steps would be required to lead to a substantial increase in the number of successful applications for City Grant. Since it is clear that the role of the local authorities was crucial in bringing forward potential schemes from the private sector, it is possible that, although their exclusion from the formal City Grant process may speed up the appraisal of those applications which are made, it may also lead to a reduction in the total number of bids which are submitted to the D.o.E., and therefore prove to be counterproductive. In view of this and the evidence that UDG had resulted in only limited job generation, it seems that City Grant may make only a modest contribution towards the regeneration of inner city areas.

In spite of these problems there are, however, some hopeful signs. It seems that UDG-assisted projects resulted in a number of benefits apart from job creation which have to date received less attention than they merit. In particular, the potential spin-offs from environmental improvements projects may have been underestimated. With the incorporation of private sector Derelict Land Grant into the City Grant regime, such impacts may now achieve a higher profile. Coincidentally, environmental improvement schemes may be the easiest projects to 'get off the ground' in more depressed regions and this may therefore help to overcome the problem of a lack of take-up of grant in these areas.

Finally, regardless of its possible shortcomings the continued existence of City Grant seems to be assured. Not only is it an attempt to lever in private sector finance in its own right (and therefore in line with the main thrust of the present Government's strategy for promoting urban regeneration), but it is also one of the main policy instruments available to the newly formed Urban Development Corporations (UDCs), which are the flagships of current inner city policy. Many of the first City Grant applications received by the D.o.E. have come from areas covered by UDCs, and this alone is likely to ensure that the programme continues to be seen as an important method of promoting local economic development in urban areas over the next few years.

REFERENCES

Bovaird, A., Gregory, D. and Martin, S.J. (1988) 'Performance measurement in urban economic development', *Public Money and Management*, Vol. 8, No. 4, pp. 17–22.

Campbell, M. (1988) 'Urban problems and policies in Mrs Thatcher's third term', *Local Economy*, Vol. 3, No. 2, pp. 79–83.

Cmnd 9143 Public Expenditure White Paper.

Cmnd 9428 Public Expenditure White Paper.

D.o.E. (1982) *FIG Briefing: Note of Topics Studied by FIG*, Inner Cities Directorate.

D.o.E. (1984) *Urban Development Grant Guidance Notes*, Inner Cities Directorate.

D.o.E. (1988a) *A Simplified Grant Scheme*, Consultation Paper, Inner Cities Directorate.

D.o.E. (1988b) *City Grant Guidance Notes*, Inner Cities Directorate.

Gregory, D. and Martin, S.J. (1988) 'Issues in the evaluation of inner city programmes', *Local Economy*, Vol. 2, No. 4, pp. 237–50.

HMSO (1988) *Action for Cities*, London, HMSO.

HUD (1982) *An Impact Evaluation of the Urban Development Action Grant Programme*, Washington, US Department of Housing and Urban Development.

Johnson, D. (1988) 'An evaluation of the Urban Development Grant Programme', *Local Economy*, Vol. 2, No. 4, pp. 251–85.

Martin, S.J. (1988a) 'Evaluating local economic initiatives', unpublished Ph.D. thesis, Aston University.

Martin, S.J. (1988b) 'New jobs in the inner city: an evaluation of the employment impacts of projects assisted under the Urban Development Grant Programme', Paper presented to the ESRC Regional and Urban Economics Seminar, Glasgow University, January.

PSMRC (1988) *An Evaluation of the Urban Development Grant Programme*, London, HMSO.

CHAPTER 4

Urban Development Corporations

Michael Parkinson and Richard Evans

INTRODUCTION: PRIVATISM AND URBAN POLICY

Three terms of Mrs Thatcher's Government have produced a sea change in policy for Britain's cities. From the rediscovery of the inner city 'problem' in the late 1960s until her accession in 1979, urban policy under both Labour and Conservative administrations rested on two shared assumptions. Firstly, policy was designed as much to provide social and welfare support services to the victims of economic change in the inner cities as to create wealth in those areas. Second, since disinvestment by the private sector was seen as the cause of many inner city problems, the public sector, including local authorities, was regarded as the natural mechanism to promote urban reconstruction.

In the 1980s, however, the Conservative Government has increasingly defined the public sector as the cause of inner cities' problems and the private sector as the solution. Apart from morally exhorting the private sector to become more involved in the inner cities, the Government has introduced a wide range of initiatives – City Action Teams, Task Forces, Enterprise Zones, Freeports, Urban Development, Urban Regeneration and City Grants, and Urban Development Corporations (UDCs) – which attempt to give the private sector a lead role in urban policy (Lawless, 1987, 1988; Moore and Pierre, 1988). Indeed 'regeneration' is now the Government's goal, as wealth creation has replaced the distribution of welfare as the aim of urban policy. This privatization of policy has led to increased emphasis upon efficiency as opposed to equity in government programmes. Equally important, the Government has decreed that local authorities are incapable of leading the recovery of their cities and is gradually stripping them of a wide range of their powers in finance, housing, education, social services, planning, and economic development (Parkinson, 1987.)

The initiative which most dramatically articulates the Government's vision – the jewel in the crown of Mrs Thatcher's urban strategy – is the creation of the Urban Development Corporations. First introduced by Michael Heseltine into the London and Liverpool docklands in 1981, Development Corporations have since been extended to Bristol, Tyneside and Wearside, Teesside, Manchester, Cardiff, Sheffield, Leeds, the Black Country, and Trafford Park. For the Conservative Government, Development Corporations are an idea whose time has come: they are designated, empowered, financed by and directly accountable to central government. They displace local authorities as the planning authorities in the areas where they operate. As non-elected bodies, UDCs are intended to eliminate the political uncertainty of local democracy which, in the Government's view, is a major deterrent to private investment in the largely Labour-controlled cities (House of Lords Select Committee, 1981). Government financial support for Development Corporations has been sustained as mainstream funding for local government has fallen during the 1980s. But this public funding is primarily intended to provide incentives to the private sector by reducing the costs and risk of investing in the inner cities.

The Government also expects the UDCs to operate in a different way from the institutions previously responsible for regeneration. Despite the broad range of goals originally allocated to the UDCs, they tend to emphasize a property-led form of regeneration which dilutes wider goals of urban policy. The model assumes a free-wheeling, entrepreneurial approach in contrast to the alleged bureaucratic style of local authorities with their traditional emphasis upon planning as development control. Equally heavy emphasis is placed upon the need for immediate action and visible results, often 'flagship' projects, to improve the environment and image of an area and, again in the Government's view, to generate the confidence needed to attract private sector investment.

The UDCs' achievements in the 1980s, especially in London, in physically transforming their docklands are constantly paraded before an international audience as dramatically successful examples of urban regeneration. But despite this preoccupation with success stories, the 'cranes in the sky' phenomenon, the second wave of Development Corporations was announced before there had been any systematic evaluation of the impact, costs and benefits of the two original UDCs. This chapter attempts to provide a preliminary assessment of their achievements.

In many respects the first two UDCs represent the extreme ends of a continuum in terms of the problem of regenerating derelict urban areas. The London Docklands Development Corporation (LDDC) was asked to regenerate an area which, no matter how physically derelict, lay within a mile of one of the largest financial centres in the world economy, and one which was about to undergo an economic explosion as a consequence of the deregulation of the domestic financial market and the larger internationalization of world financial markets during the 1980s. The Merseyside Development Corporation (MDC), by contrast, was asked to induce a private-sector-led economic recovery at the heart of one of the most economically depressed cities in Western Europe, which had suffered a massive withdrawal of private capital during the previous three decades, enduring a series of political traumas in the process (Parkinson, 1985). In this sense, Liverpool is the most testing case of the Government's strategy. But in terms of the problems facing the new UDCs, which are mainly located outside the booming South-East, it may be a more relevant guide to their future prospects than is London.

THE ORIGINS OF THE UDCs

The UDCs were created by the 1980 Local Government Planning and Land Act. The LDDC was given control of eight square miles of derelict dockland to the east of the City of London which took in parts of Newham, Southwark and Tower Hamlets. In Liverpool, the MDC was given control of a similar but much smaller and more fragmented collection of dockland areas (865 acres) spread across three local authorities. In some respects, the two dockland areas had suffered similar economic fates. In their heyday they were the two largest enclosed dock systems in the world. But shifting patterns of international trade, competition from other ports, the development of alternative modes of transport, containerization and industrial relations problems led to their rapid decline in the 1960s, with severe knock-on effects in related manufacturing industries such as food processing, chemicals and engineering. The surrounding areas consequently lost vast numbers of jobs and acquired high rates of unemployment. The physical consequences of the dock closures – extensive environmental deterioration and physical dereliction – had been apparent for many years. Redevelopment was frustrated by poor communications, fragmented patterns of land ownership and the unrealistically high 'hope' values aspired to by many of the original owners.

But there were also significant differences between the original UDCs. The MDC took control of an area which was physically isolated from the rest of the city and in which very few people lived or worked. Despite the attempts that had been made by Liverpool City Council and Merseyside County Council during the 1970s, there were no realistic development plans for the area. By contrast the LDDC inherited a very large area in which thousands of people lived and worked and for which there was already a redevelopment strategy, the London Docklands Strategic Plan, which had been agreed by the GLC, local authorities and the D.o.E. In contrast to Liverpool, community opinion in the London docklands had been given a sharp focus by the D.o.E.'s creation of the Docklands Forum in 1974, which has since continued to represent local views. Equally, local authority opinion has been mobilized through the Docklands Consultative Committee, which was set up in 1982 with the GLC to monitor the LDDC's activities. Such differences in context and political complexity have fundamentally affected the way the UDCs have operated and performed.

The Government justification for the UDCs was that the docklands needed a single-minded agency with limited objectives and operating in a closely defined area, which, using simple administrative procedures and free from political uncertainty, could regenerate the area more rapidly than could local authorities (Adcock, 1984). The UDCs were given four broad tasks: to bring land and buildings into effective use; to encourage the development of new and existing commerce; to create an attractive environment; and to ensure that housing and social facilities were available to encourage people to live and work in the same area. The UDCs were created for an indefinite period but the assumption was that they would complete their work in under fifteen years (Local Government Planning and Land Act, 1980).

UDCs have extensive land-acquisition, financial and planning powers (D.o.E., 1986). They can acquire land by either compulsory purchase or voluntary agreement. But they can also be given control of land by the Secretary of State vesting it in them. The UDCs are responsible for development control within their area and have the power to decide planning applications. They also have powers to operate outside their immediate boundaries if they think it necessary to achieve regeneration. The MDC is governed by a board of nine people, including mainly businessmen, some academics, senior local politicians and the Chief Executive of the MDC. Local authorities can nominate members but they serve in an individual capacity and do not represent the local authorities. The composition of the LDDC is similar, though with even greater private sector representation, particularly from the construction industry. The UDCs have substantial annual budgets and can also borrow from the national loan fund for commercial purposes. The MDC's annual budget has been £25–30 million annually; the LDDC's budget is £60–80 million. UDCs can also use the receipts from the sale of their land. This has become a major source of income for the LDDC in particular, amounting to £38 million in 1986/7.

EVALUATING THE UDCs

Assessing the records of the UDCs is problematic on three counts. The choice of criteria for measuring the 'success' of the UDCs is obviously critical yet they differ widely. The Government, for example, has been preoccupied with physical renewal and the extent to which public expenditure has levered in private investment. This creates a further difficulty. The UDCs have not collected adequate data for the systematic monitoring of the impact of their programmes. Finally, as other commentators have observed (Church, 1988), evaluation of the socio-economic impact of the UDCs is complicated by the coexistence of other initiatives (for example, the Isle of Dogs Enterprise Zone), the definition of boundaries, and the fact that any assessment is bound to be interim. Despite these difficulties, this assessment addresses three key policy issues.

1 *Efficiency*: what have the UDCs achieved in terms of the physical regeneration of their areas and how successful have they been in creating private sector confidence and investment?

2 *Equity*: to what extent have the benefits of regeneration, especially job creation, achieved by the UDCs been widely or equitably shared?

3 *Accountability*: how have the UDCs worked with other agencies in their area, and in particular how responsive have they been to their local authorities and communities?

The answers to those questions will allow us to judge whether UDCs are appropriate agencies for regeneration which can successfully be transferred to other areas.

Physical Regeneration and Investment

Even their critics accept that both UDCs, albeit with varying degrees of success, have transformed their impoverished and degraded physical environments in a very short time, though the LDDC has clearly had the greater success. The strength of the market demand in London has allowed the LDDC to adopt an entrepreneurial, demand-led approach where its expenditure has leveraged substantial private investment mainly for commercial and residential development. Since 1981 the LDDC claims that £440 million of public money has attracted over £4.4 billion of private sector money, a gearing ratio of 10:1 (LDDC, 1988).

In six years it had redeveloped over 2 square miles of derelict docklands. Three-quarters of the LDDC's budget has been spent on land reclamation and infrastructure, including the Docklands light railway and the city airport. This investment has paved the way for the construction of 5 million square feet of office and retail floorspace and 8,800 housing units. Major redevelopments costing in the region of £2 billion are planned for the Royal Docks complex which will provide shops, hotels, houses, leisure facilities and a science park. Most impressive of the current developments is the Canary Wharf project, currently the largest redevelopment in Europe, where planned expenditure of £3 billion will by mid-1990 result in over 10 million square feet of office space, which the LDDC claims will provide 50,000 office jobs. The LDDC and the Department of Transport plan to spend a further £700 million by 1995 on developing the transportation system of the docklands (National Audit Office, 1988).

The LDDC has already attracted a wide range of activity into the docklands, including printing and publishing, tourism, media and communication, and financial services and banking. It has dramatically diversified the housing stock in its area. Whereas it inherited 11,000 council houses which constituted over 80 per cent of its stock, over 85 per cent of the new 8,800 homes in the docklands have been built by the private sector for owner-occupation. By contrast, however, the LDDC has made very limited provision for, or investment in, community facilities.

The MDC found that major expenditure on infrastructure and reclamation of vast tracts of derelict land did not have the same effect on the private sector's willingness to invest in Merseyside. The mere provision of infrastructure has not automatically stimulated industrial demand in a depressed regional economy. For example, by 1988 £170 million of public spending had attracted only £25 million of private investment (MDC, 1988). Indeed, in the mid-1980s the absence of demand for industrial development forced the MDC to abandon its original development strategy. Originally, the MDC had designated 55 per cent of its land for industrial development and 40 per cent for commercial, residential and recreational use, with 5 per cent left for port-related activity (MDC, 1981). In 1984 lack of activity on the industrial front forced the MDC to substitute a tourist- and leisure-based strategy for its original plan. The National Audit Office subsequently criticized the MDC for this alleged vacillation in finding the right strategy (National Audit Office, 1988). But the MDC could legitimately reply that the market, rather than its own failings, constrained industrial development on Merseyside in the early 1980s.

However, there were more positive reasons for the MDC to alter its original strategy. If industrial demand proved weaker than anticipated, demand in the tourism and leisure sectors was stronger. By 1984 the tourist potential of the area had been underlined by three successful initiatives – the restoration of Albert Dock, the International Garden Festival and the International Tall Ships race – which each attracted over two million visitors. Since then the MDC has pursued a water-based tourist and leisure strategy which by 1988 was showing some signs of success. The centrepiece is the Albert Dock, the largest Grade 1 listed building in the country, which having been saved from demolition and restored at a cost of £25 million now houses the Tate Gallery, a Maritime Museum, Granada Television's news studio, and upmarket offices, shops and flats.

Equally important, the success of the Albert Dock encouraged major contracts on the adjacent Kings Dock site, which will incorporate an ice arena, shopping centre, hotel and multi-screen cinema. This is an important indicator of the leisure potential on the waterfront and is also evidence that substantial investment of public money initially may well attract future private investment. In sharp contrast to earlier developments, £5 million of public money should attract £21 million from private developers in the Kings Dock development. There have been other successes. The Brunswick

Industrial Park houses 90 small firms; a marina has been developed in the former derelict docks; about 100 low-income rental houses have been provided; and over 200 flats at the top end of the Merseyside housing market have also been sold.

A number of issues, however, remain unresolved. Many of the shops and restaurants in the Albert Dock operate at subsidized rents and their future remains uncertain as these rents rise to market level. Equally, the International Garden Festival site which successfully attracted over 3 million visitors in the initial year on a subsidized basis has since remained problematic. A private operator went bankrupt in 1985 and the MDC has had difficulty attracting further developers to manage the site which remains unused and sealed off for much of the year.

Despite these reservations, both UDCs have had major success in physically regenerating their areas, which look dramatically different from seven years earlier. The LDDC's aggressive marketing campaign has clearly transformed the poor image of the docklands and persuaded people that it is a good place to live and work. Progress in Liverpool has been much slower, although sustained public investment has now begun to attract substantial private sector interest in the area. However, future development will depend on the growing but fragile demand being sustained in the local economy. This remains a less certain prospect than in London.

Who Benefits?

If there has been substantial physical regeneration of the docklands, the next obvious question is: who has benefited from it? As the House of Commons Employment Committee rightly, if somewhat blandly, noted, 'Urban development corporations cannot be regarded as a success if buildings and land are regenerated but the local community are bypassed and do not benefit from regeneration' (House of Commons Employment Committee, 1988). The UDCs have produced three different kinds of benefit: jobs, houses, and improved amenities and environment.

Employment and Training The LDDC claims that in its first six years it increased the number of full- and part-time jobs in the docklands from 27,000 to 35,000, a net gain of 8,000 (LDDC, 1988). Despite this, however, the number of unemployed people in the area in 1988 remained at over 4,000 – more than when the LDDC was designated. Equally, unemployment rates in the three dockland boroughs remained at over 14 per cent, among the highest in London (House of Commons Employment Committee, 1988). The LDDC's own data help explain the paradox. Almost 80 per cent of the jobs created between 1981 and 1985 were in the service sector, requiring skills in office administration, printing and media services, electronics, retailing and distribution. But most local workers had skills in traditional manufacturing or dock-related industries, where the 7,000 jobs lost in the area between 1981 and 1987 were concentrated.

The problem is compounded by the fact that most of the new jobs have been taken by commuters into the area and by people who already had jobs. Indeed, 65 per cent of the 'new' jobs created in the docklands were actually existing jobs transferred from elsewhere. Future growth may help the local community equally little. Consultants have predicted that only 1,800 of the 47,000 jobs which it is estimated may be created by the Canary Wharf development are likely to go to local residents, and that over 70 per cent of them could be in part-time, low-skill jobs like cleaning (Peat, Marwick, Mitchell and Co., 1986).

The UDCs are not required to provide training directly. However, both have supported other organizations which do so. The LDDC's record of support for the retraining of local residents so that they can compete for new jobs is distinctly uneven. Despite the shortage of skilled labour in the construction industry and in technical, office and personal skills, in 1987/8 the LDDC actually supported the provision of fewer than 3,000 training places. Indeed, between 1981 and 1987 the LDDC allocated only £2.5 million in total for training. After a critical consultant's report in 1987 (Peat, Marwick, Mitchell and Co., 1987), the LDDC committed itself to boost its efforts in this field and earmarked £18 million for training over the next five years.

More generally, after this date sustained community and media criticism of its record and the realization of the growing needs for social infrastructure made the LDDC more conscious of these employment and training issues. It subsequently attempted, for example, to improve the quality of its information on training needs, to liaise more closely with the Manpower Services Commission and Local Education Authorities, and to seek to negotiate local recruitment agreements between developers and local authorities. Contracts signed with private developers and local authorities mean that a significant proportion of jobs created by the Royal Docks and Canary Wharf developments will now go to local residents. However, as the Commons Employment Committee pointed out, these relatively modest developments came rather late in the day and might have been incorporated in the LDDC's initial strategy.

The LDDC's support for existing industrial activity within its boundaries has been equally limited. It has provided only £2.5 million in grants and loans to 200 existing companies in docklands, allegedly creating 2,100 new jobs and safeguarding 1,500 existing ones (LDDC, 1988). The property-led approach adopted by the LDDC has arguably harmed indigenous industry by generating rising land values which have led many firms in the docklands to asset strip and sell out. It has also forced many out by compulsory purchase. The loss of industrial floorspace in the area has serious implications for the local community given the structure of the local skill base (Roger Tym and Partners, 1987). Equally, incentives in the Enterprise Zone have benefited property developers rather than industrialists because of their tendency to increase rents to compensate for the absence of rates (Puddephat, 1988). Again sustained criticism of its record in this field led the LDDC to shift its policy in 1987 and its future approach may differ. Nevertheless, the Commons Employment Committee subsequently stressed that the LDDC should pay greater attention to the needs both of local industry and of ethnic minorities and women in future (House of Commons Employment Committee, 1988).

The MDC's record on job creation has to be seen in a different context from that of the LDDC. The MDC operates in a much smaller area which contains very few residents and which in recent times has provided very few jobs. In 1981 there were only 1,800 jobs in its boundaries. This had increased to almost 2,800 in 1987, a net gain of 1,000 in office functions, retailing and small firms in the nursery workshops. In addition the MDC estimates that it supports over 700 construction jobs annually. The MDC also operates a grants programme which provides support to 96 firms, which it reports has created 300 jobs and safeguarded 600 existing ones. The MDC has also supported training programmes, which provided 8,000 places in 1987. Even though much of the training was short term, the MDC's record in this respect compares rather favourably with that of the LDDC.

But if job creation was the ultimate goal of MDC policy, its return on the £170 million so far invested has been small. It has created 1,700 jobs but during the same period over 800 existing jobs have been lost in an area which lies at the heart of three parliamentary constituencies with some of the highest unemployment rates in Britain. On the other hand, it can be argued that the MDC's strategy of focusing upon leisure and tourism does supply semi-skilled jobs which are more suited to the skills of the local population than those produced by the LDDC strategy. The MDC has also been more sympathetic than the LDDC to the interests of existing firms in the area. Its refurbishment of industrial units in the docks has been successful and well received. Equally, the lack of pressure for land has meant that, in contrast to the LDDC, the MDC has not had to force existing firms to quit the area.

The MDC insists that most of its original expenditure was intended not to create jobs in the short term but to physically regenerate and create confidence in the area and so attract future private sector investment. It would argue that, given the depressed local economy and derelict nature of the docklands areas it inherited, it is too soon to assess the success of its strategy. There is truth in this claim. But equally, the MDC in its first seven years was not a major generator of jobs and the individual cost of those created was extremely high. One section of the local community feels especially discriminated against by the MDC's failure in this respect. The local Liverpool black population is concentrated in Toxteth, less than a mile from the docklands. That community has always argued that the MDC was one important part of the Government's response to the Toxteth riots of 1981. However, they insist that the black community benefited very little from the MDC's regeneration of the area. It is true that the MDC has made little concerted effort either to ensure that the neighbouring black community benefited from renewal or even to monitor the impact of its programmes upon them, a criticism specifically made by the Commons Select Committee.

Housing   Housing has been the most politically controversial issue in the London docklands since the LDDC took control over virtually the entire housing land reserve of three local authorities. The LDDC's approach has proved unpopular locally for two main reasons. In contrast to existing local authority plans, the LDDC explicitly encouraged the development of private housing so as to diversify the existing housing stock which hitherto was 80 per cent council housing. This caused resentment as it focused provision at the top end of the housing market. Although it has made some effort to provide affordable housing, the strength of demand in the housing market has undermined it. Some 42 per cent of the housing built for owner-occupation at the time of sale was under £40,000. However, pressures of the housing market have subsequently forced up the market price so that only 5 per cent of that housing is reckoned to be affordable by the local community, 75 per cent of whom earn less than £10,000 a year (National Audit Office, 1988; House of Commons Employment Committee, 1988). The fact that the LDDC has no legal responsibility to rehouse those local residents who are displaced by its policies has added to community resentment. Continued criticism of LDDC policy led it to introduce a social housing initiative in 1986 aimed at providing new and refurbished housing for rent and shared ownership. But the image of highly paid incomers benefiting from a rapidly inflated housing market at the expense of low-income local people is a broadly accurate assessment of the LDDC's early record.

As with employment, the MDC's record on housing has to be seen in a different context from that of the LDDC. Liverpool docklands are essentially non-residential and the Liverpool housing market in the early 1980s was less buoyant, creating less pressure upon the MDC to provide housing. Nevertheless, the MDC does have modest plans for residential development. It has, for example, provided land for a housing association to build 100 units of low-income co-operative housing. It has also provided a handful of luxury homes near the original Garden Festival site and 200 upmarket flats in the rehabilitated Albert Dock complex. The fact that the MDC's housing programme is relatively modest, that is has a mix of public and private provision and that it has not displaced existing residents has prevented housing becoming a major political issue in Liverpool as it did in London.

The Public Environment   It can also be argued that the MDC's achievement on environmental renewal has benefited a broader public than has the LDDC. The use of the docklands as a tourist and leisure area has opened up vast stretches of the Liverpool waterfront to the public for the first time for 150 years. The provision of prestigious cultural facilities has also given the area a new focus and purpose, as well as improving the image of Liverpool with many outsiders. There is a further parochial reason why much of the MDC's achievements are locally valued. For complex political reasons, Liverpool City Council historically has had a relatively poor record in maintaining its physical environment, including its housing stock (Parkinson, 1985). The MDC, by contrast, pays great attention to environmental appearance. Expressed more generally, the MDC is a centrally imposed and locally unaccountable body which nevertheless pays considerable attention to the wishes of its consumers, whilst the elected local authority is regarded by some as having provided its ratepayers with an inferior service (Audit Commission, 1988). This contrast has muted local criticism of the achievements of the MDC despite lingering local concerns about its lack of local accountability.

By comparison the LDDC has a far more problematic local standing. Its achievements in physical renewal have frequently served to emphasize the gap between the new upmarket residents and consumers and the original low-income community by, for example, privatizing the waterfront areas. Although the LDDC belatedly recognized the need for expenditure on social infrastructure, prior to 1987 it allocated very little land for community facilities such as health clinics, leisure complexes or schools. By 1988 the amount of commercial floorspace constructed was 25 times greater than that devoted to community facilities (Potter, 1988). In fact in the whole of the docklands, apart from LEA schools, there is only one publicly financed and operated building – the Isle of Dogs pumping station. Private control of development and the environment implies that the wider public or community interest cannot be easily represented in the debate about the use of public space. Indeed, the House of Commons Employment Committee concluded that the original local residents had paid the environmental price of urban regeneration with increased traffic, escalating house prices and the dislocation caused by rapid construction, while receiving few of the benefits.

Power and Accountability

The alleged failure of the local community to benefit substantially from regeneration has to be seen in the context of the UDCs' lack of accountability to local authorities or local people. Government policy for the UDCs – part of its growing disenchantment with, and emasculation of, local authorities – emphasizes their ability to act entrepreneurially, free from the constraints under which local authorities operate. But it poses the question: to what extent does the price of this freedom constitute a loss of democratic control?

The UDCs are financed by, and report to, central government. They are effectively the planning authorities for the areas under their control. Their boards consist mainly of private sector members. Local authorities' nominees act in an individual rather than a representative capacity. The boards operate in a shroud of secrecy:

the MDC does not even publish its corporate strategy. The UDCs, however claim that they are politically accountable to Parliament, administratively accountable to the Department of the Environment and financially accountable to the Treasury. Nevertheless, it remains the case that the extent to which they are genuinely accountable locally remains entirely within their own discretion.

The fact that UDCs have a specific task of regenerating their areas within a limited time span has profoundly affected the way they liaise with external groups. The LDDC, in particular, under its first Chief Executive deliberately avoided the adoption of a master plan, opting instead for a free-wheeling development strategy which provided basic infrastructure and only occasionally reserved sites for community use. The National Audit Office agreed with the Docklands Consultative Committee in criticizing the LDDC for neglecting strategic planning and for failing to set a context for development in the docklands (Docklands Consultative Committee, 1987, 1988). This reliance on market forces produced rapidly rising land values which in turn meant that land passed to the highest bidder. The loss of industrial floorspace for residential development, 1.8 million square feet in the Isle of Dogs for example, is the clearest and most controversial example of the process.

Local authorities and local communities in both cities almost inevitably felt excluded by the imposition of the UDCs, and uncertain whether and how to relate to them. For example, the original legislation required the UDCs to agree a code of consultation which would allow local views to be represented on development proposals. Although the MDC did get one agreed, the LDDC has not managed to do so. The latter's draft code proved unpopular because it focused mainly on obtaining responses to particular development proposals rather than broad policy issues. The dialogue which took place revolved around highly controversial private-sector-led initiatives and became increasingly acrimonious as local authorities and community groups sensed that the LDDC was engaging in public relations exercises rather than genuine consultations. A High Court judge reviewing the Canary Wharf proposal insisted that the code did not 'constitute even a promise of consultation' (House of Commons Employment Committee, 1988). The belief that they could not influence the LDDC's decisions eventually led two of the three docklands authorities to reject a seat on the board.

Relations with the local authorities have improved recently as the LDDC tacitly admitted that it had a wider responsibility than solely the enablement of private sector development. Nevertheless, the

Commons Employment Committee was extremely critical of the LDDC's failure to integrate these wider issues into its strategy until it had been over five years in existence. Relations with neighbouring communities range from sceptical to hostile, with the Docklands Consultative Committee remaining adamant that the Corporation must adopt a broader strategy. Equally, attempts to extract community gain, for example by incorporating local labour clauses in major construction projects, are laudable but not enough on their own. Developers are in a powerful bargaining position because they can threaten to take their investment elsewhere. Also individual authorities can be played off against each other with costs to the wider area. For example, Newham has accepted a retail development in the Royal Docks redevelopment scheme but there is concern that this could damage retailing in other parts of inner London (Docklands Forum, 1988).

The intense pressures for development in the London docklands have produced bitter conflicts between the LDDC and the surrounding local authorities and communities. In Liverpool, the slower pace of development and the lack of residents in the area has produced less charged relations between the MDC and local organizations. Political relations have never been as strained as in London. Despite original opposition to the principle of the MDC, all three local authorities have taken a place on the board. Although Liverpool withdrew when Labour took control of the city in 1983, the new administration became preoccupied by its dispute with the Thatcher Government and virtually ignored the MDC. By contrast, the MDC and local authority officials have consistently maintained good working relations, which is hardly surprising since many of the MDC's plans and personnel were drawn from local authorities. There have been very few disagreements over major planning issues, and there has been surprisingly little explicit community opposition to the MDC, except from the black community in Toxteth. The obvious success of the MDC in opening up the docklands for mass-market consumption has also restrained opposition.

CONCLUSION

The Government's extension of the UDC model to a further eight cities assumes that the first two have been successful and ought to be emulated. What does the record in London and Liverpool suggest? As we have seen, judgements depend upon one's definition of

[79]

regeneration, the goals of urban policy and the criteria employed to assess them. In many respects the UDC experience confirms the administrative adage that form follows function. Narrowly defined institutions have produced a narrow set of solutions. The UDCs have used their very extensive powers and privileges – direct access to central government resources and influence, relative autonomy and freedom from local political accountability – to achieve what Government required of them.

There is no doubt that both UDCs' achievements are physically and visibly impressive, although the more buoyant London economy has inevitably meant that the LDDC's achievements are on a much greater scale than Liverpool's. Substantial public pump-priming through expensive major infrastructure and aggressive marketing is transforming the image and status of London's, and now even Liverpool's, docklands from that of neglected backwater to stylish and fashionable environment. London docklands are witnessing the largest redevelopment project in Western Europe. The Liverpool waterfront is becoming a major tourist attraction and an international property company is planning to build a five-star hotel, which would be the first of any quality to be built in the city in over a decade.

However, physical change, no matter how dramatic, is only one measure of successful regeneration. This assessment has shown that on two other measures, the distribution of social and economic benefits and accountability to local communities, the records of the UDCs are more uneven. The LDDC record is particularly problematic. The benefits of much regeneration, in terms of jobs created, housing built or environmental improvements, have not flown to the original indigenous low-income community. Rather, that community has borne many of the costs of regeneration. The regeneration of the London docklands has in many ways increased inequality in access to both private and public goods in the area. This inequality of access reflects the inequality of power between the LDDC and its surrounding local authorities and community. The lack of direct local accountability has meant that the LDDC has been able to neglect local concerns and give preferential treatment to private sector interests.

By contrast the MDC, although less successful in attracting private sector interest, has a less controversial record on equity and accountability issues. Its tourism and leisure strategy has meant that the service sector jobs it has created, although limited in number and perhaps in quality, may be more appropriate to the skills of the local community. It has displaced relatively few existing firms. There were virtually no original residents to displace. The improvements in the environment, in contrast to London, have opened up large stretches of the waterfront formerly sealed off from the public. To some degree the relative success of the MDC in this field explains the lack of political controversy so evident in London.

By 1988 the MDC had become an institution opposed by many in principle but often approved of in practice. Nevertheless those principled objections remain. The MDC is not accountable to the local community, which cannot easily influence its priorities. Equally important, throughout the 1980s the MDC has been financially protected by a government which has dramatically cut resources to Liverpool City Council (Liverpool City Council, 1987). The Liverpool waterfront is being regenerated but the loss of public money for the physical and social infrastructure of the city as a whole threatens to undermine the Government's alleged commitment to urban regeneration. The MDC may be improving the city's front door. The risk is that Government cuts may lead the rest of the house to crumble (Parkinson, 1988).

These reservations have been reinforced by the Government's decision in 1988 to expand considerably the MDC's boundaries on both sides of the river. This will involve the MDC in areas where the local authorities do operate in providing the full range of services – schools, houses, training and social services. In other words, the task of the MDC will change from the solely physical to broader issues of social and human regeneration. Ironically, the experience of the LDDC also confirms that UDCs cannot avoid those larger issues: training, enterprise and business development, and the provision of housing and community facilities. The concentration upon physical regeneration alone became an inadequate response.

As the first two UDCs broadened their strategy, they had to form more elaborate working relationships with other agencies in the field. This clearly has implications for the way in which the new wave of UDCs will operate. They may find it difficult to operate as single-purpose agencies, exclusively pursuing physical regeneration with little regard for other policy goals. Indeed, the initial evidence from at least Sheffield and Teesside is that some new UDCs are defining their goals more broadly than London and Liverpool originally did and are making efforts to develop early alliances with their local authorities to complement their economic regeneration efforts. The local authorities also seem to be attempting to accommodate the new UDCs. In fact, in both London and Liverpool the realities of Government policy and resource allocation also encouraged local authorities to come to terms with the UDCs, however reluctantly, in the later years.

Such accommodations may make the original and new UDCs more effective in the future than in the past. But they also raise the question as to whether UDCs were necessary in the first instance if they eventually operate more like traditional institutions. This is reinforced by the observation that public–private partnerships to achieve urban regeneration have emerged in many cities during the 1980s without UDCs being 'imposed'. In other words, the Government's end of changing institutional relationships might have been achieved through different means, thus avoiding a damaging confrontation with local government.

The experiences of Liverpool and London also suggest that the nature of the local economy is crucial. The LDDC attracted substantial private sector investment primarily because of its unique location close to the city of London. The simple declaration of a UDC does not guarantee economic success if the local economy is not buoyant, as the Liverpool case powerfully demonstrates. The economic performance of the new UDCs will inevitably be affected by the market potential of the areas they inherit. In this respect at least, Liverpool not London may be a better guide to future UDC performance. The experience also confirms that although development in the UDCs is private sector oriented it is public sector led and financed. The case is obvious in Liverpool, but even in London private sector investment has been underwritten by massive public subsidies (Docklands Consultative Committee, 1988). Indeed, private sector demand for public subsidization of social and physical infrastructure in London docklands is actually increasing.

Most importantly, the UDC experience so far demonstrates that urban regeneration requires a wider vision and a larger package of programmes for finance, education, training and social provision than an agency devoted to physical regeneration of a narrowly defined area can assemble. UDCs may achieve limited goals. But they are not expansive enough to create balanced social and economic as well as physical regeneration. And they risk the creation of islands of private affluence amidst seas of public poverty. The UDCs have energized the debate about agencies and policies for urban regeneration. But they have yet to provide adequate solutions. The debate must continue.

REFERENCES

Adcock, B. (1984) 'Regenerating Merseyside Docklands: the Merseyside Development Corporation, 1981–4.' *Town Planning Review*, Vol. 55, No. 3, pp. 265–89.

Audit Commission (1988) Untitled report commissioned by Liverpool City Council.

Church, A. (1988) 'Urban regeneration in London Docklands: a five year policy review', *Environment and Planning C: Government and Policy, 1988*, Vol. 6, No. 2, pp. 187–208.

Docklands Consultative Committee (1987) *National Audit Office Study of Urban Development Corporations: A Response from the DDC*, London, Docklands Consultative Committee.

Docklands Consultative Committee (1988) *Six Years in London Docklands*, London, Docklands Consultative Committee.

Docklands Forum (1988) *Community Implications of Public/Private Sector Agreements*, London, Docklands Forum.

D.o.E. (1986) *Urban Development Corporations: Powers and Functions – Background Note*, London, HMSO.

House of Commons Employment Committee (1988) *The Employment Effects of the Urban Development Corporations*, Vols 1 and 2, London, HMSO.

House of Lords Select Committee (1981) *Report on London Docklands Development Corporation (Area and Constitution) Order 1980*, London, HMSO.

Lawless, P. (1987) 'Urban development', in Parkinson (1987).

Lawless, P. (1988) 'British inner urban policy post 1979: a critique', *Policy and Politics*, Vol. 16, No. 4, pp. 261–75.

Liverpool City Council (1987) *Merseyside Development Corporation: The Liverpool Experience*, Liverpool, Liverpool City Council Planning Department.

Local Government Planning and Land Act (1980) C65 Part XVI, Schedules 26–31.

LDDC (1988) *Annual Review, 1987/8 1*, London, London Docklands Development Corporation.

MDC (1981) *Initial Development Strategy*, Liverpool, Merseyside Development Corporation.

MDC (1988) *Annual Report and Financial Statements, 1987/8*, Liverpool, Merseyside Development Corporation.

[83]

Moore, M. and Pierre, J. (1988) 'Partnership or privatisation? The political economy of local economic restructuring', *Policy and Politics*, Vol. 16, No. 3, pp. 169–78.

National Audit Office (1988) *Department of the Environment: Urban Development Corporations*, London, HMSO.

Parkinson, M. (1985) *Liverpool on the Brink*, Policy Journals, Hermitage.

Parkinson, M. (ed.) (1987) *Reshaping Local Government*, Policy Journals, Hermitage.

Parkinson, M. (1988) 'Urban regeneration and Development Corporations: Liverpool style', *Local Economy*, August, pp. 109–18.

Peat, Marwick, Mitchell and Co. (1986) 'The financial and economic impact of the proposed Canary Wharf Development'. Report never officially published.

Peat, Marwick and McLintock (1988) 'Review of LDDC education, training and employment initiatives', unpublished report referred to in House of Commons Employment Committee (1988).

Potter, S. (1988) 'Inheritors of the new town legacy?', *Town and Country Planning*, Vol. 57, No. 11, pp. 296–301.

Puddephat, A. (1988), 'Docklands: the sharks move in', *Chartist*, Vol. 123, pp. 19–22.

Roger Tym and Partners (1987) *The Economy of the Isle of Dogs in 1987*, London, Isle of Dogs Neighbourhood Committee.

CHAPTER 5

Government Urban Economic Policy 1979–89: Problems and Potential

Graham Haughton and Peter Roberts

INTRODUCTION

The recent evolution of national urban policy in England is now well charted (see, for example, Hasluck, 1987; Stewart, 1987; Lawless, 1988a, 1988b). There is a considerable similarity between most of these overviews in that most of the judgements which have been passed by academics have concentrated on the problems of urban policies, especially in terms of their *product* (achieved impacts) and the level of policy co-ordination achieved between different government agencies. In contrast, the policy-specific evaluations which have been carried out for government departments have been much more positive about their product, largely restricting criticisms to ones of *process*, that is management (see, for example, JURUE, 1986; PA-CEC, 1987; PSMRC, 1988). If there is a consensus between these two types of study, it is that there is a lack of co-ordination between different grant regimes and between different government departments.

In this chapter, in contrast to both of these approaches, we argue that the criticism of lack of co-ordination, though warranted, is not a central issue. There are more fundamental issues which need to be dealt with, especially those relating to the definition and identification of urban problems and potentials. We would also argue that many of the existing commentaries have been insufficiently political, not in the sense that political views have not emerged from the reviews, but rather that they have not taken sufficient account of the political objectives of the Government's urban economic policy. In this chapter we examine some of the criticisms which have emerged from the 'right', the mainstream and the 'left', in the process attempting to give a more accurate picture of the pressures which have been and are being exerted on national urban policy.

It is also important to note at the outset that much of what is referred to as 'urban policy' is, in reality, a set of often fragmented policies for the inner areas of towns and cities. Whilst this may represent a justifiable focus on the core problems which confront urban areas, it also portrays a view of policy that divorces a consideration of the *problems* of urban areas from the *potentials* for their resolution. In addition, as the belated attention paid to the economic, social and environmental problems of outer city, peripheral public housing estates has shown, inner city policy runs the risk of displacing the narrowly defined (inner) urban area problem to the suburbs and periphery and then judging the problem of the (inner) urban area to have been solved. Although it is not argued that such a success has been claimed, it is, none the less, important to see the urban problem as a whole. It is essential for any spatial policy to be considered within the context which is provided by a wider view of the occurrence of problems and of the potentials for their resolution.

THE POLITICAL ECONOMY OF INNER CITY POLICY

Problem Definition

This chapter is mainly devoted to an evaluation of the overall effects of post-1979 Government policy for English inner urban areas, in spite of our belief that there is a need to integrate inner city policy with broader urban and regional policies. The success of policy is judged here largely according to central government's own explicit and implicit objectives for the future of the city, and in relation to the success of policy in alleviating, as opposed to displacing, inner city problems and in creating areas of potential. Where other studies have criticized urban policy from an alternative political perspective, we seek to examine the much more difficult question of whether urban policy has been successful in the Government's own terms.

Inevitably we must have some misgivings about this approach, if only in terms of evaluating the *overall* effectiveness of policy. 'Effectiveness' is a critical word in evaluation. Following the Financial Management Initiative, introduced in 1982, all government bodies have had to consider their expenditure in terms of the famous 'Three Es': economy, efficiency and effectiveness. Value For Money (VFM) became the key catchphrase, one used as a mantra by a certain type of civil servant, usually in obfuscation. Though laudable in itself – how can one argue against a 'better' utilization of public money? – this initiative has had some untoward consequences in relation to the ways in which policies are devised and implemented. Nowhere is this more obviously so than in the case of inner cities policy. Qualitative measures of success seemed to become overlooked in the remorseless numbers game of quantification, shortsightedly and unforgivably relegating in importance measures such as business confidence, quality of urban living and health. The main problem, though, is the one of the missing 'E' ingredient. Unmentioned is equality – who benefits from government policy. Worst of all, effectiveness has been very narrowly construed, too often perverted to mean effectiveness in, for instance, levering private sector investment into the inner city. (There are of course other 'E' words in the emerging vocabulary of the inner cities, most notably empowerment and emancipation – the latter usually as in 'from government', definitely not 'by government'!)

In embarking upon this evaluation it is important to recognize that many of the issues raised here have been dealt with in the past, only quickly to lose favour in official circles. In particular, the SNAP Report (McConaghy, 1972) outlined many of the key items then missing from the agenda for many inner city areas. This report built upon the earlier partial, often sectoral, analyses which had been converted into policy action, such as the Plowden Report (1967) on education, and the early work of the Community Development Projects (1969–78) programme. The message of SNAP was that an effective inner city policy should be conceived and implemented within the context of broader urban change and that it should be locally rooted. National government should concern itself with creating an administrative infrastructure and providing resources for effective policy. The locality should determine policy itself and exercise control over its implementation. So it can be argued that over and above the problem of evaluating the success of inner city policy, there remains the prior unanswered question of how best to construct and apply policy for urban areas. Recent experience in the United States confirms the SNAP diagnosis, strongly suggesting that locally rooted and determined strategies and policies have proved to be powerful instruments for effecting urban change (Sorkin, Ferris and Hadak, 1984).

Problem Identification

Problem inner city areas are spatially defined by local authorities in consultation with the Department of the Environment (D.o.E.). The D.o.E. does not publish the criteria by which it ranks urban areas for inclusion in its list of urban policy areas. However, it is possible to gain some idea of how these areas are administratively defined and evaluated from the published census notes, one of whose stated aims was 'to provide information about deprivation at the local level to help guide expenditure under the urban programme' (D.o.E. 1983). In these census notes, eight key variables are defined, drawn from the 1981 Census of Population, now outdated and inadequate for the purposes of inner city policy. Given the data constraints which undoubtedly do exist, the variables adopted do provide at least an indication of the areas which should be assisted. What is most disturbing, however, about these 'problem' variables is that with at least three of them it is difficult to evaluate the success of inner city, or indeed any other, policy by measuring their changes. Population change by the mid-1980s had taken on new complexions, requiring detailed social class or similar disaggregation. The influx of better-off people into certain very limited inner city districts had not just counterbalanced existing tendencies for inner city residents to move outwards, but also had, in part, created depopulation. Similarly, lack of basic amenities is much less important as an indicator of urban problems following mass urban housing clearance and rebuilding schemes. The problems of 1960s housing in particular are much less to do with (internal) amenities such as toilets, and much more to do with poor construction (physical deterioration of the building, use of asbestos, etc.) and external amenities and environment (safe passage, play areas, etc.). Finally, ethnic minorities are scarcely a problem *per se*. Certainly without disaggregation the category as a problem indicator is meaningless: in particular, it is necessary to be more place- and gender-specific. But more than this, to regard the category itself as a problem rather than the problems faced by (many of) those within it is to invert the problem. Therein lies the nub of resolving the inner city problem: *identifying the causes of the problems, and from this which groups are most affected.*

[88]

It is only from such an understanding that successful policy can emerge – and there is no indication that either the Enterprise Zone or the Urban Development Corporation policies emerged from such an understanding. Rather the opposite: both policies are posited on a belief that economic growth rather than overall urban development should be the prime objective of policy, and if this be either via or at the expense of disadvantaged groups then this might have to be tolerated. Politically, this could be justified by an under-researched belief in the trickle-down effect – that is, that no matter if the primary beneficiaries of government policy are the better-off, the secondary benefits will 'trickle-down' to the less well-off.

In a report to the D.o.E. (unpublished but publicly available in the Marsham Street library), ECOTEC (1987) point to the very limited range and quality of data available to policy makers. In particular, the inevitable heavy reliance on the Census of Population quickly becomes untenable as the data become outdated. The classic case is the London Borough of Wandsworth, which experienced a rapid turnaround in economic fortunes subsequent to the 1981 Census, and yet in 1989 still remained one of the 57 Urban Programme authority areas in England. This points to the very acute problem of assessing the *overall* impacts of government urban policy without data which are adequate, frequently collected and rapidly released.

A prerequisite to better government inner city policy making and evaluation is that better data are systematically and regularly collected and made available to policy makers. In addition, there is a need to think through much more thoroughly the causal relations in the creation of urban problems and the mechanisms for releasing urban potential. This latter aspect is particularly important in order to improve the effectiveness of government spending: we may have to move away from a single-minded obsession with problem identification to combine this with new measures and procedures for identifying areas of potential. But to do this requires movement from relatively static variables (for example, per cent of skilled workers/unemployed) to more dynamic ones (for example, change in per cent of skilled workers/unemployed). For this, more broadly ranging, more frequently collected and more detailed data are absolutely essential.

THE POLITICAL AGENDA FOR URBAN POLICY

The 'right-wing' critique of inner city policy is a much more power-ful one than most academic commentators have admitted, and it is certainly influential. We concentrate on this political critique here because it has directly influenced recent urban policy. Rather than impute motives based on an assumption that the policy agenda steps straight out of the assumptions of neo-classical economics, we focus on one of the most thorough right-wing critiques of policy produced to date, that by Sir Nigel Mobbs (n.d., c. 1987) of Aims of Industry, and on the most telling critique of inner city research, that by Marsland (1987).

According to Mobbs, the inner cities, if they are to be revived, need to become areas which can generate greater profits for the private investor. Emphasis should be placed on creating new busi-nesses, not propping up old ones. The role of government is to facilitate the process of profit creation, principally through creating a climate of confidence and an acceptance of enterprise (p. 13). Government at all levels has to move away from a climate of 'politi-cal inertia and 'opportunism' and 'bureaucratic oppression and over-regulation' (p. 11). In addition, government must begin to target its funding better. This is in tune with the general change in philosophy, from government being seen as part of the inner city solution to it being regarded as one of the problems: 'All administrative impediments to investment must be removed' and 'Direct investment by public agencies will crowd out private involvement' (p. 17).

Mobbs also supports a strengthening of government policies to create greater diversity in housing tenure, particularly to support a revival of private sector renting at the expense of public sector housing. The Urban Development Corporation programme should be continued, and the land market be freed up, particularly with release of public land and relief from capital gains tax liability for private sector land sales. Interestingly, Mobbs provides strong support for state financial inducements to increase investment in the inner city, primarily through non-selective tax breaks, whilst also arguing for a greater focus on local job creation and on achieving high leverage ratios of public to private investment. For instance, he recommends that VAT should be dropped on repairs and redevelop-ment projects in the inner city and never imposed on new buildings, whilst the mortgage relief threshold for the inner city should be increased from £30,000. The new, robust private sector has not yet quite shaken off the free hand-outs mentality – alternatively it may be being realistic about the scale of some aspects of the urban regeneration problem and of the potential for government intervention. The private sector then seems (slightly) less willing to marginalize government than central government itself is.

There are, of course, some notable omissions from Mobbs' critique and set of recommendations. Social considerations are limited to the statement that 'the economic differential between work or being on welfare needs to be widened', ignoring the particular problems of, for instance, ethnic minority workers trying to get access to paid employment. As with Marsland, to whom we turn next, the social problem for Mobbs essentially stems from planning and over-municipalization in the inner cities, leading to the creation of a dependency and anti-enterprise culture. Not surprisingly perhaps, neither makes any mention of the growth of an anti-authority culture, and both analyses are wholly gender and race blind.

Marsland (1987) provides a critique of some of the major pieces of inner city writing, relying heavily on current government thinking and also taking some issues further. For instance, he berates the antagonistic response of government ministers to the highly critical *Faith in the City* report (Church of England, 1985) as being, if anything, too mild. The report itself is chastised for being 'thoroughly tendentious and one-sided' (p. 7), starting from unchallenged socialist philosophies and being 'in the domain of ideology rather than research' (p. 12). At times it is 'exaggerated, oversimplified and deeply misleading' (p. 9) both in its use of material and in its analysis.

Marsland is also highly critical of Paul Harrison's book *Inside the Inner City* (1983). This, he claims, is based on poorly specified research techniques, is largely specific to just one area in London and is throughout emotive and judgemental rather than balanced, rational and rigorous in analysis. Harrison is claimed to suffer from 'hysterical pessimism' and a 'jaundiced eye' and to indulge in 'a torrent of ill-considered left socialism' (p. 4).

Several other targets are aimed at, albeit more hastily and less successfully, including Hausner and Robson's *Changing Cities* (1986). Interestingly, their work is said to overstate the importance of government in creating/failing to resolve inner city problems, whereas *Faith in the City* is criticized for underemphasizing the achievements of government policy. Marsland ends with 37 'critical questions', many of which appear ill-defined and obscure, defying meaningful analysis. A flavour of the arguments is portrayed using his final 'critical question': 'Why do inner city researchers remain the last bastion in social science of faith in planning?' (Marsland, 1987, p. 19). This is a perfect illustration of the bizarre approach adopted: planning is in the same breath assumed to be bad/unnecessary and anti-free market. Indeed most of the criticism levelled at others could equally be used against Marsland himself, especially the accusations of over-emotiveness, lack of balance, prejudgement of the agenda and lack of any original supportive research.

These two pieces of work set out the thrust of the right's critique of inner city policy and research. At an operational level this critique is taken further in the analysis presented by Anthony Stern (1988) and his colleagues. As in many of the analyses, the arguments presented in favour of Public Land Utilization Management Schemes (PLUMS) are compelling in terms of the diagnosis, that the public sector has hindered urban regeneration through the unnecessary sterilization of development land, and in terms of the prescription: divest public agencies of their surplus land holdings and inject them with the urgency which private management can provide. In reality, similar solutions to the problems of the underutilization of land could have been achieved through reforms to the public ownership of land, or through constructive amendments to the now repealed Community Land Act (1975). Meanwhile the problem of private owners of land who 'sterilize' it by holding on to it looks set to grow if local authorities are effectively discouraged from 'liberating' land by buying it themselves.

EVALUATION: POLICY PRODUCT AND POLICY PROCESS

From this analysis of problem definition, there emerge two remaining key areas on which to concentrate policy evaluation. Firstly, there is *policy product*, the concrete, observable outcomes of government policy on inner city areas. We are careful here to allow scope for gauging the impacts both of specifically urban policies and of non-urban policies. Given the relatively small amount of money put into explicit inner city policy, it is quite often the impacts of non-urban policies in the spheres of, for instance, health, social security, education and labour markets which exert the greatest impact on inner cities. The key questions in policy product evaluation centre on what, where and who. *What* are the specific outcomes (for instance the numbers and types of job created, the acres of land reclaimed and the managed workspace places made available)? *Where* do the benefits accrue (for instance primarily within the inner city itself through high local business multipliers and high levels of jobs, houses, etc. for locals)? *Who* actually benefits (in terms of priority target groups such as ethnic minority populations, the long-term unemployed and young people)?

In answering these questions caution must be exercised in order correctly to ascribe cause and effect. For example, it is not necessarily the case that jobs created in the inner city will automatically equal jobs for inner city residents (Haughton, Peck and Steward, 1987). Also, there is evidence of displacement rather than additionality occurring in certain projects, notably in retailing and manufacturing schemes. An example of this effect is in the claimed displacement of existing town centre retailing by superstores located in adjacent Enterprise Zones.

In this necessarily brief review we are concerned less with measured impacts[1] than with the *style* and *range* of the government assessments which have been made. For instance, no substantial official evaluations have been published covering the impact of policy on ethnic minorities or women in the inner city, and the impact of Urban Development Corporations. Just as serious is the lack of work on the 'trickle-down effect' which is so often assumed to operate and has provided a justification for policy. Knowledge of how policies such as Enterprise Zones and UDCs work through to particular target groups is essential to good policy making. Policies could often be better targeted by additional integrative measures – for instance, much earlier training for local people might have helped forestall the chronic local skills mismatch which became evident from 1987 onwards with the growth of London docklands construction activity.

The second area which there is a need to examine concerns issues of *policy process*. The key questions here are how and by whom. *How* is policy implemented, and *by whom*? These have emerged as major issues in recent years, particularly in the case of new, innovatory urban policies such as City Grant. The management of urban policy has long been a key issue within government, and the changes introduced have had enormous repercussions for urban policy outcomes. With a few honourable exceptions (Stewart and Underwood, 1983; Stewart 1987), the importance of this dimension of policy has been considerably underestimated.

The management of urban policy immediately following the 1978 Inner Urban Areas Act was seen largely as a partnership venture between local and central government. This is best illustrated in the

Urban Programme, where local management is the primary responsibility of the local authority, individual project selection is subject to the scrutiny of the regional offices of the Department of the Environment, and the overall direction and strategies of the programme are vetted by head office at Marsham Street in London.

However, questions remain as to the ability and capacity of those involved in the local co-ordination of the Urban Programme, especially in conurbation areas following the demise of the metropolitan county councils, actually to create and implement a coherent spatial strategy for the development of the overall urban economy. In this sense at least the Government might claim a success. The Urban Programme with its growing emphasis on economic projects has succeeded in 'bending' the mainstream spending of local authorities, the requirement of providing a 25 per cent matching contribution to the D.o.E.'s 75 per cent very effectively limiting the money locally available to implement more locally based and more radical economic initiatives. This was especially effective given other Government capital spend policies, on for instance the housing vote, which meant that the Urban Programme became an increasingly important source of overall authorized capital expenditure for some local authorities.

In 1985, anticipating criticisms from the National Audit Office, the Urban Programme Management Initiative (UPMI) was set in motion (Aldridge and Brotherton, 1988). The intention was to specify objectives more clearly at the level of individual projects and overall inner urban programmes and to make clearer the areas of management responsibility for each of the key actors. Adopting output measures issued from Marsham Street, each project has to set clear quantifiable objectives and monitor performance against these. As a result of this a large amount of data is generated, though surprisingly little use appears to be made of it. The annual report for the Urban Programme sums up the overall impact for all 57 Urban Programme authorities (D.o.E. 1988). Beyond this little effort has been made, until a recently commissioned research project, to, for instance, assess average unit costs for job creation or land reclamation and to identify acceptable parameters for such unit costs across the country. UPMI illustrates a merging of the concerns of policy product and policy process, and in particular, along with the tranche of evaluation studies commissioned by the Department of the Environment from 1984 onwards, demonstrates a growing concern with gauging policy impacts and value for money.

There is, however, a much more fundamental issue in urban

policy management which has been creeping onto the policy agenda in recent years. This can be referred to as the *privatization of policy strategy and implementation*. This first became evident as a policy priority in February 1981 when Michael Heseltine, the then Secretary of State for the Environment, insisted that the private sector should be consulted on the Urban Programme strategies produced by local authorities, though it should remain aloof from participating through management committees (*Hansard*, 9.2.1981, 998 (43), col. 603). Since then, there has been an increasing move towards integrating the private sector even more thoroughly into both the policy-making and policy-implementation processes.

Despite attempts to involve the private sector more fully, the inherent weaknesses of a national policy for tackling essentially local problems remain. The ability to create effective public–private partnerships is still limited and has, in turn, led to the use of such policy instruments as Urban Development Corporations in an attempt to create a framework within which private and public investments can be better integrated.

Significant markers in the development of policy, and especially its 'privatization' have been the creation of Enterprise Zones, the encouragement of Enterprise Agencies through Business in the Community and small business support generally, Urban Regeneration Grant, Urban Development Grant, City Action Teams, Inner City Task Forces, Local Employer Networks, City Technology Colleges, Action for Cities 1987, Education Compacts, City Grant and Action for Cities 1988.

The initiation of the Urban Development Grant in late 1982 to lever greater private sector resources into the inner city followed a private sector working paper report to the Government that was highly impressed by a similar United States scheme, which aimed to lever out private sector funding with minimum state funds. This was merged in February 1988 with the newly available Urban Regeneration Grant, to form the single City Grant. City Grant is appraised for the Government by private sector secondees and is awarded to private developers directly rather than through a local authority intermediary.

Laudable though the overall objective is of getting private enterprise to invest in the inner cities and to begin to accept some additional social responsibilities, there remain some very real fears that this has in practice imposed unacceptable reductions in the powers of local authorities in particular.

POLICY SUCCESSES AND FAILURES

Urban policy has been criticized in the past for its inertia and its tendency to bring about changes in policy direction in an incremental rather than radical manner (Stewart and Underwood, 1983). In this section we operate a primary distinction between innovatory and incrementally changed policies, though it should be noted that in a sense even the innovatory policies have often been incremental in terms of shifting the overall emphasis of inner city policy. *Innovatory policies* are those introduced by the Conservative administrations since 1979, most notably Urban Development Corporations, City Grant (and its forebears, the Urban Development and Urban Regeneration Grants), Task Forces, City Action Teams, Enterprise Zones and Garden Festivals. *Incremental policies* are those policies inherited in 1979, albeit altered to varying degrees since. The most important of these are the Urban Programme (1969), Section 11 grants (the only programme specifically targeted to ethnic minorities, 1966), Industrial Improvement Areas (1978) and the Derelict Land Grant Programme (1966). Interestingly, although political preferences between the various policy arms have altered, only the innovatory policies have been (or appear to have been) jettisoned. Community Development Projects (1969–78) and Comprehensive Community Programmes (1974–76) had already been abandoned by the previous Labour administration.

Innovatory Policies

Government-sponsored studies have been undertaken of the impact of Enterprise Zones and Urban Development Grants, whilst studies are currently under way for Garden Festivals and Task Forces. City Grant is too recent an initiative to have been formally evaluated yet. UDCs contentiously remain unevaluated by government itself although, as Parkinson and Evans note in Chapter 4 of the present volume, various reports have been published which have been highly critical. Rather than review these studies, it is our intention to note the impacts of the non-quantifiable, non-explicit political agenda. In our comment on right-wing documents on the urban question, we noted several key elements of shared ground: over-municipalization was in itself considered a problem, hence local authorities had to be either tamed or marginalized; planning had not worked and needed to be taken in hand and shifted away from over-regulation, helping to release enterprise; enterprise and curbing anti-social behaviour would also be helped by moving away from a dependency culture, bringing the private sector into a more pivotal role in the process. With the possible exception of Garden Festivals, all of the innovatory policies have assisted in moving local economic development away from local authority control and in the process have severely undermined the role of planning as a regulative, 'negative' force, recasting it as an expansionary, 'positive' force. In this light, it may well be that the apparent decisions to abandon the designation of further Enterprise Zones, Task Forces, City Action Teams, Urban Development Corporations and Garden Festivals is less an acknowledgement of failure than a recognition that the main political battles have been won and that, in the light of criticisms of their cost-effectiveness, they can already be discarded.

The political success lay in changing the agenda, in changing the attitudes of business towards the inner city (though rarely those of long-standing residents) and in a demonstration effect – something *could* be done. The political failure lay in introducing policies which, even in the Government's own preferred cost-per-job terms, were far from economic efficient and effective. Enterprise Zones, Urban Development Corporations and Garden Festivals have all been expensive, and have all been criticized for being poorly targeted to meeting the needs of inner city residents.

Incremental Policies

The main inner cities programme which attempts to provide a multi-directional approach to inner cities problems is the Urban Programme. The four main categories of expenditure – economic, environmental, social and housing – are indicative of the main areas of direct control. In fact, on the ground, it is one of the most successful of the inner city programmes, albeit hampered by a shift towards economic projects (currently over 40 per cent) which bring about considerable overlap with other government initiatives. Politically, its success for national government has been in providing some salve to the continuing calls for greater attention to environmental and social projects, and yet hiding under its general banner the fact that spending on both these categories has been cut back (see below).

However, the greatest criticism of the Urban Programme has concerned the move towards a 70/30 per cent capital/revenue split for the programmes of individual area strategies, which according to Hasluck (1987) has actually caused an accentuation of the urban problem by displacing labour with capital. This criticism actually seems rather harsh for this aspect of urban policy, which has not concentrated on, for instance, machinery in manufacturing. Capital tends to be a much broader category including, for example, buying a building for a community centre, whilst revenue might cover the community workers' wages. If anything it is the problem of time expiry for projects (usually three years), and the impact of this on projects which rely heavily on labour inputs, which is most disturbing. Too many worthy projects have collapsed because of this, in spite of large-scale initial capital expenditure. It seems patently absurd to help build community centres only to end up leaving them empty because there is no one to run them. This area of policy has the look of a Treasury own goal, wasting public money under the blandishments of the need to spend it more effectively by raising capital spending at the expense of revenue support.

As we have already indicated, some local authorities have identified exhaustion of funds as a key issue in circumstances where the need to allocate sufficient of their resources to provide a contribution to urban initiatives has reduced their capacity to pursue their own economic strategies (Roberts *et al.*, 1986). Consequently, support for national government's urban policy may have actually diminished the chance of success of unconstrained, locally determined economic development strategies. Although it would be churlish to deny the success of many schemes funded through the Urban Programme, it is possible to postulate that the same results might have been achieved, and have had a wider impact, if local authorities, working with the private sector, had been allocated additional resources through the Rate Support Grant or other mechanisms in order to fund their own programmes.

Finally in this section, we touch on the Derelict Land Grant programme. This is a long-standing programme which recognizes that the process of deindustrialization has left considerable tracts of land which were too despoiled to be brought back into use without considerable cash injections to help rehabilitate them. Much of the problem in inner city areas in particular has been that land owners have retained unrealistic expectations of the value of their land, which have hindered its being rehabilitated purely within the market. Indeed many parcels of land should effectively have had negative values – as some Urban Development Corporations have discovered. Our intention in pointing this out is not to undermine what is generally an effective policy within the framework of a mixed capitalist economy. Rather, we want to indicate the incongruity here with government attitudes to unemployed labour, which is regarded as having priced itself out of the market. In labour market policy, instruments such as Employment Training and the Youth Training Scheme have been used to drive down 'unrealistic' wage expectations (Finn, 1987). A parallel policy for land markets would have been interesting, to say the least.

GAPS AND OVERLAPS: CO-ORDINATION OF POLICY

A common proposal has been for a more co-ordinated approach to urban policy, one which stretches across all government bodies (Hausner and Robson, 1986; Lawless, 1988b). In fact, as we noted in our introduction, this may well be something of a red herring. There is no real indication that a more co-ordinated approach will, in itself, generate more government money, or even necessarily spend what money there is more effectively. On the contrary, a more co-ordinated policy may prove to be a vehicle for the continual incrementalism which has dominated urban policy since the 1970s. Better co-ordination of fundamentally poorly conceived and implemented urban policies is in itself largely irrelevant. Co-ordination presupposes that the elements of policy that are the subject of co-ordination are sufficiently well defined. Our overview suggests that this may well not be the case, and that a more fundamental examination of the *purpose* of urban economic policy is required. In so far as we do accept, none the less, the need for some better co-ordination, it does appear to be inherently contradictory to attempt to resolve this through the very partially applied 'solution' of Task Forces and City Action Teams, present in some cities but not all, and in some neighbourhoods but not others.

The SNAP Report (McConaghy, 1972) argued the case for an integrated policy for the economic (and social and environmental) regeneration of our cities. In particular it noted that:

● the inner city is part of the wider urban context and should not be considered in isolation;

● the inner cities have traditionally served a useful economic and social function;

● that the wider urban context for the inner city has suffered from massive structural industrial decline;

[99]

● the problems resulting from this general decline are at their peak in the inner cities.

From this analysis, which was well supported in terms of a detailed study of conditions in the Granby area of Liverpool, the report proposed a solution through 'another chance for cities'. This new chance was not framed, in the words of the report, as a 'set piece solution', but rather was designed to create an integrated and flexible long-term programme of action that is relevant to the individual area.

Given this general view, there remain some notable gaps and overlaps in central government policy. Key amongst the *gaps* are policies which: specifically seek to help to improve the quality of women's working and home lives; attempt to plan for labour market expansion through dedicated training schemes; attempt to move, on a large scale, public-expenditure-related jobs, including the civil service and defence contracts, to inner city areas; aim to bring ethnic minorities more fully into mainstream employment and to combat their tendency to gravitate towards low-paying jobs or unemployment; and finally, seek to tackle, on an adequate scale, the problems of a poor-quality public sector housing stock. This is clearly a rather personal shopping list, and is meant to be indicative rather than definitive.

Broad areas of *overlap* perhaps inevitably exist between programmes and between government departments. The most worrying aspect of overlap is in fact the general one of a move towards economic expenditure, rather than more specific overlaps in particular project types. With the partial exceptions of Garden Festivals and the inner city Task Forces, all of the major new initiatives have been economic in orientation.[2] The existing incrementally changed programmes, such as the Derelict Land Grant and the Urban Programme, have also taken on a more economic dimension (Aldridge and Brotherton, 1988). In addition, the private sector has been encouraged to get more involved in the inner city, usually relying on enlightened self-interest and from this mainly developing commercially viable economic projects. All government departments have started to target their economic policies to the inner city, especially following the publication of *Action for Cities* (Cabinet Office, 1988). Finally, local authorities are encouraged to get involved in local economic development, albeit under new restrictions announced in December 1988. One specific consequence of this is that many local authorities find that they are required to 'buy' social projects under the Urban Programme with often marginal economic projects (Sills, Taylor and Golding, 1988), as the supply of the latter dries up or is supported by other government-sponsored or encouraged programmes.

The end result is an unbalanced economic-oriented urban policy that assumes a trickle-down effect to improve the housing, environmental and social problems of the inner cities, and ultimately to benefit the less well-off. This, in part, reflects what Hambleton (1981) regarded as the shift of government urban policy from being essentially a tool for redistributing wealth to one for creating wealth. None the less, government rhetoric, at least, has never lost sight of the need to spread the benefits of urban regeneration to all. There are, however, very real problems in assuming that job creation of the type which is now seen in London docklands will benefit local residents (Church, 1988). There is also the much broader question of whether job creation is a policy which can directly help the large numbers of elderly, children, one-parent families, disabled and others who cannot fully participate in the labour force. The nature of the urban problem is widely acknowledged, even within the Government, to be multifaceted, which makes it nonsensical to attempt to move assistance increasingly towards just one policy arm. This said, it is incumbent upon supporters of non-economic projects to ensure that there is an explicit acknowledgement of the broader benefits of directing government money towards them, and of the interrelationships of improved environmental, social and housing conditions with improving local economic confidence and buoyancy.

ACTION FOR TOMORROW?

In this concluding section we outline where we think national inner city policy is going in the near future, and also provide some pointers for how it might be successfully reorientated.

In examining the performance of urban policy during the past ten years it would appear that two issues still require detailed attention. First, there is the need to consider whether policy is truly relevant to the needs of the individual local area or whether it is dominated by a centrally determined view of what should exist. The essential gap in the current content of policy reflects the concern expressed in a recent OECD (1987) review of urban economic policy, which asked, 'do urban policies add to overall economic performance or merely redistribute resources within a nation?' On the evidence which is available it could be claimed that redistribution has dominated and, as Buck and Gordon (1987) have noted, significant redistribution is only likely in the context of overall employment growth.

The second issue that requires more detailed attention is the question of local policy relevance and accountability. Conventional wisdom in Whitehall suggests that local authorities cannot be relied upon to foster the changes that are required in the urban economic system. Whilst local government may not, in itself, be able to deliver all of the changes in attitude and performance that are required, it does offer a basis for the integration of policy measures and a mechanism for ensuring that a degree of accountability is maintained.

As policy has moved much more into the domain of the private sector, almost inevitably there has been and will continue to be a move towards 'areas of potential', that is development potential. The critical issues which arise are: whether and how the economic approach which is central to this can solve the multiple problems of the inner city; the problem of allowing cities to expand incrementally in response to short-term profit opportunities without a long-term perspective; and the problems of giving an unelected private sector the power of veto or sanction over policy implementation. In this sense the move towards an increasingly privatized, economic urban policy seems both blinkered and short-sighted, especially if it simply increases social polarization within urban areas and creates new frustrations alongside the new opportunities. Indeed, more generally, national inner city policy seems to be creating new tensions, including those with local authorities, whilst doing very little about existing tensions, especially those involving the unemployed and ethnic minorities in the inner cities.

Partial political success though has come about for the Government, in tandem with other non-urban policies, in terms of changing the political agenda: bringing actors from the private sector to the fore, whilst moving to marginalize (and indeed abolish) what it perceives to be extreme-left local authorities. The process of 'blaming the victim' has become virtually concreted into national mythology. Individuals are held to blame for their own problems, and just as tellingly there has been a blaming of the institutional victim. Local authorities, often rate-capped, are said to have created their own problems by overspending and providing poor services. Giving with one hand and taking with the other remains a central, if hidden, feature of government inner city policy (LGIU, 1987).

Policy gaps and overlaps do exist and will continue to occur. However, the resolution to the confusion of purpose and action that now exists in many aspects of urban policy is unlikely to be achieved by adding fresh policies and agencies to the current log-jam. A more reflective and appreciative approach to policy review and the fundamental purpose of urban policy might well benefit from a consideration of the principles outlined in the SNAP Report in particular. Unfortunately for the long-term prospects for cities, a veneer of enterprise and progressive change may have been applied to the urban economy without attending to the fundamental structural weaknesses that continue to exist. The variable, but often unmeasured, successes of urban policy may well be attributed to the innovative nature of the new measures introduced – the Enterprise Zones, Urban Development Corporations, and City Action Teams to name but a few – but the question remains: do these individual – and area-specific initiatives really amount to an urban policy?

These issues lie at the core of any overall evaluation, and require serious attention if future urban policy is to consist of any more than a series of *ad hoc* measures. The call for integration and the generation of a more local, city-wide dimension in urban policy should not be seen as supporting a return to local bureaucracy or providing a rationale for left-wing policies. Evidence from the United States (and GEAR in Glasgow) has indicated the value of local, consensus-based urban strategies, which have proved to be an effective means through which to channel central government resources (Sorkin, Ferris and Hadak, 1984). Greater efficiency and spatial relevance need not be in conflict; rather they can be seen as mutually beneficial and compatible objectives which can be expressed through longer-term programmes for the redevelopment of the urban economy. The compelling need is to rethink urban policy in terms of local needs and priorities and within a framework of local responsibility, one which does not seek to write out key actors from the partnership, be they the private sector or the local authority.

Overall, whilst urban policy has provided a procedure for allocating additional resources to the inner cities it has, in some cases, created the conditions for development *in* the inner cities rather than *of* them (Turok, 1987). To this extent, whilst inner city policy may have avoided some of the problems of competition and co-ordination, it may have failed to provide the necessary spatial integration which would enable it to become a policy relevant to the entire urban system.

[103]

To conclude, urban policy in the last decade has been strongly political in ambition; indeed this was true long before Mrs Thatcher's famous election night promise in 1987 to 'do something about those inner cities'. The change in 1987 was, none the less, fundamental as the Government sought to gain political control of the inner cities, promote a commercially based development policy for the inner cities, and abandon any lingering concerns with equity. It represents growth of the pot at almost any expense and with all haste, with no real attention to the issues of who should benefit from the contents. That this could be done so openly and rapidly is indicative of at least the *political* success of the previous eight years of urban economic policy.

NOTES

1. There are a variety of government-sponsored evaluations of specific policy instruments which do attempt to gauge readily quantifiable impacts. See for instance PA-CEC (1987) on Enterprise Zones.

2. We exclude from this the Education Compacts and the Home Office Five City Security Scheme announced in 1988, both of which appear to require little government expenditure.

REFERENCES

Aldridge, M. and Brotherton, C.J. (1988) 'Being a programme authority: is it worthwhile?' *Journal of Social Policy*, Vol. 16, No. 3, pp. 349–69.

Buck, N. and Gordon, 1. (1987) 'The beneficiaries of employment growth: an analysis of disadvantaged groups in expanding labour markets', in Hausner, V. (ed.) *Critical Issues in Urban Economic Development*, Vol. 2, Oxford, Oxford University Press.

Cabinet Office (1988) *Action for Cities*, London, HMSO.

Church, A. (1988) 'Urban regeneration in London Docklands: a five year policy review', *Environment and Planning C: Government and Policy, 1988*, Vol. 6, No. 2, pp. 187–208.

Church of England (1985) *Faith in the City*, London, Church House Publishing.

D.o.E. (1983) 'Census information note 2: urban deprivation', London, D.o.E.

D.o.E. (1988) *D.o.E. Inner City Programmes 1987–1988: A Report on Achievements and Developments*, London, HMSO.

ECOTEC (1987) 'Review of data sources for urban policy', report to the Department of the Environment, available at the library, 2 Marsham Street, London.

Finn, D. (1987) *Training Without Jobs: New Deals and Broken Promises*, Basingstoke, Macmillan Education.

Hambleton, R. (1981) 'Implementing urban policy: reflections from experience', *Policy and Politics*, Vol. 9, No. 1, pp. 51–71.

Harrison, P. (1983) *Inside the Inner City: Life Under the Cutting Edge*, Harmondsworth, Penguin.

Hasluck, C. (1987) *Urban Unemployment: Local Labour Markets and Employment Initiatives*, London, Longman.

Haughton, G., Peck, J. and Steward, A. (1987) 'Local jobs and local houses for local workers: a critical analysis of spatial employment targeting', *Local Economy*, Vol. 2, No. 3, pp. 201–7.

Hausner, V. and Robson, B. (1986) *Changing Cities*, London, ESRC.

JURUE (1986) *Assessment of the Employment Effects of Economic Development Projects Funded Under the Urban Programme*, London, HMSO.

Lawless, P. (1988a) 'British inner urban policy post 1979: a critique', *Policy and Politics*, Vol. 16, No. 4, pp. 261–75.

Lawless, P. (1988b) 'British inner urban policy: a review', *Regional Studies*, Vol. 22, No. 6, pp. 531–42.

LGIU (1987) 'City swindles: urban policy in the eighties', *LGIU Special Briefing*, No. 21 (May), London, Local Government Information Unit.

McConaghy, D. (1972) *SNAP 1969-72: Another Chance for Cities*, London, Shelter.

Marsland, D. (1987) 'Against enterprise: concepts and values in inner city research', SRA Annual Conference, December.

Mobbs, N. (n.d., *c.* 1987) *Inner City Challenge*, London, Aims of Industry.

OECD (1987) *Revitalising Urban Economies*, Paris, Organization for Economic Co-operation and Development.

PA-CEC (1987) *An Evaluation of the Enterprise Zone Experiment*, London, HMSO.

Plowden Report (1967) *Children and Their Primary Schools*, Central Advisory Committee for Education, London, HMSO.

PSMRC (1988) *An Evaluation of the Urban Development Grant Programme*, London, HMSO.

Roberts, P., Collins, C. and Noon, D. (1986) *Economic Development in the Shire Counties*, Manchester, Centre for Local Economic Strategies.

Sills, D., Taylor, G. and Golding, P. (1988) *The Politics of the Urban Crisis*, London, Hutchinson.

Sorkin, D.L., Ferris, N.B. and Hadak, J. (1984) *Strategies for Cities and Countries: A Strategic Planning Guide*, Washington DC, Public Technology Inc.

Stern, A. (1988) *Public Land Utilisation Management Schemes* London, Conservative Political Centre.

Stewart, M. (1987) 'Ten years of inner city policy', *Town Planning Review*, Vol. 58, pp. 29–45.

Stewart, M. and Underwood, J. (1983) 'New relationships in the inner city', in Young, K. and Mason, C. (eds) *Urban Economic Development: New Roles and Relationships*. London, Macmillan.

Turok, 1. (1987) 'Continuity, change and contradiction in urban policy', in Donnison, D. and Middleton, A. (eds) *Regenerating the Inner City*, London, Routledge and Kegan Paul.

·PART 3·

Local Government Policy

Public-Private Partnerships in Urban Regeneration

Enterprise Boards: An Inside View

Recent Developments in Local Authority Economic Policy

Evaluating Local Economic Policy

CHAPTER 6

Public–Private Partnerships in Urban Regeneration

Alan Harding

Of all the themes examined in this volume, public–private partnerships are the least easily defined and the most under-researched.[1] It is not possible, as is the case for many other types of initiative, to point to particular administrative regulations or statutes which underpin them; they are not characterized by distinct fiscal regimes, organizational structures or modes of operation; nor do they fit all that easily into the central–local typology used to organize the text. Yet if there is one clear thread which runs through post-1979 central government attempts to promote programmes which aim to tackle the problems of urban economic decline and employment loss, it is the desire to involve the private sector more fully in the policy process and in substantive programmes. Moreover the theme of the increasing involvement of the private sector in local economic policy is one that in many ways runs like a thread through many of the chapters in this text.

This chapter examines this field of public–private partnerships by posing a series of interrelated questions. Why has the notion of public-private partnership entered the political vocabulary over recent years? What forms have public–private partnerships taken, and what factors have encouraged their formation? What is the experience of public–private partnerships in the United Kingdom and also in the United States, the latter being the country which is often cited as the model which the UK is trying to follow in this field? Is the replication of the American model of public–private partnerships in the UK either possible or desirable? A short conclusion sums up the difficulties which are faced in attempting to answer such questions given the current state of research and suggests options for further study.

THE RISE OF PUBLIC-PRIVATE PARTNERSHIP AS AN ISSUE

The emergence of the notion of public–private partnership in political vocabulary in the UK since 1979 must be seen in the context of the ideological vision of state–economy relations promulgated by central government in the period and its rather more pragmatic application to urban regeneration policies. Post-1979 Conservative Governments have routinely rejected what they see as the inadequacies of the interventionist, social democratic state in favour of an approach which stresses the role of the market in promoting and sustaining economic well-being. The newly constrained role of the state ideally aims only to secure the basic conditions under which private sector profitability is encouraged. With regard to urban regeneration, previous initiatives, like the reformed Urban Programme inherited from the previous Labour Government, have been criticized as giving too little weight to economic development and wealth-creation objectives, and as being unduly dominated by public sector agencies (D.o.E. 1981, 1985).

New government initiatives since 1979 have sought to address this perceived problem and to ensure that representatives of the private sector are involved to a greater degree in defining 'the urban problem', in developing solutions, and in operationalizing them. The importance of the issue of urban regeneration has been underscored by general economic trends which have seen the economies of many urban areas, particularly those reliant on old manufacturing bases, both contract rapidly in the recession which coincided with the early period of Conservative office and fail to benefit substantially from the subsequent economic recovery. The attendant waste of human and physical resources in urban areas, in combination with the urban rioting which affected a number of towns and cities in England in 1981 and 1985, has kept the issue on the political agenda.

Whilst the process of economic restructuring in urban areas is common throughout the Western industrialized nations (Feagin and Smith, 1987; OECD, 1987), responses inevitably differ according to locality. In the UK, the rationale for encouraging public–private co-operation in urban regeneration draws on both historical and contemporary models. Some evidence on the latter, the experience

[109]

of American initiatives, is examined briefly below. It is instructive to note, however, that the form of public–private co-operation which is considered useful is borrowed from a society wherein the state is relatively weak and non-interventionist, rather than the stronger forms of partnership, based on tripartism which offers a key role to organized labour, that exist in a number of European countries.

The other model often mentioned in ministerial speeches harks back to what is seen as the golden age of privately led urban development, Victorian Britain. A romanticized view of Victorian urban society is offered which stresses the philanthropic leanings and civic pride of local economic élites and the benefit of their actions which, it is alleged, filtered down to other groups in the locality.[2] Irrespective of whether this reading of history is accepted, it is clear that the underlying conditions which operated in Victorian times have undergone fundamental change. The extension of the franchise, the rise of a working-class political party, the suburbanization of economic élites, the development of the welfare state and of local government's role within it, the professionalization of both public and private sectors, the development of limited companies and their extension into national and multinational operational spheres – all these factors have contributed to the economic, political and social transformation of urban areas. Consequently an attachment to the Victorian model bears rather more testimony to the importance of ideology in recent attempts to promote public–private co-operation. Appeals are made for a radical change (or reversion) in values in the hope of recreating Victorian-type civic consciousness and locally committed élite networks in the absence of the societal structures which sustained them in earlier times.[3] Entreaties to key actors are only a part of a government's armoury, however. The next section deals with the more practical attempts which have been made to create public–private partnerships and a climate in which they are more likely to develop.

RESHAPING THE POLICY ENVIRONMENT FOR PUBLIC-PRIVATE PARTNERSHIP

Use of the term 'public–private partnership' in urban regeneration, whilst common, presents a number of definitional problems. At the most general level it could be taken to mean any action which relies on the agreement of actors in the public and private sectors and which also contributes in some way to improving the urban economy and the quality of urban life. Such a definition strips the term of any conceptual value, however, since the interdependence of public and private sectors in realizing their respective aims in this field is so extensive as to make the concept virtually all-encompassing. Many academic accounts of public–private partnership sidestep wider definitional problems by concentrating on particular organizational entities established jointly by the public and private sectors, or by the private sector in the hope of mobilizing public sector support for particular strategies or projects, in a particular urban or metro-politan area. The latter formulation is the one which informs much of the work conducted in the USA and, since it offers the benefit of comparative simplicity, is the one used here for examining the bulk of secondary literature. However, the danger in choosing such an exclusive organizational focus is that it takes the wider environment, which in the USA proved conducive to public–private partnership, as a given. In the British context it is also important to look at the ways in which the policy environment has changed, or has been manipulated so as to give greater prominence to partnerships of this kind.

As noted above, the Conservative Government in 1979 inherited a revamped Urban Programme which, whilst it stressed the impor-tance of economic factors in urban decline for the first time and hoped for the involvement of local private and voluntary sectors in programming, was largely dominated by public sector actors. Central government provided the general framework within which local authority professionals were responsible for assembling yearly bids for resources. Clearly, if the private sector were to be given a leading role in urban regeneration policy, there needed to be sub-stantial changes in the 'policy universe' – that constellation of organizations and actors who feel motivated to make a contribution to policy formulation and implementation. The perceived narrow-ness and unsuitability of a local-authority-dominated programme became an increasingly important issue as relations between central and local government deteriorated rapidly after 1979. Central determination to limit local authority expenditure and, increasingly, to erode local authority involvement in direct service delivery played a vital role here. However, central government uneasiness with local authorities was also heightened by the development of more radical economic strategies by some urban authorities which urged more direct intervention into private decision making in order to pursue redistributive as well as developmental ends. Whilst the develop-ment of planning agreements on aspects such as equal opportunities, trade union membership and training between local authorities, or associated agencies, and individual companies can be seen as forms of public–private partnership, they clearly did not sit easily with the free-market ambitions of central government.

The reshaping of the policy environment attempted by central government has thus been characterized by ambivalence toward the role of local authorities and the need to create or encourage organizational capacity sufficient to deliver programmes at a local level. Whilst the influence of central government over programmes has increased, there has been general consistency with a tradition of decentralized service delivery and non-executive central government. This has been achieved by the use of positive and negative incentives to cajole the private sector into greater self-organization and involvement, and to either constrain local authority programmes within limits acceptable to central government or curtail their involvement completely.

In attempting to create a new policy infrastructure, the Government was aided by a small, pre-existing revival in the notion of corporate social responsibility (Richardson, Moore and Moon, 1985). Companies like Pilkingtons in St Helens began to realize that the effects of economic change on local communities, resulting in some part from their own operational restructuring and consequent redundancies, were potentially destructive and that initiatives to promote new economic activity could help limit social disruption, enhance corporate image and improve the business climate in which they worked. Pilkingtons' reaction was to form the first Enterprise Agency in 1978 with support from local firms, the local council and trade unions. The St Helens Trust provided a growing number of services to new small businesses, ranging from advice and consultancy to provision of premises and financial support, drawing on resources from participating organizations as well as other levels of government (national, EEC). Concurrently, the CBI was trying to co-ordinate corporate responses to government training programmes through its regional network. Government efforts to fuse together such attempts by the private sector to be more pro-active in local economic affairs were made via support for more research on corporate social responsibility and seminars on business–community relations.

One Anglo-American conference, held in 1981 shortly before outbursts of urban rioting, was particularly important in developing the Enterprise Agency concept and led, in 1982, to the creation of Business in the Community (BIC). A national umbrella organization with wide corporate membership and a sprinkling of other interests, BIC, and its sister organization in Scotland (ScotBIC), have played the key role in the development of a national network of Enterprise Agencies and Trusts (EAs, ETs), aided by secondments from central government departments and regional offices (the SDA in Scotland's case), grants, and tax exemptions for company contributions. They have also helped energize corporations into urban regeneration efforts at national and local levels. Before BIC had been created, however, urban social unrest had prompted a further governmental response to the perceived need to involve the private sector in the policy process.

The Financial Institutions Group (FIG) was a hastily assembled *ad hoc* group of leading financiers and seconded senior civil servants charged with examining the role that such institutions might play in urban regeneration and identifying the sort of public sector incentives which would be needed to facilitate it. Disbanded in 1982, FIG, through a number of working groups, nevertheless developed a number of themes and initiatives which were subsequently acted upon. These include: public pump-priming grants modelled on the American Urban Development Action Grant (UDG, URG, City Grant), the leading public role within which, as explained elsewhere in this volume, has been appropriated by central government; the formation of Inner City Enterprise, a property service company established by leading financial institutions which seeks out development opportunities and finance packages for individual projects; and a number of ideas regarding derelict land development and the development control system. Further corporate interest in responding to central government appeals came in 1986 with the establishment of Phoenix, a national organization dominated by construction interests which acts as a lobbying agent and information broker to central government and which has been active in promoting area initiatives. In 1987 the CBI launched its Task Force initiative with similar purposes, and in 1988 British Urban Developments (BUD) was launched. The latter, established with equity contributions from eleven major building and property development corporations who together dominate the British construction market (and incidentally include key donors to the Conservative Party political fund), has also developed local partnership arrangements and appointed a former policy adviser to the Prime Minister as its Chief Executive.

Consultation with the private sector, via local Chambers of Commerce, has also been made a condition of the procedure for making

Urban Programme submissions. Private sector representatives have been appointed directly to key agencies created by central government since 1979, for example Urban Development Corporations (UDCs) and Task Forces which are examined elsewhere in this volume. The extent to which the local public sector is involved in these bodies tends to depend on the pre-existing degree of public–private collaboration in the designated areas, but it is always possible for these agencies to go their own way.

The logic underlying all these developments appears to be that private sector participation is seen as critical to the process of urban regeneration and that local authority involvement is desirable but ultimately optional, depending on time and place. A range of changes have been introduced which attempt to limit local authority responses and to ensure that they are supportive of, or at least do not oppose the expressed or imputed needs of, the private sector.

The more radical and extensive local authority initiatives were effectively destroyed when the councils which developed them – the GLC and the metropolitan county councils – were abolished in 1986. Reviews of the statutory power most commonly used by local authorities to finance local economic initiatives have also been undertaken. Whilst the local authority associations' resistance to central interference here has helped head off changes thus far, legislation to limit local authority action in this field seems imminent as a result of the Government's response to the last inquiry into the issue conducted by the Widdicombe Committee (HMSO, 1988a). Changes to the statutory planning system have forced or encouraged local authorities into a greater presumption in favour of development. These include: Enterprise Zones (EZs) which are negotiated with planning authorities but offer incentives which they can find difficult to refuse in return for a relaxation of development control; Simplified Planning Zones (SPZs), similar to EZs but lacking any subsidy element; and greater power of direction on planning matters to the Secretary of State and to UDCs which completely strip local authorities of their development control functions. Possible moves to force local authorities to dispose of municipal land have been floated, but inducement to sell has in any case been provided by reductions in central revenue and capital support and by the outlawing of lease-leaseback deals with developers. Contracts compliance procedures, through which some urban councils tried to influence company decisions on recruitment of minorities, training, trade union recognition, wage levels and so on, were made illegal early in 1988 and further legislation has been introduced following a discussion paper which deals with reducing local authority interests in companies (D.o.E., 1988).

The results of these manipulations of the policy environment have been twofold. First, there has been an often striking shift in attitudes on the part of local authorities which have seen their independent room for manoeuvre reduced and the incentive to achieve at least some of their objectives through co-operation with the private sector increased. Second, there has developed within the private sector greater organizational capacity for the common development of urban regeneration schemes. In combination with the post-1983 economic upturn which has increased the possibility of profitable investment in urban areas, these factors have helped prepare the ground for a new wave of local public–private partnerships in recent years.

EXPERIENCE OF PUBLIC–PRIVATE PARTNERSHIPS IN THE UK

The development of locally based public–private partnerships in the UK can roughly be divided into two phases. The first, dominant to the mid-1980s and still important, was largely characterized by small business development. This has been augmented, since around 1985, by a wider range of initiatives, including new property-based schemes. In each phase the influence of national private sector organizations was important in galvanizing the local private sector into self-organization as a precondition to the building of agreements with local public sector agencies, although in some cases it has been public authorities which have taken the lead role.

The first phase saw the development of a network of Enterprise Agencies and Trusts on the St Helens model, largely as the result of the efforts of BIC and ScotBIC and encouragement by the D.o.E. and the SDA. In most cases these have been supported, financially and/or through administrative assistance, by local authorities, many of which were already active in this area, although the more radical urban authorities with a critical stance on the role of small businesses in the economy were careful to distance themselves from such agencies (GLC, 1982). Nearly 300 EAs and ETs are now established, having received a total funding of £300 million, split roughly fifty-fifty between public and private sectors. Their core activities continue to be small business counselling and information services, some providing additional services in business training, provision of workspaces and financial assistance (BIC, 1988). The agencies tend to be small and rely substantially on secondments from the private sector for staffing.

The growth of BIC and ScotBIC, and the greater contact between local private sector interests which local agencies have facilitated, have been a factor in the recent expansion in the range of private-sector-led initiatives. These include the creation by BIC of Target Teams on a range of issues such as recruitment practices, purchasing policies, voluntary sector activities and property development which will promote model projects locally. Six neighbourhood partnerships have also been established between BIC member companies and voluntary groups to develop community employment and training schemes and community facilities. Three newer BIC activities relate directly to public–private partnership. The first, the Compact scheme, brings locally based employers into direct agreements with local education authorities. Modelled on the Boston (Mass.) example, first developed as a way of counteracting a crisis in confidence in the secondary schooling system, the Compacts are drawn up between particular sets of employers and schools and offer employment guarantees, or further training leading to employment, to pupils who meet standards agreed between the two sides. Compacts, or Education/Business Partnerships established with the intention of developing them, are currently planned in 30 inner city areas and financial assistance from the Training Agency has recently been made available.

The two other BIC initiatives, local Business Action Teams and One Town Partnerships, function more like those undertaken by the CBI Task Force and Phoenix and differ from the earlier phase in so far as they put more emphasis on physical development and edge participants toward a form of strategic planning for particular sub-city areas. A feature of such efforts is that they attempt to establish a critical mass of locally based firms who can form the basis for a partnership initiative and organize and lobby for public sector support. BUD tends to rely to a greater extent on the local presence of its chosen partners and to co-ordinate the efforts of its members centrally. The lobbying role, particularly of Phoenix and BUD, should not be underestimated. The Phoenix initiative emerged from a report, sponsored by prominent building and property development interests, which examined the US experience of partnerships and argued precisely that the system of state incentives available to private developers there was more effective and should be replicated in Britain (Cowie, 1985). Some of the work carried out in association with Phoenix restates traditional pleas for increases in capital/infrastructural spending and tax incentives for developers, albeit in a more subtle form.[4]

Other partnership efforts have been led by the public sector. Examples here include: Sheffield City Council's Industrial Regeneration Committee, established with the Chamber of Commerce following a dramatic change in the local authority's approach to the city's economic problems; the Birmingham Heartlands initiative where the same organizations were again the prime movers; Glasgow Action, which builds on sustained development work by the local authorities and the SDA (Boyle, 1988); and Aberdeen Beyond 2000 where the SDA and the councils are again major contributors. Central government nervousness with local authorities was further illustrated with regard to Sheffield's plans for the Lower Don Valley, and in the case of Phoenix schemes being drawn up with councils in Manchester and Bristol, when UDCs were designated in each of the areas in 1987/8. Irrespective of the prime mover, partnerships share the characteristic that each side needs to organize itself and bring to a newly created forum particular ideas which would be unlikely to be acted upon if each side acted independently but which, as a result of internal bargaining and compromise as well as the added powers, resources and contacts of the other partner, can become implementable programmes. The leading characteristics of the more recent forms of partnership are examined below.

Membership

With the partial exception of BUD's local schemes, this inevitably varies according to the local economic structure. Due to the massive centralization of higher-order functions in London, only rarely do private sector representatives include corporations with headquarters in particular areas (Pilkingtons in St Helens and the Halifax Building Society in Calderdale are amongst the rare examples). For the most part they are drawn from indigenous firms and local branches of larger concerns, be they the branches of national financial institutions common to most cities or more specialized, international corporations like the oil companies involved in the Aberdeen programme. In some instances they are dominated by particular development entrepreneurs (such as John Hall, of Gateshead Metro Centre fame, in the CBI's Newcastle Initiative, and Ernest Hall, who developed Halifax's Dean Clough workshop complex, in the Calderdale Partnership). Local authorities are the most common public sector members although the SDA figures prominently in Scotland and UDCs are thus far the favoured partners of BUD due to their powers of land assembly, compulsory purchase, development control and gap financing (BUD, n.d.).

Resources

Whilst the mix of interests present at local level does not necessarily include all those needed for the successful prosecution of projects, association with the national private sector organizations arguably gives greater access to external resource networks. Local authority involvement too is encouraged by the possibility of gaining additional political credibility, and further resources, from central government. BUD alone of the national private sector bodies holds substantial funds independent of those used by its members in particular local projects. These are used for land assembly and servicing before resale to targeted developers. In virtually all cases public sector resources are critical in supporting potentially profitable investment, particularly in property schemes. Many rely almost entirely on the attraction of pump-priming central grant.

Scale and Location

Scale varies widely, from cases like the Ravenhead Renaissance project in St Helens which covers 40 acres of land, to Birmingham Heartlands (1,850 acres). Locations vary considerably too, from an exclusive focus on central city sites, to city centre fringes, waterside locations, and degraded industrial land, each offering different potential advantages in terms of marketing. Others (for example, Aberdeen) have little spatial focus at all, dealing in sites only when they are crucial to specific sectors, as city centres generally are for tourism.

Mode of Operation

Most partnerships are formed with the intention of generating projects and strategies acceptable to the range of partners, and preparatory work, carried out in-house or by consultants, is commonly needed. In examples like Hull's Victoria Dock Company, formed by the city council and Bellway Urban Renewals Ltd, partnerships are established with particular projects in mind: in this case management of a redevelopment scheme, based on a £17 million City Grant, to provide 1,200 homes and associated facilities. In others, a flexible framework is established within which particular projects can be fitted after marketing. In some cases, such as Aberdeen (Aberdeen Beyond 2000, 1988), this entails a fairly sophisticated, long-term view of the potential development of the local economy. In others, such as Newcastle (Newcastle Initiative, 1988), the 'vision' is more limited and concentrates on specific medium-term property developments and themes: in this case the provision of a range of Japanese facilities to spur inward investment. Others are far less strategic, comprising a collection of disparate projects and themes which are of interest to participants. One common theme, however, is 'place marketing' and attempts to create a climate of business confidence. For local authorities, this marks a reversion to a more traditional, competitive approach which is more in keeping with the national political climate, there being a feeling that attempts to present areas as 'deserving' of central government support on the basis of needs indicators is now counterproductive and that cities need to sell themselves as potential 'winners', both politically (to central government) and economically (to the private sector).

Impact

It is far too early to establish what economic or other effects partnerships will have in Britain, since most have been running for less than two years. Little evaluation, or even accounts, of the process and operation of partnerships has yet been attempted. However, there is very limited evidence that partnership action, particularly on property schemes, is being targeted toward particular social groups. Phoenix, for example, describe the potential benefits accruing to local communities as 'the new and exciting prospect taking shape around them' (Phoenix, n.d.): along with BUD they aim explicitly at increasing profitability on physical development schemes (retail, commercial, leisure and housing), albeit over longer than usual timescales and with the private sector assuming some responsibility for pump-priming work. Some initiatives take local labour market issues and community views more seriously. This is the case to a limited extent with the BIC partnerships in Blackburn and

Calderdale where local discussion forums are being established and where projects include Compact and small training schemes. Birmingham Heartlands too, unusual amongst the property-based initiatives, has conducted local consultations and includes community health issues and improvements to council housing and training programmes to foster local take-up of associated job opportunities as elements in its package (Birmingham Heartlands, n.d.).

THE US EXPERIENCE

Public–private partnerships in the USA comparable to those described above date back to the early post-war years and are better documented than those in Britain (Fosler and Berger, 1982; Jezierski, 1988a, 1988b; Whelan, 1988; Coleman, 1986; Vogel, 1988; Krumholz *et al.*, 1988). Whilst detailed analysis cannot be attempted here, a number of relevant themes relating to their operation and to the differences between US and UK circumstances can be drawn out.

The first major feature seen as separating the USA and the UK in the ease with which local partnerships are formed is the decentralized nature of American capital. The existence of regional financial institutions, and of corporate headquarters in many cities, ensures that the resources and expertise needed for private sector development schemes are more readily available. It is also a factor in the greater awareness of and interest in local economic well-being in the private sector, and in the existence of social networks linking major business people, such as the clubs and/or foundations of Chicago (Cafferty and McCready, 1982), Portland (Barbour, 1982) and Cleveland (Krumholz *et al.*, 1988). Where these factors are absent, as in St Louis, partnerships have been slower to form and prove less effective (Whelan, 1988). Faced with signs of economic crisis, the locally based private sector in the USA has therefore had a basis for self-organization. In many cases this led to the formation of associations, either independently or jointly with the local public sector, which aimed specifically at creating a consensus for development plans. Economic crisis, though important, is not the sole motivating factor. The Minneapolis/St Paul area offers an example of a highly organized indigenous private sector with the ability to anticipate the need for future economic diversification (Brandl and Brooks, 1982).

In the earlier post-war examples, such as the Allegheny Conference on Community Development in Pittsburgh and the Greater Baltimore Committee, private sector activism was particularly vital in providing policy-making capacity to a highly fragmented public authority system which lacked the organizational sophistication to become involved in economic planning. Effectively, these organizations took on a strategic planning role and then negotiated with public authorities for support. In later examples city governments which are organizationally better geared have been more influential partners from the start. However, it can be argued too that the fragmentation of US metropolitan government gives impetus to a highly competitive struggle for new development, in which the need to provide a stable business climate is particularly important (Peterson, 1981).

Nevertheless, the effects of governmental fragmentation and of intergovernmental financial transfers are not straightforward. There are examples of partnership strategies, such as the Renaissance 2 programme in Pittsburgh, which are prepared solely on the basis of capital bids to higher levels of government. Federal grant regimes dating back to the civil rights period in the 1960s and the Carter presidency have also had an important impact on local programmes. Indeed one clear benefit of partnerships is the advantage which they can offer in bidding for and securing non-local funding support or state legislative backing. On the other hand, the greater reliance of US urban authorities on locally raised finance generates greater political sensitivity to local economic buoyancy.

Programmes of the 1960s, channelled directly to neighbourhood groups, created countervailing political forces to the Democratic Party base in cities and resistance to the wholesale dislocation of disadvantaged communities which had occurred in city redevelopment, sometimes as a result of partnership action. Particularly in cities where this neighbourhood empowerment ultimately had an impact on electoral fortunes, as in the election of populist mayors unbacked by business élites in Cleveland (Swanstrom, 1985) and Atlanta (Henson and King, 1982), partnerships lost much of their legitimacy influence, leading to adjustments in their role ranging from virtual breakdown in communication to strategies to incorporate leading community critics (Jezierski, 1988b). The political stability on which many partnerships rested has thus been tested in recent years, although a degree of ideological congruence between stable, largely Democratic city government and business (largely Republican) élites still survives in many cities. Private sector membership of partnerships has shown considerable continuity, although domination by charismatic individuals, both public and private, has tended to give way to more bureaucratic leadership. The Carter programmes were more explicitly supportive of economic development programmes and provided extra resources and impetus to partnerships. Not all partnerships have been keen to attract federal funding, however, precisely because it limits the autonomy of local groups. It can also be argued that the federal cut-backs introduced under Reagan have made local public–private co-operation even more critical.

In the earlier phase, partnerships contributed to governmental fragmentation in being the key proponents of special purpose development agencies, established with city government and private sector support but insulated from the formal democratic process (Sbragia, 1988). Whilst these agencies introduced much-needed executive capacity, and are generally favoured by the private sector since their decision-making procedures are closer to those of the business community, there has been considerable disquiet about their lack of accountability and neighbourhood groups commonly object to the somewhat skewed representation of local interests.

The degree of tension between community interests, in terms of residential redevelopment and access to new employment opportunities, and those of partnerships differs according to the social and political make-up of individual urban areas and the extent to which partnerships encompass sectional interests. Taken as a whole, however, the earlier period of urban renewal in which partnerships were active was almost entirely dominated by the physical redevelopment of downtown districts, this despite the fact that many partnerships in principle cover metropolitan-wide areas. The newer wave of partnerships, notwithstanding the greater political organization of non-business interests, exhibits only limited signs that the agenda has been widened to incorporate issues such as low-income housing or local labour market considerations. The most heralded achievements associated with partnerships continue to be the physical adaptation of the built environment to new economic processes, particularly the shift from manufacturing to services (leisure, commerce) and residential restructuring which can attract the more prosperous workers in the service sector. There is no doubt that the economic fortunes of certain urban areas have been transformed as a result of this process, and that public-private co-operation helped smooth it. What remains open to considerable doubt is the precise contribution of partnerships; whether the benefits have accrued to groups other than the local and non-local business community and middle-to high-income groups; and whether the political and economic logic of partnerships can facilitate this outcome.

CONCLUSION

Could public–private partnerships become the driving force in UK urban regeneration programmes and mirror developments in the USA? And if so, what pattern of outcomes can we expect? Current research can provide only partial answers. We can suggest that US partnerships appear to have been important components in the physical transformation of city centres, bringing increased economic activity in their wake. However, despite stronger legislation on positive discrimination in employment and on contracts compliance procedures which allow the targeting of disadvantaged social groups, the reported US experience does not indicate that this model is capable of addressing distributive issues to any great degree. We can also point to a range of differences which make the replication of the US model in Britain difficult, including spatial differences in the organization of capital, differences in governmental structure and intergovernmental fiscal relations, and differences in party systems and ideological characteristics.

Such factors notwithstanding, it is certain in the short to medium term that further stress will be put on encouraging private-sector-dominated solutions to urban problems in the UK, with particular emphasis on physical redevelopment and the attempt to reverse the long-standing trend of suburbanization which has seen more affluent social groups desert the cities in large numbers. The basis of a new policy infrastructure is now in place and will be augmented over time, a contemporary example being in training where local private sector groups are, through the creation of new Training and Enterprise Councils, being given responsibility for public programmes (HMSO, 1988b). Conflicting national political demands will not, however, ensure that central government will be wholly supportive of partnerships. The introduction of the poll tax in 1990 and the concomitant nationalization of the local business rate, for example, will reduce rather than enhance incentives for local authority participation in partnerships. Moreover, it is by no means clear that the private sector construction lobby will maintain their interest in urban development should further subsidy programmes not be forthcoming. How effective future arrangements will be in tackling a range of urban problems can ultimately be gauged only be adequate research.

The agenda for such research would need to be considerably wider than that evident in the US literature examined here. Even allowing for the highly qualitative nature of the studies which try to link institutional inputs to particular economic and social outputs, we can form no firm impression as to the real contribution of public–private partnerships as yet. Whether some cities have achieved successful economic adjustment without the need for any institutional mechanism or others failed despite developing such a mechanism remain open questions. If the critical issue is the extent to which actors in the public and private sectors are able to anticipate future economic trends and act entrepreneurially to ensure that particular localities adjust successfully and to mutual benefit, an institutional focus, however convenient, will not cover the range of bargaining processes involved.

Area-based public–private partnerships in effect try to counter two sets of constraints by a process of coalition building and bargaining. The 'objective' constraints, based on the assumption that investment is inherently rational, concern profitability and lead to attempts to encourage risk sharing between participants. The opposite assumption, that investment decisions are not rational, leads to responses which suggest that investors will respond favourably to information which points out irrationality in resource allocation (hence place-marketing), or to appeals to trade off profit levels in the name of some higher good (social responsibility). Each element is represented in UK efforts at present. Testing the adequacy of each assumption in particular localities would be a useful first step in the evaluation of partnerships.

Future work must also examine the contribution of various factors which influence partnership building. These include: the level of autonomous decision-making capacity available to actors in the local public and private sectors and their ability to gain access to non-local resources through their respective networks; the influence of national organizations, both public and private, particularly the impact of national public policy and private sector umbrella groups; the range of participants and their respective motivations – the more encompassing US concept of 'growth coalitions' (Logan and Molotch, 1987) offers considerably more scope here although allowance should be made for the greater role of national organizations in the UK given the greater levels of economic and political centralization; the process of bargaining, goal setting and institutional development; the policy tools used; and performance evaluation of partnership-inspired projects, measured against both stated objectives and wider indicators of urban deprivation in order to assess the redistributive potential of partnerships. These are the bare bones of a research programme which should be subject to wider debate, but sustained empirical work is essential if discussion about partnerships is to rise above its current politically charged and rather superficial level.

NOTES

1.   The few studies include Law, C.M. (1988) 'Public–private partnership in urban revitalisation in Britain', *Regional Studies*, Vol. 22, No. 5 (1988) pp. 446–51; and Moore, C. and Richardson, J. (1986) 'Shifting parameters: public/private partnership in local economic regeneration', *Public Policy and Administration*, Vol. 1, No. 1, pp. 33–49.

2.   For a detailed account of élite power in Victorian society, see Garrard, J. (1983) *Leadership and Power in Victorian Industrial Towns 1830–80*, Manchester, Manchester University Press.

3.   A wider discussion of governmental appeals for a revolution in values can be found in Marquand, D. (1988) *The Unprincipled Society: New Demands and Old Politics*, London, Fontana, Ch. 3, pp. 63–88.

4.   See, for example, North-West Group of Eight (1987) *Renaissance North-West: A Plan for Regional Revival*, Manchester, North-West Group of Eight.

REFERENCES

Aberdeen Beyond 2000 (1988) 'Initial plan', Aberdeen, Aberdeen Beyond 2000.

Barbour, G.P. (1982) 'Portland, Oregon: A balance of interest in public–private co-operation', in Fosler and Berger (1982).

BIC (1988) *The Future of Enterprise Agencies*, London, Business in the Community.

Birmingham Heartlands (n.d.) *A Strategy for the East Birmingham Inner City Renewal* and *Fact Sheets Nos. 1–9*, Birmingham, Birmingham Heartlands.

Boyle, R. (1988) 'Private sector urban regeneration: the Scottish experience', in Parkinson, M., Foley, B. and Judd, D., *Regenerating the Cities:*

The UK Crisis and the US Experience, Manchester, Manchester University Press.

Brandl, J. and Brooks, R. (1982) 'Public–private partnership for urban revitalisation: the Minneapolis and St Paul experience', in Fosler and Berger (1982).

BUD (n.d.) *The Partnership Enterprise Zone*, London, British Urban Developments.

Cafferty, P.S.J. and McCready, W.C. (1982) 'The Chicago public–private partnership experience: a heritage of involvement' in Fosler and Berger (1982).

Coleman, M. (1986) 'Examination of public/private co-operative response patterns to regional structural change in the Pittsburgh region', Paper to Regional Structural Change and Industrial Policy in International Perspective Conference, Spryer, W. Germany, 24–7 April.

Cowie, H. (1985) *The Phoenix Partnership: Urban Regeneration for the 21st Century*, London, National Council for Building Material Producers.

D.o.E. (1981), 'Review of inner cities policy: ministerial guidelines', Press Notice 59, 9, London, Department of the Environment.

D.o.E. (1985) 'Urban Programme: ministerial guidelines for partnership and programme authority areas, London, Department of the Environment.

D.o.E. (1988) 'Local authorities' interests in companies: a discussion paper', London, Department of the Environment.

Feagin, J.R. and Smith, M.P. (1987) 'Cities and the new international division of labour: an overview' in Smith, M.P. and Feagin, J.R. (eds) *The Capitalist City: Global Restructuring and Community Politics*, Oxford, Basil Blackwell.

Fosler, R.S. and Berger, R.A. (eds) 1982 *Public–private Partnership in American Cities: Seven Case Studies*, Lexington, Mass., Lexington Books.

GLC (1983) 'Small firms and the London industrial strategy', Economic Policy Group Strategy Document No. 4, London, Greater London Council.

Henson, M.D and King, J. (1982) 'The Atlanta public–private romance: an abrupt transformation', in Fosler and Berger (1982).

HMSO (1988a) 'The conduct of local authority business: the Government response to the report of the Widdicombe Committee of Inquiry', Cm 433, London, HMSO.

HMSO (1988b) 'Employment for the 1990s', Cm 540, London, HMSO.

Jezierski, L. (1988a) 'Political limits to development in two declining cities: Cleveland and Pittsburgh', in Rothschild, J. and Wallace, M. (eds)

Deindustrialisation and the Economic Restructuring of American Industry, Vol. 3, Greenwich, Conn.: JAI Press.

Jezierski, L. (1988b) 'Neighbourhoods and public-private partnerships in Pittsburgh', Paper to American Sociological Association Meeting, Chicago, Ill., August.

Krumholz, N., Keating, D. and Metzger, J. (1988) 'Cleveland: post-populist public-private partnerships', Paper to Urban Affairs Association Conference, St Louis, March.

Logan, J.R and Molotch, H.L. (1987) *Urban Fortunes: The Political Economy of Place*, Berkeley, Calif., University of California Press.

Newcastle Initiative (1988) 'Initial plan', Newcastle, Newcastle Initiative.

OECD (1987) *Revitalising Urban Economies*, Paris, Organization for Economic Co-operation and Development.

Peterson, P.E. (1981) *City Limits*, Chicago, Ill., University of Chicago Press.

Phoenix (n.d.) 'Urban regeneration for the 21st century', publicity leaflet, London, Phoenix.

Richardson, J., Moore, C. and Moon, J. (1985) 'Politicisation of business: corporate responses to unemployment', Paper to Politics and Business in Western Democracies Workshop, ECPR, Barcelona, March.

Sbragia, A. (1988) 'The American investment state: entrepreneurship, restriction and circumvention', Paper to 'L'Etat aux Etats-Unis' Conference, Chantilly, January.

Swanstrom, T. (1985) *The Crisis of Growth Politics: Cleveland, Kucinich and the Challenge of Urban Populism*, Philadelphia, Pa., Temple University Press.

Vogel, R.K. (1988) 'Dynamics of business-government relations in the community: towards a typology of public-private decision making systems', Paper to Urban Affairs Association Conference, St Louis, March.

Whelan, R.K. (1988) 'New Orleans: public-private partnerships and uneven development', Paper to Urban Affairs Association Conference, St Louis, March.

CHAPTER 7

Enterprise Boards: An Inside View

John Gunnell

INTRODUCTION

Enterprise Boards, economic development companies set up by local authorities to provide corporate investment, are an unintended product of the early years of the Thatcher Government. The sharp decline in employment over the period 1979–81 not only focused attention on the need for urgent economic redress in urban areas, it also led to an electoral swing to Labour so that in May 1981 big gains in the local elections gave the Labour Party workable majorities in many counties including all six metropolitan county councils and the Greater London Council.

There are upwards of 70 local authority economic development companies, the majority of which are directly involved in investment or other joint activities with the private sector. Enterprise Boards are, however, a relatively small grouping distinguished by the scale of their staff and funding and by their common involvement in corporate investment. No clearer definition is possible as Enterprise Boards are not statutory bodies and nor, except as companies limited by guarantee, do they have common articles and memoranda.

This chapter covers six companies which have promoted themselves individually, and to some extent collectively, as enterprise boards: Derbyshire Enterprise Board (DEB), Greater London Enterprise (GLE, formerly GLEB – Greater London Enterprise Board), Lancashire Enterprises Limited (LEL), Merseyside Enterprise Board (MEB), West Midlands Enterprise Board (WMEB) and

Yorkshire Enterprise Limited (YEL, formerly WYEB – West Yorkshire Enterprise Board). It examines their methods of corporate investment, their control and funding, and the other services they provide.

Each of the six companies originated in authorities which Labour had gained in 1981; five were created by administrations elected in 1981 (the exception, the DEB, being created during Derbyshire's second Labour term of office), four by authorities abolished in 1986 by Act of Parliament. Significantly, the two metropolitan county councils which remained in Labour control throughout their existence did *not* create parallel structures, while the administration taking control in the remaining metropolitan county, Greater Manchester, inherited a company set up by the Conservative administration. The Greater Manchester Economic Development Corporation (GMEDC), although it has called itself 'the first metropolitan enterprise board', operated from a property rather than finance base. The Greater Manchester district authorities kept the GMEDC in operation without major change, and investment in local industry has remained a minority part of its work.

Although the Enterprise Boards were themselves an innovation, they owed much to the previous experience of key individuals who themselves had been involved in local 'interventionist' strategies. Michael Ward, newly elected to the GLC, had pioneered early economic development work as a Wandsworth borough councillor. Jim Mason, a former Lancashire county councillor, was not only a director of the Co-operative Bank but for four years had been chairman of Warrington Development Corporation. Geoff Edge, elected to the West Midlands County Council, had served as an MP during the period in which Labour set up the National Enterprise Board. They all believed that their councils (who could raise significant sums of money through their Section 137 2p rate) could provide a more radical form of local government intervention in industry than had hitherto been the case. The 1981 Labour manifestos in West Yorkshire, Lancashire, London and the West Midlands contained a commitment to establish enterprise boards or industrial investment companies as a major response to rapidly rising local unemployment.

Despite their manifestos the authorities proceeded with caution on election as legal uncertainties were raised by officers. Could local authorities hold shares in companies? Was an Enterprise Board able to do anything that the council itself could not do?[1] Some advantages were easily recognized: rapidity of decision making, confidentiality, flexibility of approach – all advantages that are difficult to accommodate in the council committee system. Detailed investigation revealed others: the scope for raising private sector finance to part fund the operations of an arm's-length company limited by guarantee, and the potential for recruiting the kind of corporate finance staff who would not be attracted by jobs in local or central government. The dates of incorporation of the earliest Boards do indicate, however, that extensive work was needed before the key officers within the authorities evolved a structure which satisfied their proper concern for legality, prudence and accountability (Table 7.1).

MODELS OF ENTERPRISE BOARD: BEFORE AND AFTER 1986

Although each Enterprise Board cited job creation and preservation as the rationale for its existence, both the theoretical models on which intervention was based and the ways in which the Boards operated once running differed widely. Rather than considering each Board individually a comparison between those that differ most widely will illustrate the range of thought and practice. The words used to justify the setting up of the GLEB and the WYEB bear little resemblance to one another. The scope of services offered by the LEL is in sharp contrast to the narrower remit of the WYEB/YEL. The approach to the process of investment itself in the WMEB is very significantly different from that in the WYEB/YEL.

In London, the GLEB was intended to promote a new socialist market economy. Investment was to create 'high quality long term jobs . . . welded to the specific social priorities' of the GLC. While economic viability was a 'major concern . . . priority is given to areas, industries and social groups most affected by unemployment

Table 7.1 Key dates in the formation of the Enterprise Boards (month/year)

	DEB	GLEB	LEL	MEB	WMEB	WYEB
Committee approval for setting up an Enterprise Board	6/86	8/81	12/81	3/83	7/81	6/82
Managing director appointed	2/87	6/82	5/82	1/84	2/82	9/82
Open for business	4/87	10/82	5/82	4/84	4/82	11/82

and industrial decline'. The particular needs of 'women and ethnic minorities', 'workforce participation', 'new forms of industrial ownership and control' are all significant within the 'new approach to investment' launched by Alan McGarvey, the first chief executive. In this he accurately reflected the promises of the election statement. The West Yorkshire manifesto, by contrast, was tentative. The commitment to the setting up of an 'industrial investment board . . . hopefully on a commercial basis' was one of a number of measures aimed at ameliorating unemployment and economic decline in the county. The practical concern was paramount; the theoretical underpinning largely absent. If the GLEB was a fully formed embryo before election day, the WYEB still had much gestation ahead.

When the WYEB was established it was complementary to, but quite separate from, the economic development unit of the county council. In contrast, the economic development unit of Lancashire County Council became LEL. Until abolition the WYEB provided corporate finance but no other service: it was only as YEL from June 1987 that it set up White Rose Training Ltd and widened its activities. From the start, however, LEL was not only providing investment but also handled property, training, promotion, sponsorship (for example of Technology Centres), the Lancashire Co-operative Development Agency and even the county's applications to the European Commission for grants from the European Regional Development Fund (ERDF) and the European Social Fund (ESF). LEL therefore merged those parts of economic development which were subsidy oriented with those which might reasonably expect to be profitable. By isolating corporate investment, the WYEB left the county council itself to operate a subsidy-giving policy while the Board held the potentially profitable work.

Even in their approach to the process of investment major contrasts existed between the Enterprise Boards. Faced with the rapid decline of some traditional industries, the WMEB undertook sectoral studies in order to take a pro-active role. This information was to be used as a basis for selective investment aimed at restructuring and reviving important industrial sectors. The resources required for any significant impact, however, proved to be beyond those available. The approach of the WYEB/YEL, on the other hand, was reactive. Although the West Yorkshire area has dominant traditional industries (coal and textiles) there is none the less a diversity of smaller industries. The Board's existence and remit was advertised but no attempt was made to approach specific companies or to concentrate on any particular sector.

The abolition of their parent bodies, with a consequent reduction in public funding, has changed the perceptions of some boards. GLE, for example, owned by a consortium of London boroughs, lost over 90 per cent of its public funding and therefore needed access to private sector monies in order to continue its role. This has meant not an abandonment of its social remit, nor of the breadth of its activities, but a more commercial orientation towards its key corporate investment role.[2] Similarly, the WMEB and the MEB had to accommodate to the less certain public funding of district councils, while YEL accurately assessed before abolition that it would get no funding at all from the district councils in its area. Having operated preabolition in a wholly commercial manner, there was no need for change in either its style of operation or its approach to investment. The company was fully aware that its survival was dependent on the survival and success of its client companies.

CORPORATE INVESTMENT: A CASE STUDY OF WYEB/YEL

Rationale for the Board's Existence: The Funding Gap

The entry of the public sector into the realm of venture capital was, in itself, a response to market forces – whatever the motivations, political or otherwise, of some of the people involved. Without a valid *financial* reason for intervention the setting up of an Enterprise Board could not succeed.

At the end of 1982 when the WYEB opened for business the rationale was clear. The early 1980s were not flowing with funds for investment. The control over almost all potential money was based in the City of London. Financiers were not averse to inner city or regional investment provided that propositions were of a sufficient size to yield a good, preferably rapid, rate of return. So, ironically, it was easier to borrow large sums of money than small ones. There were thus viable proposals for potentially successful businesses which were unable to go ahead just because they wanted relatively small investment sums (less than £250,000). In the regions it was believed that the 'City men' did not think it worth the travelling effort to analyse such proposals. Thus the WYEB was promoting its services as an answer to the 'funding gap'.

The record of the WYEB/YEL might, in itself, suggest the validity of this rationale. Offering finance as equity, loan, convertible loan, mortgage or lease, £20 million had been invested when at the end of 1988 the WYEB/YEL's hundredth completion took place. Additionally, the company had achieved recognition and respect in the regional market place, had proved a reliable partner in co-investment with established institutions, and had even seen its own success reflected in the number of other venture capital firms which had become interested in direct work in Yorkshire and Humberside. YEL's record and reputation, however, owes as much to the company's way of operating as to its results.

Staffing

At the beginning of 1983 the WYEB employed only four people – a managing director, two investment managers and a secretary – but already crucial decisions of style had been taken. The managing director was recruited from the private sector because of the breadth of experience he had to offer in corporate finance work as well as in having run his own businesses. He recruited the other members of the team from a similar background. The company's staff has expanded as its business has grown – 15 by April 1986, 26 by October 1988 (including a secondee) – but the same principle has been applied. The 'case workers' in YEL have remained the investment managers with required business experience. They were soon backed up by a group of investigating accountants, coming from private sector accountancy firms, and an in-house legal team, enabling propositions to proceed as rapidly as possible towards completion. Within the regional financial world the quality of staff affects not just the viability of the proposals completed, but also the reputation of the company itself as respect for the style of operation and the record of individual managers circulates in a relatively tight community. The investment team of YEL have more than once found themselves subject to block headhunting.

Political Consensus

The initial decision to create the WYEB aroused controversy both within the county council and in the West Yorkshire business community. Yet such was its style of working that after the first resolution no other proposal concerning the Board failed to get

Conservative as well as Labour support. The decision to have cross-party representation on both the membership and the directorships meant that the early progress and priorities of the company reflected a consensus. Attitudes in the business world showed a similar and rapid shift. When government consultation papers on the proposed abolition of the metropolitan counties were silent on the issue of Enterprise Boards, the Leeds Chamber of Commerce publicly called for an assurance that the WYEB would remain because of its contribution to business in the region.

The WYEB/YEL has remained free from party political controversy. In its work with local authorities it has formed joint companies not only with Labour-controlled authorities but with the region's only Conservative-controlled authority, North Yorkshire County Council. Its advocates in the region span a complete range of political viewpoints. This consensus also applied to more significant decisions taken first by the county council and later by the company. From the outset WYEB operated quite independently of the County Council and in 1984, well satisfied with the progress made in its first two years of life, the county council made provision for the WYEB to be a wholly independent company. Nevertheless the working relationship between WYEB investment staff and the county's economic development team on matters of common interest continued. In 1986, with the demise of the council, the WYEB widened its geographical remit to include the whole of the Yorkshire and Humberside region, and in a partnership deal with all five West Yorkshire metropolitan district councils – and with the Departments of the Environment and Employment acting as midwife – set up the West Yorkshire Small Firms Fund Limited (WYSFF). In 1987, recognizing the growing amount of business emerging in those parts of the region outside West Yorkshire, the company changed its name to Yorkshire Enterprise Limited (YEL).

Range of Investment Size

If the motivation for creating the WYEB was the loss of jobs in the county, its strength now is the record of 'jobs with profits'. Not only are thousands of people employed in companies in which the WYEB/YEL has invested but YEL itself has been able to generate a profit on its activities.

In its first full operating year YEL invested £1.1 million in twelve companies, for the most part those in the traditional industrial sectors that are strongly represented in West Yorkshire: engineering, textiles and clothing, and printing. Initially, many of the enquiries that were referred to the WYEB were for a 'lender of last resort'. However, it was soon recognized in the local business community that no company would get WYEB backing unless it could show itself to be a commercial proposition with every prospect of long-term viability. It was realized that jobs can always be sustained by subsidy but that profitability must be achieved without subsidy in order for a company, or the jobs, to have any permanence. The quality of propositions improved as the reputation of the WYEB's investment team grew. Initially, the WYEB offered funding in the range of £50–250,000 but was always willing to respond to a one-off investment opportunity (for example, see Profile 1 on Optare).[3] Today, it ranges from £3,000 to over £2 million.

WYSFF was a government-supported 'takeover' of a small firms employment fund successfully operated by West Yorkshire Metropolitan County Council from 1982. The five existing staff transferred to the new subsidiary company, their resource costs being shared between the five district councils. Capital was provided by the WYEB and the fund was formally launched by David Trippier MP, then minister for small firms, in May 1986. WYSFF has proved a very popular resource for the starter and very small business. Offering low-interest, unsecured loans in sums of up to £15,000 it had offered its millionth pound by the end of 1988. The money actually taken up by 31 October 1989 amounts to £973,300 and the number of firms helped to 164.

With WYSFF catering for the risk-finance needs of the smallest businesses and YEL offering equity and loan funding in sums of up to £0.5 million, a further logical step in developing YEL's core business was to create a mechanism for supporting firms needing larger sums. In February 1989 South Yorkshire and West Yorkshire superannuation funds approved proposals to invest £6 million each in a new £15 million Yorkshire Fund in which YEL is also an investor. This fund is managed by a new joint subsidiary company set up with York Trust, the Leeds-based merchant bank, and provides risk finance in sums up to and in excess of £2 million. Already some £5 million is committed. If the Yorkshire Fund proves successful there is a provision to increase its size to £25 million.

Profile 1 **Optare**

In 1984 British Leyland decided that it was going to close its Charles H. Roe bus-building plant in Leeds. The workforce invited a former manager at the plant to lead a buy-out and asked YEL to provide the financial backing. Between September 1984 and February 1985 the plans were laid for a rebuilding of the business as a specialist bus builder. With finance from YEL and from the employees of the new company through an employee share ownership plan (ESOP), Optare moved into the old Charles H. Roe works in February 1985.

In a chaotic market where bus operators were uncertain, because of impending deregulation, which way to jump, Optare designed and launched its 25-seat City Pacer. The bus was a runaway sales success, quickly emulated in style and size by other manufacturers. Four years on from its uncertain birth Optare has capitalized on its early success with further new product launches. City Pacers are now in use all over the country, as are increasing numbers of the larger Star Rider and single-deck Optare Delta.

Indeed, the wheel has now come full circle with Optare once again building double-decker buses. It was the dependence of Charles H. Roe on double-deckers and the collapse of demand for that product that prompted British Leyland to close Charles H. Roe in the first place. Optare has maintained the reputation for quality earned by Charles H. Roe and has added to it a flare in design and a diversity of product that has allowed a build-up in the workforce to 200 plus, with the prospect of more jobs to come.

Joint Companies

Recognizing that the county council itself was soon to disappear and perceiving the strength derived from linking the commercial expertise of WYEB staff with the local knowledge of the economic development units in the local authorities, steps were taken to establish joint companies. This move enabled councils in the region to extend the range of services offered to businesses within their own areas. Underpinning this initiative was an arrangement with the Yorkshire Bank to make up to £20 million available in loans against guarantees from the WYEB and the local authority involved.

Bradford Metropolitan Enterprises Limited (BMEL) was the first such company established and by 1988 another five had been formed, including one in which there is a third party involved. North Yorkshire County Council first determined the nature of the company they needed and then interviewed prospective teams, choosing a combined team of YEL and York Trust. Each joint company has one of the YEL investment team with a particular remit for its area.

The reputation of YEL in the market-place is a reflection of two factors: its success in making a profitable business out of an activity that had been abjured by other financial institutions; and, the key to that success, its hands-on management style. The logic, right from the outset, was that if YEL was to survive in a market that other finance houses were not prepared to enter, then it would have to provide something extra as part of its service. That extra is the management input that is made through YEL non-executive directors to the deliberations of client company boards of directors. The practical business experience of YEL's investment managers is thus made available to the management of client companies. If necessary and appropriate, YEL's involvement will go further than the provision of advice, including active participation in the day-to-day running of the business.

The five investment managers are YEL's salesforce. It is their responsibility, with whatever help is needed from other members of the client-support team, to carry out an appraisal of a prospective client and to pull together, if it is proposition they would wish to back, a funding package that suits that particular company's circumstances. That package will seek to accommodate the differing interests and requirements of the client managers themselves, the secured lenders (i.e. the High Street banks), and the risk-capital providers including YEL itself.

Once a week all investment proposals are reviewed at a meeting involving all of the investment managers and investigating accountants. If proposals to invest and the funding packages designed pass the scrutiny of this meeting, a pre-offer letter is sent to the prospective client. If the company in question accepts, the proposal is taken to the board of YEL or to the board of, say, the North Yorkshire Investment Company Limited for approval. Once approval has been given, a formal offer letter is sent to the prospective client and the legal work begins in earnest.

Whilst the decision process is fairly straightforward, the in-depth analysis that is carried out, what might be called a highly focused sector study, can mean that it may take up to six or eight weeks to conclude an investment. On occasions, where YEL has been forced to make an emergency response, this rigorous analysis and investigation has had to be abandoned in favour of gut feelings and quick decisions. The norm, however, is for YEL to try and protect its downside risk by identifying all of the problems before the investment is made.

Downside risk is also reduced through maintaining, post investment, a close involvement with client companies. Built into the investment agreements are a series of controls that allow YEL's non-executive director, normally the investment manager who carried out the appraisal, to take control of a client company *in extremis*. Because YEL is interested in job creation, the primary concern apart from matters of financial prudence has been in ensuring that companies retain and expand jobs within the region and so structure employer–employee relations that both productivity targets and trade union and other individual rights are safeguarded. The trade unions have taken the view that it is not up to YEL to promote trade union membership in client companies but rather to ensure that the unions themselves are able to present their case for membership.

With its strong commitment to client company aftercare many of the problems faced by companies that are seeking to grow can be satisfactorily addressed. Even so, YEL has had its failures. To date it has lost thirteen of its clients in receiverships (including Keighley Foundries, see Profile 2), though only one of the businesses has failed to re-emerge in one form or another. Against these failures, as YEL's investment portfolio reaches maturity so there is an increasing flow of realizations (including Hotwork International, see Profile 3). At present the balance between profitable realizations and losses through company failures is enough to secure a profitable return for YEL itself. On average, for every £4 made YEL loses £1 on its divestments.

The three company profiles illustrate YEL's investment role. Hotwork International was brought from near closure to profitability. Keighley Foundries and Optare were both former British Leyland companies: Optare has succeeded against the odds, whereas Keighley Foundries has gone into receivership.

Training

In 1987 YEL made its first move to diversify out of its core role, corporate finance. In the autumn of that year a training consultancy service was set up. It was recognized at the time that it was important to develop the hands-on management philosophy so that YEL could

Profile 2   **Keighley Foundries**

One of YEL's earliest investments was at Keighley Foundries, a management buy-out from British Leyland. Employing over 150 people making castings for the automotive industry, the company appeared, in its first few months of independence at the end of 1983, to be operating profitably. However, it quickly transpired that many of the profits were of a one-off nature, that costs inherited from the previous owner were going to be a substantial burden to the company, and that margins on a number of fixed-price contracts negotiated in the early days were negligible to non-existent.

With help from YEL, costing systems were built up and efforts made to boost productivity. But the foundry industry in general was in a very depressed state and this prevented any significant improvement in margins. In the space of a single year there was flooding when the River Aire burst its banks, an explosion that blew part of the roof off and then further flooding following torrential rain, after which optimism began to fade.

Despite these setbacks further investment was committed in a bid to reduce the cost of sales. In the event this further investment did not generate returns quickly enough to avoid a final slide into receivership in 1986. The business was subsequently bought out of receivership by a major plc. Additional heavy investment coupled with a recovery in the market for automotive industry castings has brought the former YEL client back to profitability.

promote its services as having 'added value' by comparison with its growing number of competitors. Servicing the interface between client companies – many of whom do not have their own training manager – training providers and funding agencies, YEL's training consultancy service has become an important back-up resource to its investment managers. Comprehensive training audits have been carried out in client companies, recruitment problems have been resolved, and training programmes have been devised to answer specific needs at management, supervisory and shopfloor levels.

As YEL itself does not provide the training, it can take an independent view on behalf of the client, putting together packages that combine the best of what is available from private sector providers, further education colleges, polytechnics and other bodies. Demand for the service offered has expanded much more quickly than was anticipated. In July 1988 the Yorkshire Open College Consortium (YOCC) was launched. This brings together YEL, the Open College

Profile 3 **Hotwork International**

In early 1986 over 200 jobs were on the line when Dewsbury-based Hotwork International ran into financial difficulties. While highly regarded for its technical ideas and engineering ability in the manufacture and installation of burners for the metal-melting and glass-producing industries, the company had been poorly managed in a business sense. With the company's bank on the point of putting in a receiver, YEL was asked if it would back a management buy-in.

A fortnight later a financial restructuring had been agreed and the new chief executive, backed by an investment manager and an investigating accountant from YEL, were beginning to reshape the business. A labyrinthine structure of 22 companies was reduced to four UK companies and one overseas company. With a management buy-out taking 30 jobs in a peripheral subsidiary out of Hotwork International, the company was left with 176 employees.

Within a year the attack on overheads and the refocusing of the business had allowed a £1.4 million overdraft to be wiped out and a trading loss to be translated into a substantial trading profit. With support from YEL, through its non-executive director on the Hotwork International board, the company steadily built up its reputation and profits. On the back of this success, in January 1989, the management team recruited by the new chief executive bought both him and YEL out.

and six further education colleges scattered across the region. Through YOCC and its other links, YEL's training consultancy service has already provided help to more than 80 companies.

Whilst YEL, like any other commercial organization, must make a profit to survive, it has a wider objective, to sustain and create long-term job opportunities within the Yorkshire and Humberside region. Backing growing companies that show good prospects for viability and continuing commercial success is the means to this end. Past and present YEL client companies employ over 8,000 people. WYSFF, the partnership company of YEL and West Yorkshire local authorities, has provided finance to firms capable of sustaining, with the investment they have received, almost another 1,800 jobs. Given that YEL is playing its job creation role and making a profit at the same time, and that the only cost to the public sector of WYSFF's operation relates to salaries of staff and other associated overheads, there is a logic to the replication of the

YEL/WYSFF model in those remaining areas of the country where the Enterprise Board approach has yet to be adopted.

Perhaps the most significant evidence of YEL influence is the change in availability of finance within the region. When the WYEB/YEL opened for business in 1982 there was only one other significant player, at the local level, in the provision of risk finance to the small business: Investors in Industry. In 1989 Investors in Industry (or 3is, the name the company now uses) remains by far the largest provider of development and venture capital in Yorkshire and Humberside. But because of the pioneering effort of the WYEB/YEL in backing propositions that were not attractive to 3is or City-based venture capital companies, a wider selection of equity providers have emerged to take an interest in the small firms sector in Yorkshire and Humberside. The resulting competition is, clearly, to the benefit of firms seeking risk finance.

WIDER ROLES OF THE BOARDS

Venture capital activity is the distinguishing feature of Enterprise Boards and many aspects of YEL's operation are closely paralleled in each of the other Boards. Tables 7.2 and 7.3 show the investment records of the Boards both in their mainstream activities and also in the help given through different mechanisms to small firms.

Whilst there are differences in the post-investment mechanisms developed, the packaging of funds for an individual proposition will be on similar lines whichever Board is involved. The more

Table 7.2 Enterprise Board mainstream corporate investment

	DEB	GLEB[1]	GLE[2]	LEL	MEB	WMEB	YEL
Funds invested in companies up to 31.12.88 excluding grants given (£m)	1.1	17.0	6.4	11.2	4.4	17.8	20.0
Number of client companies benefiting up to 31.12.88	6	120	24	54	47	50	100
Number of employees in past and present client companies	240	2,000	450	5,850	2,300	6,500	7,000

Notes: [1]Period to 31 March 1986.
     [2]Period from 1 April 1986. Includes pension fund monies managed.

Table 7.3 Enterprise Board investment in small firms

	GLE Business Incentive Scheme	LEL Rosebud Fund	MEB Small Firms	WMCOF	WYSFF
Funds invested in companies up to 31.12.88 excluding grants given (£m)	0.2	0.42	0.25	1.01	0.8
Number of client companies benefiting up to 31.12.88	49	53	35	53	136
Number of employees in past and present client companies	100	438	220	n/a	1,400

Note: GLE in a joint enterprise agency venture with Barclays Bank has made 49 loans totalling £213,000 to start up ethnic minorities businesses.

notable differences lie in the breadth of the role given to the Board: property renewal and development, an extended role in training, programmes of technology and new product development, the development of co-operatives, and advocacy have all been tackled successfully.

Property

All local authorities own and manage property. Major councils for historic reasons often possess much land of strategic significance in their urban centres: at abolition West Yorkshire Metropolitan County Council owned some 28,000 sites and the land holding of the GLC was reputed to be worth approaching £10 billion. The utilization of this resource is critical not just to the finances but to the urban regeneration policies of the authority.

Three Boards have chosen to develop a property portfolio: GLE, LEL and the DEB. In Greater London GLE inherited, on abolition, property from the GLEB much of which was overvalued in its accounts. Initially it had to rationalize and reduce the holding, retaining for its own property division those sites for development which fitted its overall policy objectives. Now it works primarily within those boroughs which are in membership to provide workspace for small and medium-sized companies through a 'turnkey' service package involving purpose-building to meet the requirements of the individual client. GLE's total portfolio is now valued at £14.5 million and it has set up a joint venture company with

Rosehaugh plc to purchase industrial sites which GLE then manages.

LEL in its first year of operation purchased two development sites, renovating them to create units for small to medium-sized companies. By 1984/5 it owned 1 million square feet in fourteen sites and by 1987 25 sites totalling over 1.5 million square feet. LEL has concentrated on sites the development of which carries forward its strategic economic work, as illustrated in the profile of White Cross, Lancaster (Profile 4).

Training

YEL's training role is limited to the provision of a consultancy service to client companies, a marked contrast to the approach of other Boards. Those which are part of an ongoing county authority – LEL and the DEB – offer a wide training provision as the authorities choose to use the Boards to implement their requirements. Those which have no parent body have adopted a more specialist approach to serving the business community. Each of the services offered claims success: the WMEB for a training centre which serves the local community at Tyseley as well as wider business needs; GLE for the newly created Enterprise Training Centre, opened by Prince Charles in 1988.

LEL through many different schemes has established over 3,000 training places within the county. It has also shown the value of linking training with investment. A particular example is the securing by Lancashire of the UK plant set up by Sanko Gosei of Japan. They chose Skelmersdale as a location because in addition to the Regional Selective Assistance grant, which the DTI would have given them for going to any Assisted or Development Area, LEL offered a £1.12 million training programme.

Technology and New Product Development

Finance for new product development is available in many local authority areas. In general, the sums provided are small, intended as 'seedcorn' and given as grants. A number of the Boards have worked in this field: the WMEB primarily through links with Aston University; LEL, recognizing the subsidy element, through gaining private sector sponsorship for a specific 'investment' fund; and GLE through its concentration on technology initiatives (Profile 5).

[143]

Profile 4   **White Cross, Lancaster**

One of Europe's most ambitious inner city regeneration projects began with a telephone call from the manager of a rubber products business. Its parent company was drawing up plans to close down its entire operations at White Cross with the loss of 650 jobs. The manager believed his division had a viable future and approached LEL for finance for a management buy-out. The deal appeared doomed, however, when the parent company demanded vacant possession of the entire site.

Rather than see a good business fold, LEL brought the entire 15-acre site for £1 million. And backed with a £60,000 investment from LEL, White Cross Rubber Products Limited was launched in the summer of 1983. The company has since doubled its workforce and an £8 million programme of redevelopment has transformed the once near-derelict White Cross site.

The new company required only 50,000 of the available 1,000,000 square feet and an urgent review was needed to put the remainder of the site back to use. Extensive demolition of the more dilapidated buildings within the complex was instigated, clearing more than half of the site to improve access, car parking and the environment. The redevelopment plan outlined four separate zones – office, industrial, housing and social – which would breathe new life into the remaining buildings. With the involvement of the private sector, a canalside pub and restaurant has been opened and new homes built. The historic Grade II-listed former barracks building is now the prestige entrance to an extensive commercial complex and the industrial zone is complete and fully let.

Today, White Cross is the address for more than 60 businesses, together employing more than 500 people in activities ranging from heavy engineering to television broadcasting. When the site is fully developed, 400,000 square feet will have been brought to the market in the heart of the historic city of Lancaster. White Cross, which once stood empty and on the verge of dereliction, is now a classic example of what can be achieved with the necessary commitment and expertise, and the right mix of public and private sector investment.

Support for Co-operatives

The co-operative movement itself recognizes intrinsic difficulties in commercial investment by external companies in a co-operative. Schweke (1989) argues that the current legal structure:

> means that equity capital is almost impossible to attract due to the prospects of fairly low returns; that preference shares can

Profile 5   **Greater London Enterprise technology**

Not only is there a shortage of hands-on venture capital, appropriate premises, and skills training in our national and regional economies, there is also a clear need for more funding of innovation. Greater London Enterprise considers that its technology initiatives play a key role in supporting innovative developments which also feed into venture capital, property and training programmes.

In 1986 GLE became prime contractor for a £4.5 million EEC contract to develop human-centred computer integrated manufacturing systems – putting the skilled operative back into computerized production systems. This work has been conducted with partners in Germany and Denmark, and BICC and Rolls-Royce, along with universities in Manchester, Sheffield and London. GLE has invested £425,000 in a small London company which was the subcontractor for the project in the UK. As a result of the commercial development of the project, GLE's investment is now valued at £1.5 million.

GLE's engineers helped design a new more efficient plant layout for Plessey in Lewisham, enabling it to relocate in the borough. GLE's property specialists are now involved in the development of the property.

GLE has also secured an EEC contract to develop training technology for reskilling during industrial change. This will be conducted with partners in Italy, Greece and Portugal.

Finally, commitment to product development has led GLE to invest in the development of robotic vision systems – or robots that can see – along with advanced computer systems. Again investment in this area has seen the value of GLE's stake in a company double as a result of new investors now coming in at a much higher price.

---

be sold only by designing complicated additional legal subsidiaries; and that there is a lack of individual member equity or debt contributions to the firm ... To a private lender this entails that the firm will be always too highly geared in its equity to debt ratios and that there are not enough signs of genuine in-house financial commitment to the enterprise.

The historic relationship of the co-operative movement to the labour movement means that a number of Boards are expressly committed to working with them. Doing so requires mechanisms separate from the normal investment processes, as illustrated by West Midlands Co-operative Finance Limited (Profile 6).

Profile 6 **West Midlands Co-operative Finance Limited**

When a British-based lingerie company rationalized its operations 40 people lost their jobs. Ten of them in Cradley Health, West Midlands, decided to use their knowledge and skills in clothing manufacture to set up a co-operative. Their company, Topstitch, began in 1987 with £1,000 in redundancy pay from each of the ten and £8,000 from West Midlands Co-operative Finance (WMCOF). Buying the plant at a favourable price, the company is now performing 50 per cent better than its target and has added two extra staff.

WMCOF, set up in 1984, has over a period of four years provided loans totalling over £1 million to more than 50 companies. Its judgement in investment is based on the realism and accuracy of the company's financial projections, the market for the product and the people in key positions. After-investment care is a feature of the fund's work and includes a factoring service. WMCOF purchases sales invoices from co-operatives, advancing up to 75 per cent of the face value with the balance payable when the customer pays.

The success of WMCOF is illustrated by the region now having a relatively strong co-operative sector, in marked contrast to the situation of the early 1980s. Losses on the loans made amount to 12.7 per cent, a rate which compares favourably with lending to starter businesses generally.

The Co-operative Development Agency has developed a 'model' equity participation model. In practice, however, co-operatives will not consider giving up a slice of their equity. Schweke argues for equity participation by members of the co-operative on an employee share ownership plan (ESOP) basis. ESOPs have proved a controversial issue within the labour movement and there is no consistent view of them among the Boards. YEL has three involvements in companies with wide workforce ownership: Optare (Profile 1), Rodley Engineering, and its one Unity Trust-backed ESOP, RFS Industries at Doncaster, a management buy-out from BREL when the Government enforced privatization of the company. The commitment of the workforce in these companies suggests that ESOPs will play a larger role in the future. At Doncaster the money for the workforce percentage of the company was provided by Unity Trust, the trade union bank. The three YEL clients where ESOPs have been introduced each employ more than 100 people; the suitability of the ESOP structure for a smaller co-operative has not been demonstrated.

While no other Board has participated to date in a Unity Trust-backed ESOP, support for co-operatives under the existing structures has been strong. In Lancashire the Co-operative Development Agency, which in its fifth year of operation helped its fiftieth co-operative to set up, could by 1989 count over 330 employees within the existing businesses. In Merseyside, where there are 25 trading co-operatives, the small loans fund was specifically committed to helping this form of business.

Advocacy

The abolition of the metropolitan counties has prevented a comparative study of the effectiveness of housing the venture capital service within or outside the framework of the local authority economic development structure. The evidence from Lancashire is that there is added value from an integrated approach because the finance arm can be linked not just with other service functions but with the public responsibility which an authority has as a voice or advocate for its area. Thus liaison with the EEC over grant funding both through ESF and ERDF, and the development of trade links with China for the benefit of Lancashire companies, are properly within the scope of LEL.

The regeneration of the economy along the length of the Leeds and Liverpool Canal (Profile 7) is the most dramatic and visionary work of LEL, involving as it does EEC and urban programme funding and the active participation of the British Waterways Board, Wigan Metropolitan District Council and each of the district councils along the route, as well as the private sector. Lack of a strategic tier of county government prevents a similarly comprehensive scheme developing on the Yorkshire side of the Pennines.

CONTROL AND FUNDING

Each of the six Enterprise Boards was started by a local authority using money available under the Local Government Act 1972. Each Board initially had a relationship of accountability to its parent authority. But the only statements which apply to all six companies are historical: today they are controlled and financed in significantly different ways, with the likelihood that by the date of

Profile 7   Leeds and Liverpool Canal Corridor

The Leeds and Liverpool Canal was heralded as one of the greatest civil engineering achievements of its era when it was completed in 1816. Linking the Port of Liverpool with the pioneering towns of Britain's industrial revolution, the canal was the longest man-made waterway in Britain.

But what started life as a symbol of prosperity for the North-West has since become a monument to the region's industrial demise as the industries which created the boom years faced massive and continual decline. Entire industries like coal, textiles and quarrying have almost completely disappeared along with the related heavy engineering which followed them. The Leeds and Liverpool Canal was lined with dereliction and decay. The mills that were a testament to the drive and energy of a bygone era stood mostly empty, crumbling into disrepair.

It was no surprise when a detailed survey commissioned by LEL in 1985 revealed that the communities along the Leeds and Liverpool Canal were among the most deprived in Europe. Unemployment was far in excess of national averages. In terms of derelict land, 6 per cent of England's total fell within the canal corridor.

To meet this challenge, LEL brought together a consortium of local authorities and other bodies like the British Waterways Board. From the outset, the consortium recognized that all available resources – both public and private – had to be involved. In 1986 an economic development plan was completed, listing pilot projects along the Leeds and Liverpool Canal with a total investment cost of £80 million.

Within two years, this total had to be revised to a conservative £300 million as the private sector climbed aboard the redevelopment bandwagon. The first of the pilot projects was completed in 1988 when a business development centre was opened at Eanam Wharf, Blackburn, which included starter units, a craft centre, a textile technology unit and a pub and restaurant. A nationwide marketing campaign launched early in 1989 produced an avalanche of interest from the private sector in areas ranging from tourism to industry and from housing to commerce.

The project was meeting its objectives. By bringing together the best of the public and private sectors, some of the worst examples of inner urban decay in Europe could be transformed into a thriving mixed economy.

implementation of the Local Government and Housing Act 1989 they will be even more diverse in their arrangements.

The major distinction currently is between those Boards orphaned in 1986 and those which remain part of the local authority. LEL and the DEB, as integrated economic development arms of their county councils, have boards of directors and parallel council committees. The remaining Boards have directorships based on different terms of membership and, post-abolition, different structures of control and accountability.

In Greater London a transformation of the company was inevitable. With the huge rate base available to the GLC the company had received funding of some £20 million per year until the final year of the council when, with funding now controlled by central government, there was a long delay before continued funding was denied. If the company was to survive, a major revaluation of roles was essential. The social priorities of the GLEB were never specifically abandoned but, with future funding running annually at less than 10 per cent of the earlier budget, insistence on a wholly commercial approach was necessary for survival. The directorships reflected the change to funding from thirteen London boroughs, and GLE as a new company distances itself from the record of the 1982–86 GLEB.

In the West Midlands there were few immediate changes to the Board but by 1989 its composition reflected a transfer of responsibilities. A less dramatic change of company outlook was needed and, as the company moved towards self-financing stability, directorships altered as the West Midlands district councils became more directly involved in the work. Geoff Edge, the chairman, had been a member of both the county council and Walsall Metropolitan District Council before abolition and provided the essential continuity in a period of transition.

The MEB and WYEB were given independent status by their parent authorities prior to abolition. Each chose to work directly with its local authorities – in the case of YEL with local authorities throughout the region. Changes within the directorships at the MEB brought greater district council involvement. This, sadly, has not brought with it sufficient additional funds from those local authorities to guarantee a future for the MEB. In October 1989 it was announced that the MEB would be wound up. At YEL the composition of the main board remains unchanged. However, where joint companies have been established YEL's local authority partners have come to play a vital role in the investment decision-making process.

It is impossible to arrive at a real comparison of the cost-effectiveness of each of the Boards. Those, like LEL, which combine subsidy-oriented and commercial activity are not profit-maximizing bodies. The proper comparison would be between, on the one hand, the costs and outputs of LEL and, on the other hand, the costs and outputs of a combined WMEB/West Midlands District Council economic development service. Even then the differing circumstances of a shire (LEL) and a metropolitan county (WMEB/West Midlands District Council) would invalidate the comparison.

All six Boards were started with funding over the period to April 1985. The GLEB received approximately £60 million (only £20 million remained when GLE was formed), the WMEB £16 million, the WYEB £10.5 million and the MEB £2.2 million. LEL, which still receives capital annually from the county council, had taken a total of £17.3 million by March 1988 but had also had the benefit of interest-free loans of £7.1 million. The DEB in its first thirteen months to March 1988 received grant funding of £1.25 million.

The WYEB in 1984 became the first of the Boards to seek and receive external funding with a £10 million loan secured from the Bank of Nova Scotia and guaranteed by the county council. This was followed by the acquisition of a £20 million line of credit from the Yorkshire Bank for investment taking place through the joint company structure. Other Boards have followed parallel paths – LEL having a facility through Rothschilds – while several Boards have formed unit trusts jointly managed with private sector institutions. The first of these was that formed between the WMEB and Lazard Investors – the West Midlands Regional Unit Trust (WMRUT). The trust, which invests in both quoted and unquoted companies, has proved a vehicle through which pension fund monies can be applied within the region. As of June 1988, 28 per cent of its investments were in unquoted companies with major interests in the region and the emphasis in quoted investments was also on those regionally based. The value of the trust at the 1988 year end was £9.4 million. A similar mechanism has also enabled the WMEB to extend its geographical remit – Oxfordshire, for example, participating as an investor through its pension fund. At the smaller investment level, the WMEB has joined with the local authorities to set up specific area-directed funds such as the Black Country Venture Capital Fund. A further advantage of funds of this nature is that, if managed by the Enterprise Board staff, they provide a fee income.

THE FUTURE

In YEL, realizations form an increasingly important part of the company income. The company has remained both profitable and able to invest four years after it last received public funding because, like other venture capital companies, it has made investments which have been very successful in commercial terms as well as in retaining jobs.

In the future this may well prove to be the only way forward for the Boards. Although each is different from the others, they all face two simultaneous challenges. Their financial role is now threatened by competition because of growth in the venture capital industry and a more aggressive stance by High Street banks. If they do not adapt to market needs and competitive pressures they will not survive. Additionally, the activities of local authorities and their successors through company structures are being curtailed. The Widdicombe Report commented on the area of local authority companies, and the legislation resulting from that inquiry will bring in new mechanisms which will affect many already in existence.

The Local Government and Housing Bill 1989, shortly to receive royal assent at the time of writing, creates classes of 'controlled' or 'influenced' local authority companies. Companies falling into these classes could find their expenditure counted against the capital allocations made to the constituent local authorities themselves. The bill places powers in the hands of the Secretary of State for the Environment which will allow him or her to categorize individual companies and to include or exclude them from the powers of the bill as he sees fit. As the rules under which companies will operate are to be contained in regulations yet to be published, the effect of this bill on the Boards when enacted and in operation in April 1990 is as yet uncertain.

The thrust of the legislation would seem to be forcing individual companies to make the choice between operating from a public sector base and operating from a private sector base. Enterprise Boards have raised substantial amounts of bank and pension fund finance to fuel the expansion of their activities. In the future it may be necessary for them to look exclusively to these funding sources, cutting or greatly diminishing the links that they have retained from the days of their inception within the world of local government.

ENTERPRISE BOARDS: SUCCESS OR FAILURE?

Those who brought the Boards into existence had high hopes for them. The potential for the progressive local authority to contribute to and influence its local economy through direct intervention seemed high. Application of social cost–benefit techniques might bring a new and liberating form of capitalism, concerned with jobs, conditions, unionization, and the social value of products as well as with profits. Some believed that it would be possible to restructure a given sector within a regional economy; others that the success of the Boards would lead to pressure for their existence throughout the regions. In practice, the external circumstances of the 1980s have made these dreams quite unrealistic as the Boards have operated on a limited scale and in a climate hostile to interventionist policies. They have seen few attempts to create new Boards and now encounter legislation which threatens their own existence.

Nevertheless there are some distinct achievements suggesting that the provision, but not necessarily the management, of venture capital is a proper and positive role for those local authorities with a large resource base. These achievements can be seen both at the individual company level (illustrated by the profits) and at the broader policy level. That YEL without public funding has still expanded its remit and enlarged its turnover shows that on market criteria there is a role for it. The success of investments made by the Boards has heightened the interest of other venture capital companies in the regions. Some of those successes have blurred the distinction between social and commercial investments: who can really predict whether a given case is or will become either social or commercial? This can only lead to more help for viable but border-line propositions.

For the local authority, venture capital provision is clearly a way of directly influencing the local economy. Acquiring or working alongside staff with a different experience and background may help to sharpen the approach in economic development as a whole for an authority. The strengths which come from linking venture capital with other work and with the advocacy function of the council have been clearly demonstrated. That few authorities have chosen to create Enterprise Boards following the experience of those set up in the 1980s may seem an indictment of the experience. It is more likely that there was an early recognition that in order to be successful in the market a Board must have a substantial resource base and a large catchment area in which to operate.

The Boards themselves had expected that their experience would be reflected in national policies. Yet even within the Labour Party election statements of 1987 they had only fleeting mention. Instead the Labour Party put forward 3is as a vehicle for regional investment. The emphasis now within each of the opposition parties is on future regional structures of government. Most models see the regional economy as a major area of devolved responsibility, and the provision of regional venture capital is cited as a necessary part of this.

The Enterprise Boards have shown that there is a very practical role to be played in improving market mechanisms in the supply of capital to the smaller firm at the sub-national level, and as a result their influence on future structures is bound to be significant. In the shorter term, pension funds may well take up the investment role pioneered by the Boards. Already a number of them, including some of the local authority pension funds, are active in the corporate finance field, investing in small unquoted companies. For some current Board clients there may perhaps still be the mechanisms to help. But the expensive process of investment analysis will be detached from the pension fund itself. There is unlikely to be an ongoing relationship between the client and the pension fund, and so that distinctive feature of YEL which, above all, has given it success is unlikely to form part of a pension fund provision.

NOTES

1. Officer advice that a separate company would add nothing to a council's ability to effect economic development was presented to elected members in both West and South Yorkshire. Abolition of the metropolitan counties was not even on the horizon at the time so the decision to proceed with the setting up of an Enterprise Board in West Yorkshire was in no way conditioned by worries as to the future of the county council itself.

2. 'Unlike YEL, GLEB/GLE represents historically two different enterprise boards' (GLE private communication, February 1989).

3. Each of the seven profiles in this chapter has been produced by the Board involved in the company or project described.

SELECT BIBLIOGRAPHY

Clarke, A. and Cochrane, A. (1987) 'Investing in the private sector: the enterprise board experience', in Cochrane, A. (ed.) *Developing Local Economic Strategies*, Milton Keynes, Open University Press.

Cochrane, A. (1988) 'In and against the market: development of socialist economic strategies in Britain, 1981-86', *Policy and Politics*, Vol. 16, No. 13, pp. 1-13.

DEB (1988) *Investing in Derbyshire: Annual Report and Accounts, 1987/8*, Chesterfield, Derbyshire Enterprise Board.

Edge, G. (1986) *Priorities for Economic Regeneration in the West Midlands: The Future Role of the West Midlands Enterprise Board Ltd Group of Companies*, Birmingham, West Midlands Enterprise Board.

Enterprise Boards (1986) *The Regional Alternative for Jobs and Industry*, joint publication, Preston, Lancashire Enterprises Limited.

GLE (1986) *An Introduction to Greater London Enterprise: Our New Approach*, London, Greater London Enterprise. *Annual Report and Accounts*, London, Greater London Enterprise.

GLEB (1983) *A New Approach to Investment*, London, Greater London Enterprise Board.

GLEB (1984) *Saving Jobs ... Shaping the Future*, London, Greater London Enterprise Board.

Green, C. (1987) 'The new municipal socialism', in Loney, M., Bocock, R., Clarke, J., Cochrane, A., Graham, P. and Wilson, M (eds) *The State or the Market: Politics and Welfare in Contemporary Britain*, London, Sage.

LEL (1983-8) *Annual Report and Statement of Accounts*, Preston, Lancashire Enterprises Limited.

Mackintosh, M. and Wainwright, H. (eds) (1987) *A Taste of Power: The Politics of Local Economics*, London, Verso.

Marks, S. (1987) *Enterprise Boards: Their Contribution to Economic Development and Investment*, Manchester, Centre for Local Economic Strategies.

Mawson, J. and Miller, D. (1986) 'Interventionist approaches in local employment and economic development: the experience of Labour local authorities', in Hausner, V. (ed.) *Critical Issues in Urban Economic Development*, Vol. 1, Oxford, Oxford University Press.

MEB (1984) *MEB Ltd: Policy and Procedures*, Liverpool, Merseyside County Council.

MEB (n.d.) *Investing in the People of Merseyside*, Liverpool, Merseyside Enterprise Board.

Millward, T. (1986) 'Future priorities for the Greater London Enterprise Board', Paper for ALA Labour Group.

Newman, I. (1986) 'Greater London Enterprise Board: vision and reality', *Local Economy*, Vol. 1, No. 2, pp. 67–78.

Schweke, W. (1989) 'Grown up model causes alarm', *New Co-operator*, Vol. 31, No. 3 (winter 1988–9).

WMEB (1984–8) *Annual Report and Accounts*, Birmingham, West Midlands Enterprise Board.

WMEB (1988) *West Midlands Regional Unit Trust Report and Accounts*, Birmingham, West Midlands Enterprise Board.

YEL (1986–8) *Annual Report and Accounts*, Leeds, Yorkshire Enterprise Limited.

CHAPTER 8

Recent Developments in Local Authority Economic Policy

Allan Cochrane

INTRODUCTION

Over the past decade local authority economic development work has both expanded steadily and been a source of major policy innovations. Lessons learned have been shared across the political spectrum of local authorities, above all in the move towards public–private partnerships. There has been a displacement of industrial policy from the centre towards the local level, whilst the decline of nationally sponsored regional policy has also left most policies of spatial redistribution to the local level. Broader strategic thinking is being developed within local government, using intervention to bargain and negotiate with the private sector but also defining a wider range of activities as part of the process of economic development, including culture, education and training. There are also some signs of a move away from industrial development towards elements of employment planning, through labour market intervention. Despite centrally imposed restrictions, local-authority-based economic development policy remains a centre of innovation whose importance is likely to grow in the 1990s. Indeed, every new obstacle seems to encourage a renewed search for ways around it.

THE DEVELOPMENT OF LOCAL AUTHORITY ECONOMIC POLICIES

There have traditionally been no general statutory powers of 'economic development' in any local government legislation.[1] Until relatively recently, a few authorities did have private Act powers to undertake specified forms of economic development activity (expressed, for example, in the Tyne and Wear Act 1974, Parts III and IV) but government hostility, Labour as well as Conservative, meant that these were allowed to lapse in the early 1980s and attempts by other councils to gain similar powers were also resisted. Yet at the same time councils were becoming more and more involved in economic development activity. Each seemed at least to have its own industrial development officer, or equivalent, and many councils were setting up units and/or committees concerned with economic development. By the mid-1980s, according to Chartered Institute of Public Finance and Accountancy (CIPFA) estimates, over £250 million was being spent annually out of revenue budgets on economic development and promotion by local authorities in England and Wales, while their capital spending was around £150 million p.a. These amounts rival the level of central government spending on regional policy and in any case substantially underrepresent actual spending on economic development, since some is buried under other (mainstream) budget heads. Whilst the most noticeable trend over the past decade has probably simply been the continued expansion of activity (Mills and Young, 1986; Martinos, 1988), this tells us little about the nature and implications of the policies and strategies actually adopted at local level.

In the 1970s the dominant forms of local authority economic development activity were the provision of land and premises to developers and businesses, and of related information about the availability of land and premises in the private sector, coupled with extensive promotional campaigns to attract industry from elsewhere. In a few cases small amounts of financial assistance were offered, usually in the form of grants, sometimes loans and mortgages. Close relationships often existed between property agencies and industrial development officers. At local level, small firms were the main targets for assistance and success was measured in terms of factory units constructed and enquiries from potential customers. Little serious attention was paid to the numbers or nature of jobs created. Industrial development officers were frequently employed as 'experts' who understood the private sector and, in a sense, were

[157]

expected to act as its representatives in a way that orthodox local government officers could not (for a discussion of this period, see Boddy, 1984). The expansion of activity in the late 1970s in response to rising unemployment was not at first accompanied by any change in policy direction. Blunkett and Jackson summarize this period well. Local councils, they say:

> were adapting the traditional economic role of British local government which offered inducements in the form of grants, free loans, and publicly subsidised infrastructure, and no request for reciprocal involvement with the community, in order to attract industrial and commercial concerns which were looking for suitable sites for investment and trading. (Blunkett and Jackson, 1987, p. 110)

In other words, the initial move was towards more of the same, rather than towards new initiatives or alternative forms of intervention (for a discussion of this period, see Chandler and Lawless, 1985, Part II).

Despite this expansion, economic development remains a relatively minor part of local authority activity, at least in terms of spending. Although the existing accounting conventions encourage an undercounting of its significance, they do not completely distort it. CIPFA statistics suggest that economic development work amounts for no more than 1 per cent of local government spending and it has rarely been given the same recognition as service departments within most councils. Although there are now a few exceptions – such as Ealing, Leeds, Sheffield and Wakefield – in few cases are those responsible for economic development appointed at or close to chief officer level. This suggests also that only in a relatively small number of cases is it appropriate to talk of the development of local economic strategies, and that in general economic development officers continue to work in the 'opportunist' fashion which was typical at the end of the 1970s (Johnson and Cochrane, 1981, pp. 172–3).

But recognizing the limits of change does not mean that change has not taken place. Moreover, the direction of change and the changing context within which economic development work now occurs are also important. The increased interest in economic development work implies a different context for decision making not only for the better-known authorities, but throughout the local government system. This is reflected in the, not always welcome, publicity given to the activities of a limited number of high-profile authorities, such as the Greater London Council, its Enterprise Board (GLEB, now Greater London Enterprise – GLE) and Sheffield, and increasingly to the other Enterprise Boards and councils, including Glasgow's promotional campaigns and Birmingham's civic boosterism, from Grand Prix to the Olympic Games. Not only is economic development activity now taken for granted as part of the work of most local authorities, particularly in urban areas, but it is also increasingly accepted that the concept of economic development needs to be more broadly defined and that existing methods of intervention require reassessment.

In the past, in considering the direction of change, it has been common to draw a distinction between 'traditional' (Cochrane, 1983, 1986) or 'mainstream' (Boddy, 1984) approaches and the 'local socialist', 'radical' (Martinos, 1988) or 'interventionist' (Mawson and Miller, 1986) initiatives associated with a relatively small number of Labour-controlled authorities. Distinctions of this sort, however, are becoming increasingly less useful, both because the lessons and methods of the more radical councils have been shared more widely, and because some of their more extensive ambitions seem to have been forgotten as the importance of market pressures has been acknowledged. One reinterpretation of the 'radical' councils and their experiments in this area has suggested that their actual *practice* has tended to be 'like Gaitskell and Crosland rejecting Clause IV in favour of the Swedish approach of controlling private capital through redistributive taxation and close regulation of capital investment and working conditions' (Chandler and Lawless, 1985, p. 260). Equally important, perhaps, such distinctions tend to ignore the significance of developments initiated outside the local government sphere (for example, encouraged by business), or involving councils which in other respects would not be identified as radical or representative of 'local socialism'. The growth of local-government-sponsored economic development companies committed to the provision of venture capital, for example, has not been restricted to Labour councils (Kent Economic Development Board, and Manchester Economic Development Company are only two examples of initiatives launched by Conservative-controlled councils). The stressing of party political differences between authorities tends to encourage an underestimate of the degree of cross-fertilization between officers. If there has been a more general sharing of ideas and – more important – methods learned from the experience of the 'radical' councils, they too have borrowed extensively from the experience of 'traditional' councils. There has been a general convergence towards what Moore and others (Moore and Booth, 1986; Moore and Pierre, 1988) have called the 'modified market' model.

Moore and Pierre argue that:

> This approach places the stimulation of enterprise through private investment as the central objective in order to diversify local economies and provide sustainable long term jobs. Public intervention must be limited and targeted towards commercially viable developments in the market. The strategy accepts the 'logic of the market', but identifies areas of specific weakness where public intervention can release constraints. (Moore and Pierre, 1988, p. 174)

The significance of this is already apparent from a reading of the preceding two chapters which have discussed the development of initiatives through public–private partnerships and by Enterprise Boards. Although Enterprise Boards were initially developed by 'radical' councils, they have increasingly been used as a means of achieving public–private partnerships, and the idea of share ownership and closer involvement in investment decisions has now been taken up by a wider range of councils and development companies. Conversely, although Business in the Community was a private sector initiative (see Pelling, 1984), and although the Enterprise Agency movement has been supported by central government, the interest of local authorities of both left and right in the development of 'partnerships' has been crucially important for their expansion.

In this sense the most significant set of changes in the field of local economic development has been those of attitudes and involvement. Instead of the relatively passive and potentially responsive role, which was reflected in strategies which focused on the marketing of land and premises, there has been a shift towards closer and more consistent links between business and local authorities. Many of the activities have remained the same and expanded, but the context of policy making has begun to change, and there has been a growth of various types of agency intended to make those links more effective. As Stoker (1988, Ch. 3) notes, this has been reflected in the growth of what he calls non-elected local government – more or less autonomous bodies including Enterprise Boards, Economic Development Companies, Enterprise Agencies, and even Urban Development

Corporations. How these bodies operate, of course, is likely to vary significantly from case to case.

They may provide opportunities for private sector agencies to influence, and even direct, the process of public policy making. Such an ambition probably lies behind the Conservative Government's support for Enterprise Agencies in the hope that local employers will take the lead in decision making within them. It certainly seems to underlie its plans for the break-up of the Manpower Services Commission (later the Training Commission and, at the time of writing, the Training Agency) in order to give the key roles in determining patterns of training to local boards, the new Training and Enterprise Councils, which are dominated by employers' representatives. Scotland is already being used as a test-bed to see how such methods can be introduced more widely. On the other hand, similar forms might also be used to increase the possibility of local authorities influencing the operation of the market and mobilizing additional financial support. This is an ambition which underpinned many of the initial arguments for the setting up of Enterprise Boards and justifies the involvement of many councils in Enterprise Agencies (Moore, 1988 provides an interesting discussion of the merits of the Enterprise Agency model for councils involved in economic development).

Whatever the continuing political differences between councils, the general direction of policy development is clearly towards 'partnership' with the private sector. Central government hostility to local initiatives and towards attempts to bypass centrally determined financial constraints is reflected in the proposals of the 1988 White Paper 'Local Authorities' Interests in Companies' to restrict the possibility of setting up local authority companies. If they are implemented, such proposals are likely to make it more difficult for public and private sector to work together, despite the apparent enthusiasm for collaboration which has been expressed by both sides and, in some cases at least, even by the Department of Trade and Industry. Attempting to redraw the public–private boundaries by effectively giving business representatives direct public responsibilities is likely to make co-operation and collaboration more difficult, and so restrict the possibility of achieving a longer-term accommodation with local communities. Despite the relative success of Business in the Community, it remains unclear that there are many senior businesspeople keen to spend a great deal of their time on activities delegated to them by the state.

Traditionally economic development work, as an identifiable

policy area within local government, has concentrated on a relatively narrow range of activities, perhaps better expressed in the term 'industrial development'. The orientation has been towards the expansion and attraction of firms and investment. In many ways, this has been just as true of the more recent (and 'radical') approaches as it has of the older ones. Most of the activities referred to so far can loosely be placed under the heading of 'industrial' policy. They are concerned to support and sustain existing industry, to identify and attempt to overcome weaknesses, and possibly to encourage development in new areas to replace the decline of traditional employment. Although they can be seen as extensions of past policies, however, their extent and nature begins to hint at more substantial change. Claims are beginning to be made for local authority contributions to restructuring their local economies which go beyond the ambition of property-related activities and of attracting a little more high-technology industry than their neighbours. It is in this sense that it becomes possible to identify, in embryonic terms at least, some commitment to the development of local economic strategies.

FROM INDUSTRIAL TO ECONOMIC POLICY

Some of the policy developments in the early 1980s suggested a key role for local authorities in influencing the process of economic restructuring through intervention in the process of production itself. This was probably put at its strongest in the arguments of the Greater London Council (GLC). In one publication it was argued that 'Profit is no longer an accurate guide to the way out of economic crisis. It is like a compass which has lost its bearings and points in the opposite direction to the way in which we need to go' (GLC Economic Policy Group, 1983, p. 17). It was suggested that changing economic structures made it possible for councils to intervene on the side of labour in the process of restructuring which was taking place. Drawing on analogies from the retail sector, it was said to be possible to identify strategic points of intervention. Just as major retailers such as Marks and Spencer, Benetton and Next could place conditions on suppliers, so local authorities (or Enterprise Boards) should be able to place conditions on firms they assisted, or firms which supplied them. The aim was to shift the balance of forces between capital and labour and encourage change which not only generated and protected jobs, but would also open employment to previously excluded or disadvantaged groups, and encourage democratic planning within enterprises and in ways which involved the wider community (see also GLC, 1985, Introduction).

The GLC's approach was controversial, arousing criticism not only from the predictably hostile Conservative Government, but also within the Labour Party and from other councils trying to develop their own economic policies. But its experience also illustrated in a very sharp form the way in which local authority economic policies became *politically* important, and thus impossible to reduce solely to technical and professional questions, even if the need for the economic and financial viability of projects was always stressed. The range of publications produced by the GLC (including its massive strategy documents, GLC, 1985, 1986a, 1986b) far exceeds those produced by other councils and local agencies, but they were part of a more general move towards the publication of economic policy documents by a range of authorities – including, for example, the various local jobs plans prepared in 1987, discussed and summarized by Campbell *et al*. (1987a, 1987b).

Another sign of the increased political salience of local authority activity can be found in the significant increase in their involvement in technology policies (see, for example, Marvin, 1987; Blackburn and Sharpe, 1988; the latter argues for the development of a national strategy, but draws extensively on local government experience). There has been a genuine process of policy development, considering, responding and trying to influence identified development trends alongside narrower attempts to put together marketing strategies for science parks. Local technology policies have taken three distinct, although arguably complementary, forms. The first has been a concern with technology transfer – that is, the implementation of new technologies in existing industries, the move from the laboratory to the enterprise. One of the weaknesses identified in existing industries in many regions has been their inability to introduce new technologies, and one of the tasks identified by the more 'interventionist' authorities has been to make the diffusion of innovations easier, through advice, financial assistance and support for specialist agencies to encourage it. The second has been a concern to provide appropriate training (for example, through Information Technology Centres – ITECs) to expand the skilled labour force able to work in the growing sectors of employment, both to ensure that there are no bottlenecks in the supply of labour which might restrict growth, and to assist those who might not otherwise find employment (for example, through specialist training programmes for women and black people). Finally, there has been a concern to encourage the development of new enterprises and the growth of existing ones in electronics, communications and other technology-related areas. This has been reflected in a series of schemes to encourage the development of new products, linking the academic and production worlds, for example through technology networks in the case of the GLEB/GLE (see Mole and Elliott, 1987 for a discussion of technology networks), UDAP (Unit for the Development of Alternative Products) in the West Midlands and SCEPTRE (Sheffield Centre for Product Development and Technological Resources) in Sheffield.

Although the number of new products generated by these schemes has been modest, they suggest a more positive orientation for development than is implied by the mushroom growth of local-authority-supported science parks which has also taken place. In general, these have been set up as little more than industrial estates with a more marketable title, part of a long tradition in local industrial development rather than a new departure. But in some cases a rather different approach is apparent, bringing together workshops and projects in the early stages of development and already established enterprises in a context which is intended to encourage growth to take place in a supportive environment. Some authorities have played a catalytic role, in co-operating with institutions of higher education in the hope that product development will be encouraged, and that the longer-term manufacturing and distribution of any new products will be encouraged locally. Again this implies that active local authorities are taking on a role on a smaller scale which might otherwise have been expected to be that of central government. In Japan, for example, the initiative for developing a series of regionally based technopoles is being taken from the centre, albeit with the active involvement of local and regional authorities (see, for example, Glasmeier, 1988; Fujita, 1988).

The increased involvement of councils with various European Community (EC) schemes is another example of this. Within the UK, the driving force for taking up European Regional Development Fund (ERDF) and technology schemes – such as ESPRIT – comes from local and regional agencies (such as the Enterprise Boards and the Development Agencies). The departments of central government act either as enabling organizations or, sometimes, obstacles but they are not the initiators. A great deal of emphasis in the self-help literature of economic development puts a stress on

EC schemes and how to gain access to them, and some of the most impressive (as well as most 'glossy') literature is oriented towards persuading EC agencies of the appropriateness of providing assistance to local schemes. The case prepared by Lancashire Enterprises Limited and others, including Wigan Metropolitan Borough Council, Lancashire County Council and six other borough councils, as an Article 24 Submission to the ERDF for support in redeveloping the Leeds and Liverpool Canal Corridor is a good example of the highly professional, well-argued cases which have been put together. The initial submission moves from a summary of socioeconomic indicators, showing the extent of the problems, towards an outline of the positive potential of development and a statement of costings and other sources of finance for the preparation of a ten-year Economic Development Plan. The package includes a commitment to spending from all the authorities involved, which highlights the growing need for councils to work together on a more regional scale if they are to operate effectively in this sphere. The increased emphasis of EC programmes on the regional level and responses from that level reinforces this trend because the UK is unusual within the Community for having no elected regional institutions, and few unelected ones either, at least in England, and for having a central government with little interest in regional policy. Already, as John Gunnell has explained in Chapter 7, most of the Enterprise Boards have shifted their focus from the local to the regional scale.

One important conclusion to be drawn from this is the growth of political confidence on these issues at local level. It suggests that there has been a degree of displacement of debate on economic policy issues away from the level of national government towards the local level. The official central government attitude towards economic policy in the 1980s emphasized the need for the state to let the market determine the direction of change with little or no state interference, although in practice it seems to have been accepted that the state has a major role in making Britain 'safe for the market', as the existence of Urban Development Corporations, Enterprise Zones, the Scottish and Welsh Development Agencies, and all the training initiatives and special employment schemes suggest. The aim of withdrawal from the market has, in other words, been accompanied by significant intervention, often in the guise of urban policy and usually at local or regional level (see, for example, Moore and Booth, 1986b on the SDA itself, although the Government now appears to have decided that it has done its job and is proceeding to

[165]

dismantle it and localize activity still further). Within local authorities this seems to have encouraged, or at least to have been paralleled by, a more explicit concern with broader 'strategic' economic issues, often involving 'partnership' arrangements, and including an interest in forms of 'industrial' policy and, increasingly, labour market policies. The practice of local economic development work has also encouraged moves towards more joint activity, at regional and national levels. The withdrawal of central government from regional policy has made the need for some regional framework clearer to many local authorities involved in economic development, particularly in the context of Europe.

There has been a significant growth of agencies which bring those active in the field together to share experiences and ideas. At officer level there is now an Association of Economic Development Officers, and the Centre for Local Economic Strategies (CLES) brings politicians and officers together in debate and discussion as well as in the identification and sharing of best practice. CLES is not just a clearing house for ideas and a source of consultancy work and research, although it is clearly filling an important gap for many councils in these areas because the lack of research facilities at local level is something which was noted by many respondents to the survey reported by Mills and Young (1986). It also increasingly acts as a lobbying organization speaking for authorities engaged in economic development work, particularly those at the rather more active end of the spectrum, and as a campaigning organization, promoting the value and encouraging the spread of economic development work within the local government community. There has long been a tradition of joint regional campaigning and development companies in the North of England, and this has been more actively pursued in recent years, but regional initiatives sponsored by local governments have spread more widely. Even in the South-East of England, SEEDS (South-East Economic Development Strategy) brings together a group of authorities concerned, as the name suggests, jointly to develop strategies for the South-East and to indicate some of the particular problems and possibilities which exist there. In the late 1980s and into the 1990s, the value of adequate research highlighting local and regional economic trends, sometimes in key industrial sectors, is increasingly recognized, and resources are being allocated to it, both within individual councils and through these broader organizations. In Sheffield, for example, a Joint Institute for Social and Economic Research has been set up, bringing together the city council, the university, the polytechnic and Northern College.

THE REDEFINITION OF LOCAL AUTHORITY ECONOMIC POLICY

The growing interest in economic development has also begun to encourage a move beyond the narrow definitions of the past and to offer a means of integrating a range of local authority activities. Instead of being seen as a narrowly specialist area, it has begun to encourage a broader interpretation of the role of local authorities in general. Of course, signs of this can also be identified earlier in the history of local government: the 'gas and water' socialism of the late nineteenth and early twentieth centuries is a well-known example of local government initiative in the provision of essential infrastructure for economic development; in the inter-war years it was assumed that local government was the prime agency with responsibility for sustaining employment; and in the 1950s the reconstruction of the central areas of Britain's major provincial cities and their associated road-building programmes were aimed at economic revival and modernization. But such ambitious schemes have generally been forgotten in the process of managing the delivery of local government services, and in the face of the increasing tightness of local government finance.

There are signs of a reinterpretation of the role of local authorities which has allowed a wider focus on the processes of economic change and ways of influencing them other than by direct involvement. It is now widely accepted that the impact and effectiveness of local industrial policies is likely to be limited unless they are part of a wider national strategy, but there is also an increasing realization that the changing structure of the British economy means that a narrowly based *industrial* policy is itself unlikely to be successful. This has encouraged some councils to move towards other schemes, most obviously towards a greater sympathy for retail developments outside the central area and for mall-type developments within it. The new shopping malls are generally private initiatives even if councils have sometimes played a major part in the process of land assembly which makes them possible. They are now far more likely than in the past to be sympathetic to large-scale office development and to concentrate instead on gaining some concessions in the form and nature of the development which takes

[167]

place. There has been a revival of interest in large-scale property development as a source of growth, in part, no doubt, because there is now pressure for such development from the private sector, and because of the apparent success – at least in terms of cranes along the skyline – of the Government's Urban Development Corporations (UDCs), particularly in London's docklands. After a period of principled resistance to co-operation by many local authorities – again particularly in London, where it was reinforced by an equal reluctance and even hostility from the Development Corporation – most councils with UDCs within their boundaries are now eager to seek some accommodation with them because of the resources they command.

Some of the more adventurous councils have begun to stress the importance of cultural policies as an element in economic development. Glasgow is probably the best-known example of a city which has used the development of cultural activities to transform its image and gain external recognition for itself, for example (but not only) through the growth of its arts festival (Mayfest). It is to be the 'European City of Culture' in 1990 and, according to the Arts Council at least, 'Glasgow's regeneration has been largely arts-led, with the Mayfest and the opening of the Burrell collection all helping to change the city's image from a decaying industrial backwater to a dynamic growth area' (quoted in McKellar 1988, p. 14). Other councils have followed suit in drawing up policies and programmes for cultural development, including Liverpool, Birmingham and Nottingham. The GLC, too, made cultural policies an important part of its economic development activity, particularly in its campaigning (see, for example, Mackintosh and Wainwright 1987, Ch. 14).

In a rather different way, in its early days the GLEB stressed the direct employment potential of the 'cultural industries' (GLEB, 1986) and Sheffield has attempted to identify a 'cultural industries quarter' next to its science park, imaginatively using planning legislation with the designation of a commercial–industrial improvement area on the outskirts of the city centre. The 'quarter' includes municipally owned music and recording studios, as well as privately owned studios in the same set of buildings, studio and exhibition space for photographers and artists, and a music, dance and arts centre. It is planned to provide training for work in film, video, television and music industries in the area. This is, of course, all rather a far cry from the dominant image of economic development with its stress on the provision of 'real' jobs (that is, manufacturing – in the case of Sheffield, steel or heavy engineering). Councils are increasingly imaginative about the areas in which they are prepared to intervene.

The move towards a redefined and more strategic view of economic development in some local authorities is also expressed in an increased interest in labour market policy. Instead of focusing attention on activities which may be productive in terms of new factory units or additional local investment, they have begun to approach the problem from a different angle. There has been a growing concern about the nature of jobs in the local labour market and about access to them. Many councils now have officers responsible for encouraging the growth of ethnic minority businesses and, in some cases, there is a specific interest in encouraging the growth of women's employment. It has even been suggested that the only form of economic intervention which can be successful at local level lies in attempting to influence the labour market (Lovering, 1988, pp. 153–6). Policies which may be relevant here, for example, include the targeting of specialist training in areas where there are skill shortages and, if equal opportunities are one aim of policy, then various forms of positive discrimination could direct resources towards disadvantaged groups. Attempts have also been made through the process of contract compliance to ensure that those who supply goods to councils will agree to improve their own employment practices. Although this process has been made more difficult as a result of central government legislation, there is some possibility of applying informal pressure, and it seems widely agreed now that construction schemes in the inner cities should take on a substantial proportion of local labour. Moreover, it is still possible to lay down some conditions about the employment of ethnic minorities. Employment policies *within* local authorities may themselves also provide examples which can actively be pursued with employers in the private sector. This has been a matter of some controversy in many councils, but there has been a growing commitment to equal opportunity policies of one sort or another throughout the local government system. It is no longer merely a concern of 'radical' or Labour councils, but has increasingly been taken up within the officer structure, to the extent that, formally at least, it has almost become taken for granted as an ambition of good personnel management. The so-called 'demographic time-bomb', which will make the recruitment and retention of skilled staff on the old basis more difficult at just the time when demands on the system are increasing, is likely further to encourage such policies.

[169]

The preparation of local jobs plans, although initiated in 1987 as part of the Labour Party's preparation for the General Election, seemed to confirm a potentially important shift of emphasis because the focus of debate was on jobs and the nature of employment rather than investment and patterns of restructuring (Campbell *et al.*, 1987b). They began to make it possible to approach a much wider range of local authority activities – for example, including education – in terms of their significance for employment, as well as to relate these to a wider vision of the local economy. The experiment of the jobs plans themselves does not seem to have been developed further with local authorities since 1987, but their significance in pointing to the value of developing a more systematic approach to labour market intervention and their linking of social policy objectives to employment ones do not deserve to be forgotten. A recent CLES report (Campbell *et al.*, 1988) stresses the potential of a local-authority-related employment programme in meeting local needs, generating employment and reducing spatial divisions.

CONCLUSION

The pattern of recent developments in local authority economic policy must be seen in the context of changing national policies and, in particular, changes in local government finance and in rules on how it may be spent. A great deal of time is spent in all local authorities in trying to evade the rules or use them positively, and this is particularly true in economic development. Some activities which were possible at the start of the 1980s were no longer possible at the end. It could be argued, for example, that the most important contributions made to economic development by the GLC and South Yorkshire County Council, now both abolished, came out of their transport policies, where both were committed to cheap fares which significantly improved the mobility of those groups which found it most difficult to find work. The privatization of the buses and the reorganization of London's public transport mean that such intervention is no longer possible, and the GLC's wider ambitions for restructuring would also be impossible (see Mackintosh, 1987). The possibility of developing municipal enterprise is increasingly restricted. Reference has already been made to the difficulties placed in the way of contract compliance, and to legislation proposed to limit the possibilities of creating joint local government-private sector companies. It is possible that other limitations will arise in the next few years. But perhaps what is most striking about the 1980s has been the dynamism of local authority economic development policies and the constant pressure to reinterpret central government rules to suit the needs of the council concerned. It will not be easy for central government to draw rules tight enough to stop this. Local economic policy will continue to change its shape and move into new areas, but it does not seem likely to disappear.

NOTE

1.   Ironically, proposals to identify a specific power for economic development which are put forward in the Government's response to the Report of the Widdicombe Committee, *The Conduct of Local Authority Business* (Cmnd 433, 1988), and given statutory force in the Local Government and Housing Bill likely to be enacted in 1990, are directed towards reducing local economic development activity rather than giving it official endorsement.

REFERENCES

Blackburn, P. and Sharpe, R. (eds) (1988) *Britain's Industrial Renaissance? The Development, Manufacture and Use of Information Technology*, London, Comedia/Routledge.

Blunkett, D. and Jackson, K. (1987) *Democracy in Crisis: The Town Halls Respond*, London, Hogarth Press.

Boddy, M. (1984) 'Local economic and employment strategies', in Boddy, M. and Fudge, C. (eds) *Local Socialism? Labour Councils and the New Left Alternatives*, London, Macmillan.

Campbell, M., Hardy, M., Healey, N., Stead, R., and Sutherland, J. (1987a) 'The economics of local jobs plans,' *Local Economy*, Vol. 2, No. 2, pp. 81–92.

Campbell, M., Hardy, M., Healey, N., Stead, R., and Sutherland, J. (1987b) *Economic Sense: Local Jobs Plans*, Manchester, Centre for Local Economic Strategies.

Campbell, M., Healey, N., Stead, R. and Sutherland, J., with Leach, R. and Percy-Smith, J. (1988) *Meeting Real Needs: Creating Real Jobs*, Manchester, Centre for Local Economic Strategies.

Chandler, J.A. and Lawless, P. (1985) *Local Authorities and the Creation of Employment*, Aldershot, Gower.

Cochrane, A. (1983) 'Local economic policies: trying to drain an ocean with a teaspoon', in Anderson, J., Duncan, S. and Hudson, R. (eds) *Redundant Spaces in Cities and Regions? Studies in Industrial Decline and Social Change*, London, Academic Press.

Cochrane, A. (1986) 'Local employment initiatives: towards a new municipal socialism?' in Lawless, P. and Raban, C. (eds) *The Contemporary British City*, London, Harper and Row.

Fujita, K. (1988) 'The Technopolis: high technology and regional development in Japan', *International Journal of Urban and Regional Research*, Vol. 12, No. 4, pp. 566–94.

Glasmeier, A. (1988) 'The Japanese Technopolis programme: high-tech development strategy or industrial policy in disguise?' *International Journal of Urban and Regional Research*, Vol. 12, No. 2, pp. 268–83.

GLC (1985) *London Industrial Strategy*, London, Greater London Council.

GLC (1986a) *London Financial Strategy*, London, Greater London Council.

GLC (1986b) *London Labour Plan*, London, Greater London Council.

GLC Economic Policy Group (1983) *Jobs for a Change*, London, Greater London Council.

GLEB (1986) *Altered Images: Towards a Strategy for London's Cultural Industries*, London, Greater London Enterprise Board.

Johnson, N. and Cochrane, A. (1981) *Economic Policy-Making by Local Authorities in Great Britain and West Germany*, London, Allen and Unwin.

Lovering, J. (1988) 'The local economy and local economic strategies', *Policy and Politics*, Vol. 16, No. 3, pp. 145–57.

McKellar, S. (1988) *'The Enterprise of Culture'*, *Local Work*, No. 8.

Mackintosh, M. (1987) 'Planning the public sector: an argument from the case of transport in London', in Cochrane, A. (ed.) *Developing Local Economic Strategies*, Milton Keynes, Open University Press.

Mackintosh, M. and Wainwright, H. (eds) (1987) *A Taste of Power: The Politics of Local Economics*, London, Verso.

Martinos, H. (1988) 'Identifying local economic development research priorities', Paper presented to ESRC Conference, London, 2 February.

Marvin, S. (1987) 'Local authority technology development policies and initiatives: an overview', Occasional Paper No. 13, Technology Policy Group, Open University.

Mawson, J. and Miller, D. (1986) 'Interventionist approaches in local employment and economic development: the experience of Labour local authorities', in Hausner, V. (ed.) *Critical Issues in Urban Economic Development*, Vol. 1, Oxford, Clarendon Press.

Mills, L. and Young, K. (1986) 'Local authorities and economic development', in Hausner, V. (ed.) *Critical Issues in Urban Economic Development*, Vol. 1, Oxford, Clarendon Press.

Mole, V. and Elliott, D. (1987) *Enterprising Innovation*, London, Frances Pinter.

Moore, C. (1988) 'Enterprise agencies: privatisation or partnership?' *Local Economy*, Vol. 3, No. 1, pp. 21–30.

Moore, C. and Booth, S. (1986a) 'Urban policy contradictions: the market versus social distributive approaches', *Policy and Politics*, Vol. 14, No. 3, pp. 361–87.

Moore, C. and Booth, S. (1986b) 'The Scottish Development Agency: market consensus, public planning and local enterprise', *Local Economy*, Vol. 1, No. 3, pp. 7–20.

Moore, C. and Pierre, J. (1988) 'Partnership or privatisation? The political economy of local economic restructuring', *Policy and Politics*, Vol. 16, No. 3, pp. 169–78.

Pelling, T. (1984) 'Local government and the business sector: Business in the Community', *Local Government Policy Making*, March, pp. 43–7.

Stoker, G. (1988) *The Politics of Local Government*, London, Macmillan.

CHAPTER 9

Evaluating Local Economic Policy

Andrew Coulson

INTRODUCTION

Ex post evaluation of investment projects in general, and those associated with local economic policy in particular, is a neglected – and to some people a suspect – part of social science. It is neglected partly for political reasons: both those who invest in a project and those who implement it have little reason to wash their dirty linen in public. It is probably not a coincidence that several of the techniques used in evaluation (such as social audit, social cost-benefit analysis, impact analysis, and some approaches to action research) tend to bias the results in favour of the result the evaluator would like to report. Favourable results are well publicized. Unfavourable evaluations are pigeonholed, or their publication delayed.

A second reason why evaluation is neglected is that all evaluation methodologies are uncertain and subjective. One difficulty is that the *ex post* evaluator has the benefit of hindsight, where the original investor could only assess risk and make a judgement. So if an investment 'fails' (however failure is defined) this in itself does not necessarily invalidate the original investment decision. A more fundamental problem is that the *ex post* evaluator has to build a model which will project what outcomes would have been if the project had not been implemented; these projections are then compared with what actually happened, so producing an estimate of project 'benefit'[1] which may be compared with whatever costs can be associated with the project. This process is not objective: different evaluators would construct different models of what might have happened, and hence produce different estimates of the project's 'benefits'. Moreover, the evaluators (to say nothing of the project beneficiaries, or those who implement the project) will disagree about the importance to be given to different objectives. And since an investment project affects income distribution (that is, it makes some people better off and others worse off) then there may be no simple test of success.[2]

In the face of these problems (which strike at the foundations of social science research), the evaluation methodologies actually used and recommended are simplistic. For example, they frequently assume a single objective, or reduce all other objectives to a single objective (for example, 'profit' for many private sector investment projects; minimizing public expenditure for the Government's Financial Management Initiative; or job creation for local economic initiatives). They do not ask too many questions about what would have happened if the project had not been implemented. They largely ignore the wider social or macroeconomic context within which the investment takes place, and which must, to a large extent, determine its 'success'.

These weaknesses in methodology do not mean that we can avoid evaluation. Policy makers and officials in bureaucracies need to know what is going on in order to allocate resources effectively between activities. They need confidence and determination to follow their hunches, and then in the future must reflect upon and learn from their experiences. Evaluation is a key component in the feedback circuit of decision making that enables more resources to be fed in.[3]

Local authority economic development illustrates this process. The British Government is presently legislating to regulate and control it. Many claims have been made for its success (see Mawson and Miller, 1986 for a particular perspective). But there are also doubts and uncertainties, and close examination of many of the claims shows that they are based on very weak methodology. Yet if local authority economic development is to gain recognition as a mainstream activity of local authorities, then it has to be able to show that it can provide value for money. Quite apart from this, the local authorities concerned need to review and evaluate their own programmes as part of their regular management processes, so as to discontinue or change aspects that are not achieving, while expanding those that are successful. If evaluation and review cannot demonstrate a learning from experience, and indicate what in the future is likely to succeed, then it will not have a strong claim to resources, either nationally or locally.

EVALUATION IN LOCAL AUTHORITIES

At the present time, for the majority of local authorities, evaluation of their economic development activities is not given high priority. Of more than 300 British local authorities who responded to a recent survey,[4] more than 90 per cent had one or more staff working in 'economic development', just under 60 per cent employed three or more staff, and the average was just over seven. The figures are shown in Table 9.1. Of the local authorities which replied, 72 per cent present monitoring reports of their economic development activities to a council committee at least once a year. But only 58 per cent reported that they had any arrangements for 'assessing the performance of the economic development programme' (Table 9.2). When asked when they had last reviewed their economic development programmes, they replied as shown in Table 9.3. Table 9.4

Table 9.1 Professional staff with economic development responsibilities

No. of staff (full time)	Authorities (%)
None	5
Less than 1	2
1 or 2	33
3–5	29
6–10	14
11–20	12
More than 20	4

Type of authority	Mean no. of staff (full time) per authority
Non-metropolitan counties	12.0
Non-metropolitan districts	3.3
Metropolitan districts	29.3
London boroughs	10.6
All authorities	7.1

Table 9.2 Frequency of monitoring and assessment (%)

Frequency of monitoring reports to committee	All authorities	Authorities with:		
		5 staff or less	6–10 staff	More than 10 staff
Annually	24	24	19	25
More often	48	46	63	72
Less often	9	11	9	2
Never	15	19	9	2
Those with arrangements for assessing the performance of economic development programme	38	32	51	73
Those with no such arrangements	62	68	49	27

Table 9.3 Council's last review of overall policy for economic development (%)

Currently in progress	27
Within last 12 months	28
1–2 years ago	14
3–5 years ago	8
More than 5 years ago	3
Never	21

Table 9.4 For councils with a review, by whom conducted (%)

Officers in responding department	71
Performance review unit	8
Consultants	2
Others/combinations (e.g. management team and members)	18

shows that the great majority of reviews are carried out by officers in the responding department. There were few independent external reviews, even for the larger economic development units, that is, those with five staff or more.

The 'Rational Model' or 'Action-Research'?

Those who conduct evaluations may base their methodology on a version of the 'rational model': that is, assume that objectives can be unambiguously defined before an investment takes place, that the investment will place as planned, and that it can therefore be evaluated by whether or not its original objectives were achieved. The evaluation of Urban Development Grant, described by Stephen Martin earlier in this volume, takes such a view. The evaluators took the initial objectives of the scheme (to encourage private sector investment in the inner city; to promote activity which otherwise would not have taken place; and to create employment) and their evaluation researched the extent to which these objectives were achieved.

An alternative approach to evaluation is that of 'action-research'. Here the evaluation assumes that objectives are not fully defined at the beginning of the project, and indeed *expects* them to change as a programme matures and discovers more about what it can, or cannot, achieve. It starts from the assumption that the best solutions or approaches can often only be discovered by action, by experimentation, or by pilot projects. In this process the original objectives of a project may be altered but experience of value may nevertheless be gained. The job of the evaluator is to interpret what happened in historical terms, to assess the worth of what was actually achieved, and to make recommendations for the future.[5] There is a clear illustration of this process in one of the Department of the Environment's evaluations of the Urban Programme:

> The majority of projects have been funded for several years, and it is a particular characteristic of these projects to have modified their objectives. Increasing levels of unemployment have caused many of the projects to revise their activities or to target the young unemployed, client groups within this category, or particular symptoms of unemployment . . .
> What does emerge from the analysis and discussion of project objectives is a discernible 'gap' in many of the projects between stated objectives of a project and activities per-formed. Some projects undertake more activities than stated, others undertake different activities. This is not a sign of 'bad' practice necessarily. In part it is due to projects respond-ing quickly to new needs and issues, and this is particularly

relevant for projects benefiting the young unemployed. (Whitting *et al.*, 1986, pp. 41–2)

Objectives

The importance given to different objectives may vary not only over time, but between different individuals or institutions. For example, the objectives that seem most important from a particular local perspective may not be those that are most important to central politicians and administrators. Table 9.5 includes ten of the main (by no means the only) objectives of local economic development projects.

Most projects have more than one objective. Often these are in conflict, particularly in the short term. Thus, for example, wealth creation may conflict with employment creation; employment of ethnic minorities with employment for the rest of the population; improving the conditions of labour with creating jobs. And there are many more potential conflicts.

Table 9.5 Objectives of local economic development projects

Objective	Illustrative project with this objective
Creating jobs	Grant to start-up businesses; business training
Saving jobs	Loan to a firm in trouble
Growth, or creating wealth	Purchase of a machine that will reduce employment but raise both capital and labour productivity
Creating jobs for a specific target group	Training project for an ethnic minority, women, long-term unemployed, or residents of a particular estate or inner city area
Improving conditions of labour	Campaign against low pay, homeworking, poor safety, etc.
Giving confidence	Centre for the long-term unemployed; women's training workshop; an Industrial Improvement Area
Promoting of self-reliance	Support for the voluntary sector, or workers' co-operatives
Creating socially useful technology	Innovation centre
Demonstration projects	Project demonstrating women's manual skills or a new form of finance
Influencing central government	Campaign for railway electrification or the rebuilding of sewers.

Job Creation

Most recent discussions of the evaluation of local economic development concentrate on a single objective, job creation. It is true that several of the objectives listed in Table 9.5 involve types of job creation, or may be reduced to job creation. Thus if there is an agreed methodology for evaluating job creation, this may readily be adapted to analyse, for example, job creation for ethnic minorities. It may also be adapted to evaluate training, on the assumption (which may, however, be false) that the only objective of the training is that it should lead on to paid employment.[6] It may be applied to projects designed to create new technology, although here (as with wealth creation generally) timescale is an issue: a science park or innovation centre may offer the prospect of many jobs in the future, but only a few at high cost in the next five years. A campaign, or demonstration project, may be judged on whether it *ultimately* leads to jobs.

Difficulties remain in turning these points into practical evaluation procedures, and we should be cautious before claiming that 'considerable progress has been made towards solving some of the major technical problems involved in evaluation research' (Martin, 1989). There has, however, been widespread discussion of some of the main issues.[7]

Displacement refers to the situation that jobs may be created in one place at the expense of jobs in another place. The jobs may be lost at premises owned by the same firm (for example, if it transfers production into an Enterprise Zone), or in other firms (for example, a new shopping centre will almost certainly displace employment in other retail businesses). Employment may be displaced in other parts of the country, or the world; whether this is an issue will depend on the perspective of the evaluators and their sponsors.

Deadweight (or non-additionality) occurs when the assistance given by the public body does not affect the behaviour of the project which receives the assistance: the investment would have been the same even without the assistance.

Indirect impacts (including multipliers) are when an investment creates jobs indirectly, in the firms that supply the new project, in firms that use or sell its products, and through the spending of wages in local shops and services.

Leverage occurs when public sector investment makes possible a larger private sector investment. The 'leverage ratio' (the ratio of private to public investment) is sometimes used as a performance measure, but it has many paradoxes. In particular, it can lead to double counting if two or more collaborators on a project claim to be creating the same jobs. Figures of 'cost per job' where leverage is involved are not directly comparable with figures of the total costs of creating a job, or of costs per job where there is just one investor.

There is also the distinction between *housed* and *attributable* jobs. The number of jobs attributable to a property project is not the same as the number of people who work in the buildings constructed, since many of those jobs would have otherwise existed somewhere else.

The number of jobs created by a training project is not the same as the number of trainees who get jobs, since some jobs filled by trainees (or part-time or temporary workers) mean the loss of full-time permanent jobs. This is the problem of *job substitution*.

There is also the problem of *veracity* – of finding out the truth. Respondents have an obvious bias to report that they have used money well. They may adopt strategies to 'pull the wool over the eyes' of evaluators who are perceived as hostile. On the other hand, the sponsors of evaluations have every incentive to publicize them and take the credit if the reports are favourable. If they are unfavourable they are liable to pigeonhole them or publish them obscurely.

Then there is also the issue of what assumptions to make about *structural change* and long-term unemployment. If workers made redundant from a shipyard face years on government benefits, it may well be cheaper from the government point of view to subsidize the shipyard than to pay out the unemployment benefits. Such calculations underpin social audits of closures, which invariably recommend that the plants (or shipyards) should stay open. Governments may reject these arguments because, at least in the short term, they have other objectives (an internationally competitive economy, an economic structure with fewer very large firms and more small ones, etc.) Such evaluations have usually been ineffective (at least in stopping the closures) because of a fundamental disagreement about objectives.[8]

Another problem which evaluation research faces is, as we have seen, the fundamental problem of social science: the *counterfactual problem*. To judge whether a project is successful, the evaluator has to model (or guess) what would have happened without the project. Would the small business have expanded anyway? Would some other use have been found for the building? Would the target group of local residents (or long-term unemployed) eventually have found work elsewhere? What would have happened if interest rates had not risen sharply in 1988? Was it reasonable not to anticipate that the major industry in the area would be decimated as a consequence of high interest rates and a high pound? The evaluator has not only to project what might have happened, but also to take a view of risk and uncertainty.[9]

There is also a gradual awareness that *local labour markets* need to be understood if project interventions are to be assessed. The situation in parts of South-East England is very different from that in the North-East. A particular type of project may work more effectively in some areas than others. Hence a negative evaluation of a project does not necessarily imply that it would fail elsewhere.

PUBLISHED EVALUATIONS

We now consider published evaluations of policy in each of three groups:

● evaluations of local authority support to small businesses, derived from consultancy sponsored by particular local authorities;

● evaluations of central government schemes of assistance in which local authorities participated. The Inner Cities Directorate of the Department of the Environment has been particularly active in sponsoring and publishing such evaluations;

● action-research evaluations, by sympathetic social scientists who have followed through the changes in projects that grew and responded to changes in their environments.

Local Authority Support to Small Businesses

There are at least four published evaluations of local authority financial assistance to small businesses: Gunby and Smith (1985), Davies *et al.* (1986), Townroe and Brenton (1987), and Turok (1988).[10] The first three are concerned with very small grants or loans to very small businesses. They were conducted with minimal research resources, and all concluded that local authorities could create jobs at extremely low costs. Turok's research on Southwark's support to industry between 1978 and 1983 was concerned with larger sums given mainly to established businesses. These researchers' main results are summarized in Table 9.6.

Table 9.6 Local authority financial assistance to businesses

	Gunby and Smith (1985)	Davies, Campbell and Barnes (1986)		Townroe and Brenton (1987)		Turok (1987)
Local authority	Cleveland CC	Humberside CC		Norwich DC	Broadland DC	LB of Southwark
Scheme	Small Business Grants Scheme	Small Business Grants Scheme	Employment Subsidy Scheme	Norwich Loan Scheme	Broadland Rate Relief Grant	Southwark Fund for the Development of Industry and Commerce
Period of support (researched firms)	1980–3	March–December 1984		January 1981–April 1986		1978–83
No. of firms supported	293	219		104	152	119
Expenditure	£304,152[1]	£99,834		£279,386	£73,153	£2,920,000
Net job expansion	374	213		414[2]	245[2]	229
Expenditure per job	£813	£771	£346	£675	£298	£12,750

Notes:
[1] Calculated from expenditure figures in the text.
[2] It is not clear from the text (p. 172) if these figures derive from the authors' survey or from council monitoring procedures.

The first two surveys succeeded in contacting high proportions of the small businesses who had received assistance and were still trading (74 and 97 per cent respectively), and thus in calculating reasonably reliable figures of jobs gained in supported firms and lost in firms that subsequently ceased to trade. Townroe and Brenton achieved a much lower response rate (around 40 per cent). They too found evidence of expansion, but like the other researchers they are careful not to claim that the financial assistance *caused* the additional employment. Indeed 24 of the 40 Broadland businesses interviewed 'had either forgotten that the company had received this assistance, or this assistance was not seen as "financial aid" ' (1987, p. 176). However, in Southwark, Turok found that 19 of the 56 firms supported, employing 739 people at the time when they were assisted, had by 1984 closed or moved away from the area. By 1987 a further ten firms, employing 526 workers in 1984, had closed or moved out. The figure of 229 jobs used in the cost per job calculation is a figure of jobs created or saved *in the firms that survived*: the author implicitly assumes that the jobs lost in the other firms would have been lost anyway. The cost figure used is the sum of the grants plus the losses the council made on loans that were not repaid, in other words it is not the total sums paid out.

All these authors are aware of the theoretical difficulties with their figures. None of them calculates displacement effects, though the Humberside study discovered that over 70 per cent of its respondents made more than 70 per cent of their sales within the county boundary, and from this concluded that displacement was likely to be significant. Deadweight was probably an even greater problem. Thus the Humberside wages subsidy scheme was to assist firms which wished to expand their labour forces. The interviews were conducted within twelve months of the aid being given, so it would have been surprising if the firms concerned had not increased employment. That much of this employment was *caused* by the small grants of up to £1,000 seems unlikely. A similar, if slightly weaker, point can be made in relation to the Small Business Grant Scheme. The authors point out that:

> there is the possibility that both the receipt of aid and the employment growth are jointly caused by some other factor, most obviously superior business ability. In that case, it could be argued that the superior employment performance of the aided firms should be attributed to their superior ability, not to their receipt of aid. (Davies *et al.*, 1986, p. 49)

Or, in simpler language, these firms wanted to expand anyway, and succeeded in getting money out of the council. Of course, firms in this situation are often heavily overdrawn and a small grant at a crucial time could make a lot of difference; but in such cases it is simplistic to claim that the small grant 'caused' or 'created' a specific number of new jobs.

The Southwark cases raise other issues. The period under consideration turned out to be a particularly difficult one for manufacturing employment in London. Between 1961 and 1981 manufacturing employment in the borough fell by 62 per cent. Turok has published a separate article exploring the effects of various kinds of pressure on these firms (Turok, 1989). He provides case histories of some of the businesses assisted, and their responses to the recession of 1980–1, and concludes:

> An active policy of financial assistance to local firms was pursued to save and create employment. However, the prevailing circumstances were unfavourable. Powerful external forces and corporate weaknesses stifled employment growth and brought about decline. Piecemeal, arms-length subventions had little impact in this context ... The policy implications are that in such circumstances intervention is necessary both at the level of firms and at broader levels relating to the context within which firms operate. At the level of firms, actions affecting the immediate external environment of production (physical infrastructure, finance, etc.) are insufficient. More wide-ranging intervention in the organisation of production is required: in corporate strategies, management, investment, technology, marketing, training, recruitment practices, etc ... Conducive macro-economic conditions are obviously necessary, but perhaps more important are coordinated sectoral interventions that relate more directly to the relationships between firms, their competitors, and their markets and suppliers. (Turok, 1989)

Researchers in this area have on occasion made estimates of indirect effects, especially by using employment multipliers. Multipliers as high as 1.4 have been used, with little justification (see, for example, Davies *et al.*, 1986, p. 47; Moore *et al.*, 1986, p. 9). However, a recent study by Harvey Armstrong of just four companies supported by two different local authorities in contrasting areas shows how small local multipliers can be and how they can vary. The main results are summarized in Table 9.7.

Table 9.7 Local income impact of four district-council-assisted small manufacturing companies in Lancaster and Stockport, 1985/6

	Lancaster City Council District		Stockport Borough Council District	
	Company A[1]	Company B	Company C	Company D[2]
Annual sales (£000 to nearest £000)	2,450	162	10,355	5
Direct employment (full year equivalent employees)	22.5	8.0	255.9	2.0
Absolute increase in income (direct and indirect) resulting from annual operations (£)	423,841	180,539	3,114,157	3,401
Local income multiplier	1.163	1.183	1.120	1.195

Notes:

[1]Figures for Company A refer to the 1985 calendar year.

[2]It should be noted that in 1985/6 Company D was at an early stage in its operations, with activity and sales beginning to build up. These results are not therefore typical of a full operation year. Company D is the newest of the companies examined.

Source: Armstrong (1988), p. 25.

There may be a particular reason for a project to create additional spending within a local area (for example, a shopping centre which means that many people shop within the district rather than in the neighbouring district, or a business that brings into use a local raw material). Some small local firms make extensive use of local services, such as solicitors, accountants and servicing agents. But in general the British economy is so open that any study that uses local multipliers above 1.2 should be treated with suspicion unless specific justification for the figures is provided; and this is for multipliers on *local* spending only. A large part of any additional spending in the British economy inevitably goes abroad on imports, and these outflows should be deducted from total spending before local employment multipliers are applied (Armstrong, 1988).

Evaluations of Government Programmes

Turning now to the evaluations sponsored by central government, there have been recent evaluations of Urban Development Grants (D.o.E., 1988; see also Stephen Martin's article in this volume); Enterprise Zones (D.o.E., 1987b); economic development projects in the Urban Programme (D.o.E., 1986a, 1986b, 1986c); and a particularly interesting study of financial support for business in the Newcastle metropolitan region (Robinson *et al.*, 1987; Robinson and Wren, 1987). There is also a study of the Glasgow Eastern Area Renewal scheme, regrettably unpublished itself although a manual based on its methodology has recently been issued by the Industry Department for Scotland.

The Newcastle study examined the receipt of all aids, from central as well as local government, and its key results are given in Table 9.8. It would seem that selective assistance ('RSA/NSA') was more effective in job creation terms than the (non-selective) Regional Development Grant (RDG), although non-selective assistance evidently had other aims as well as job creation, notably the strengthening of regional and national economies – for example, nationally a large proportion of RDG went on capital-intensive chemical plants which *reduced* employment in the period by 28,000 (Moore *et al.*, 1986, p. 11), and the Newcastle study identified the same tendency (Robinson and Wren, 1987, p. 53). However, it is doubtful if the authors of this survey agreed with the Government's policy change announced at about the same time as the survey was published, which involved abolishing RDG altogether and cutting the total sums available for regional investment subsidies. Local authority assistance proved cost-effective:

> Local authority assistance comes out well in terms of cost per job despite the fact that a large minority of projects do not lead to employment creation [this mainly refers to grants to improve buildings, change premises or make environmental improvements, mainly funded under the Urban Programme] and the level of deadweight projects is relatively high. This stems from both the low levels of expenditure and also from the concentration of assistance on start-up businesses which necessarily do create employment. It should, however, be noted that the displacement effects from assisting start-ups may be higher than for other types of project. (Robinson and Wren, 1987, p. 60)

Table 9.8 'Cost per job' for assisted projects

	'Crude' cost per job					'Refined' cost per job				
						Projects where assistance from named source was 'additional'		Projects where only the assistance from the named source was 'additional'		
Column	1	2	3	4	5	6	7	8	9	10
Source of assistance	No. of new jobs associated with projects assisted by named source	Number of projects	Total assistance paid to projects from named source	Total assistance paid to projects (all sources)	'Crude' cost per job $\left(\dfrac{column\ 3}{column\ 1}\right)$	Number of new jobs	'Refined' cost per job $\left(\dfrac{column\ 3}{column\ 6}\right)$	Number of new jobs	Total assistance paid by named source	'Refined' cost per job $\left(\dfrac{column\ 9}{column\ 8}\right)$
RDG	593	122	£5,421,000	£8,287,000	£9,142	307	£17,658	72	£657,000	£9,125
RSA/NSA	522	48	£2,278,000	£6,614,000	£4,364	317	£7,186	112	£399,000	£3,563
Local authority	567	123	£1,366,000	£3,459,000	£2,400	157	£8,701	93	£201,000	£2,161

Source: Robinson and Wren (1987, p. 59) survey of (201) assisted establishments, 1985.

Notes: 1 All assistance figures are cost prices.

2 Projects receiving assistance from named source (RDG; RSA/NSA; local authorities) may also have been assisted from other sources.

3 In columns 6–10, projects where assistance was 'additional' refers to those projects which managers said would have been delayed, cancelled or have taken place elsewhere had assistance not been given.

4 The cost per job figures in column 7 include all assistance from the named source but only the jobs in those assisted projects which managers said depended upon the provision of assistance, and therefore include some deadweight spending. Column 10 includes *only* the expenditure and the jobs created in projects where the named source was additional and therefore does *not* include deadweight spending.

5 The number of projects for which the cost per job figures in column 7 were calculated are 53, 31 and 52 respectively for RDG, RSA/NSA and local-authority-assisted projects. For the cost per job figures in column 10 the respective figures are 23, 12 and 41.

The UDG study gave considerable attention to deadweight, and faced the issue of attributable (as distinct from housed) jobs. The Enterprise Zone study was inevitably concerned with displacement (especially from just outside the Zone boundaries) as well as with deadweight. Its main conclusion, that the cost per job on reasonable assumptions was of the order of £30,000 (that is, much above the Newcastle study's estimates for either local authorities or Regional Selective Assistance), may be one reason why the Government is now only prepared to designate new Enterprise Zones in very specific closure situations. The Urban Programme studies found such a variety of projects and objectives that the evaluators were forced to assess on the basis of secondary objectives (see Meyer, 1986 for a critique of this – and Bozeat's reply for a defence). The Urban Programme Monitoring Initiative subsequently introduced a very wide range of performance indicators into the management of the Urban Programme, and this has enabled figures of Urban Programme achievement to be produced and published; a more formal research analysis of this data is now being undertaken.

There are also studies of the job-creating impact of speculative factory building, especially in rural areas (for example, Hodge and Whitby, 1981). Here displacement is a key issue, since many of the jobs concerned would be created in nearby towns or cities if they were not attracted to the countryside. So their 'success' depends on the price a local council or Rural Development Agency is prepared to pay to create employment specifically in the countryside. The policy fails unambiguously, however, if too many of the units or factories remain unoccupied long after construction.

Action-Research

Action-research projects are few and far between, although Stern (1987) describes the approach and Marris (1982) provides a classic study of the Home Office Community Development Projects of the 1970s in terms of action-research, but this did not involve local authorities. There are echoes of the approach in Whitting *et al.*'s (1986) study of youth employment in the Urban Programme and Robbins (1987) uses the method in her report on the monitoring and evaluation of the European Programme to Combat Poverty. The absence of more work on these lines is as much as anything a reflection of the lack of evaluation of most local authority employment initiatives in general.

CONCLUSIONS

The fact remains that there are few published evaluations of local authority economic development initiatives; but the discussion above suggests several clues as to why this is so. It is partly because the research task is difficult. To do it well is time consuming and expensive, and the resulting policy conclusions may not make much difference to practice if this is changing anyway. Many councils can envisage the research costing almost as much as the initial investment. This is particularly a problem when the council's programme involves many initiatives, each one with only a small budget.

Where do we go from here? In the first place there are some yawning gaps to fill. Little has been published on the effectiveness of expenditure in attracting inward investment since Camina (1974) and Mason (1979), both of whom researched these policies in a very different economic climate. However, work in progress at Coventry Polytechnic, by David Noon and others, will undoubtedly contribute in this area. There is also work in progress at the Open University, by David Wield and others, on the effectiveness and impact of science parks. But little is available on the effectiveness of voluntary sector employment projects, training workshops, innovation centres, or Enterprise Board policy and investment.

Some kinds of policy can most effectively be evaluated by means of comparisons between comparable schemes in several councils. Townroe and Brenton (1987) made progress in this respect by comparing Norwich with Broadland. But it could go much farther. One could, for example, imagine a comparison of grant schemes to small firms across (say) ten local authorities in different parts of the country with different labour market properties. Such a project might be financed at modest cost by subscriptions from the councils involved, or qualify for assistance from the Economic and Social Research Council, or the Department of the Environment.

The third and final conclusion is that there is a need for more policy reviews, more qualitative evaluations of what has been achieved, and more evaluations based on action-research, both of specific projects (such as community development projects) and of the overall economic development work of councils. As the centre of gravity of policy moves away from grants to small firms and loans to larger firms, and towards the types of partnership described by Cochrane, Harding, Parkinson and Evans and others in this volume, this type of evaluation will become more necessary. Indeed, in such cases it is very doubtful if purely quantitative analyses, leading to figures of cost per job, would either be meaningful or convey more than a fraction of the information needed to judge whether the work is successful or not.

NOTES

1. Benefits may be measured in quantitative terms, or qualitatively. The latter may produce a 'balance sheet', as proposed by Industry Department for Scotland (1988).

2. For a discussion in straightforward terms of the philosophical problems associated with cost–benefit analysis, see Self (1975).

3. This is sometimes referred to as 'the project cycle', especially in the literature on project appraisal in developing countries.

4. This survey of local authorities and economic development was sent to all British local authorities in late 1988. It is being conducted by Liz Mills at the Institute for Local Government Studies, with assistance from Ken Young, Andrew Coulson and Margaret Hobson. Preliminary results are available from the author. The full survey will be published in book form in late 1989 or early 1990.

5. For expositions of this approach, see Room (1986) or Stern (1987).

6. This is the approach followed in research at the Centre for Planning, Strathclyde University, sponsored by the Department of the Environment and conducted by Ivan Turok and Urlan Wannop. This research has produced 'cost per job' figures for 31 projects in four contrasting parts of the country. The cost per job figures vary greatly, even for similar projects. The authors are very cautious about the use that should be made of such comparisons, and in particular about whether the costs per job of training programmes (that is, the capital and revenue costs of the training programme divided between the numbers of trainees who subsequently get jobs) can meaningfully be compared with cost per job figures for investment in start-up businesses, or in property.

7. Two manuals have been produced recently which should be of considerable help to practitioners. They are Coulson (1987) and Industry Department for Scotland (1988). See also *Local Economy*, special issue on evaluation, Vol. 2, No. 4, especially articles by Coulson, Gregory and Martin, Johnson, and Thomas.

8. For a discussion of local authority social audits, see Harte and Owen (1987).

9. Martin (1989) points out that the PEIDA manual (Industry Department for Scotland, 1988) is not clear on this point, and at times

seems to suggest that a project may be assessed by comparing the situation *before* the project started (using a baseline survey) with the situation subsequently.

10.   An earlier study is Cameron *et al.* (1982).

REFERENCES

Armstrong, H. (1988) 'Variations in the local impact of district council assisted small manufacturing firms', *Local Government Studies*, Vol. 14, No. 3, pp. 21–34.

Cambridge Economic Consultants (1985) *An Enquiry into the Benefits of the Government Advance Factory Building Programme*, Report to the Department of Trade and Industry, London, HMSO.

Cameron, S.J., Dabinett, G., Gillard, A., Whisker, P., Williams, R. and Willis, K.G. (1982) *Local Authority Aid to Industry: An Evaluation in Tyne & Wear*, Inner Cities Research Programme 7, London, Department of the Environment.

Camina, M. (1974) 'Local authorities and the attraction of industry', *Progress in Planning*, Vol. 3, No. 2, pp. 83–182.

Coulson, A.C. (1987) *The Monitoring and Evaluation of Local Economic Development: A Distance Learning Package*, Local Government Training Board and Coventry Open Tech Unit.

Coulson, A.C. (1988) 'The evaluator: inquisitor, comrade or spy?' *Local Economy*, Vol. 2, No. 4, pp. 229–36.

Davies, H. Campbell, J. and Barnes, I. (1986) 'An evaluation of local authority assistance to small firms: the case of Humberside', *Local Government Studies*, Vol. 12, No. 3, pp. 37–50.

D.o.E. (1985) *Five Year Review of Birmingham Inner City Partnership*, Inner Cities Research Report No. 12 (PSMRC), London, HMSO.

D.o.E. (1986a) *The Employment Effects of Economic Development Projects Funded under the Urban Programme* (JURUE), London, HMSO.

D.o.E. (1986b) *The Evaluation of Environmental Projects Funded under the Urban Programme* (JURUE), London, HMSO.

D.o.E. (1986c) *The Evaluation of Industrial and Commercial Improvement Areas* (JURUE), London, HMSO.

D.o.E. (1987a) *Evaluation of Derelict Land Grant Schemes* (Roger Tym and Partners), London, HMSO.

D.o.E. (1987b) *An Evaluation of the Enterprise Zone Experiment*, (PA-CEC), London, HMSO.

D.o.E. (1988) *An Evaluation of the Urban Development Grant Programme* (PSMRC), London, HMSO.

Gregory, D. and Martin, S. (1988) 'Issues in the evaluation of inner city programmes', *Local Economy*, Vol. 2, No. 4, pp. 237–50.

Gunby, D. and Smith, E. (1985) 'Monitoring the effectiveness of grants to small firms: the Cleveland experience, 1980-1984', in Davies, E.M. (ed.) *Economic Regeneration: The Role of 1. The Local Authority 2. Tourism*, Papers delivered at the Research and Intelligence Conference, INLOGOV.

Harte, G.F. and Owen, D. (1987) 'Fighting de-industrialisation: the role of local government social audits', *Accounting, Organisation and Society*, Vol. 12, No. 2, pp. 123–41.

Hodge, I. (1982) 'The social opportunity cost of rural labour', *Regional Studies*, Vol. 16, No. 2, pp. 113–20.

Hodge, I. and Whitby, M.C. (1981) *Rural Employment: Trends, Options, Choices*, London, Methuen.

Industry Department for Scotland/Scottish Development Agency (1988) *Area Initiatives Evaluation Handbook*, ESU Research Paper No. 16 (PEIDA Consultants), Edinburgh.

Johnson, D., (1988) 'An evaluation of the Urban Development Grant Programme', *Local Economy*, Vol. 2, No. 4, pp. 251–70.

Marris, P. (1982) *Community Planning and Conceptions of Change*, London, Routledge.

Martin, S. (1989) book review, 'Area initiatives evaluation handbook: Industry Department for Scotland and Scottish Development Agency', *Local Government Studies*, Vol. 15, No. 5.

Mason, C.M. (1979) *Industrial Promotion by Local and Regional Authorities: The Effectiveness of Advertising Material*, Discussion Paper No. 4, Dept of Geography, University of Southampton.

Mawson, J. and Miller, D. (1986) 'Interventionist approaches in local employment and economic development: the experience of Labour local authorities', in Hausner, V. (ed.) *Critical Issues in Urban Economic Development*, Vol. 7, Oxford, Clarendon Press.

Meyer, P. (1986) 'Assessing improvement area policy', *Local Economy*, Vol. 1, No. 7, pp. 35–43; and reply by Bozeat, N., *Local Economy*, Vol. 7, No. 3, pp. 71–2.

Moore, B., Rhodes, J. and Tyler, P. (1986) *The Effects of Government Regional Economic Policy*, Department of Trade and Industry, London, HMSO.

Robbins, D. (ed.) (1987) *Monitoring and Evaluation of Local Programmes to Combat Poverty*, Birmingham, Institute of Local Government Studies.

Robinson, F. and Wren, C. (1987) 'The impact of urban and regional policy on economic development: a case study of the Newcastle Metropolitan Region', *Local Government Studies*, Vol. 13, No. 3, pp. 49–62.

Robinson, F., Wren, C. and Goddard, J. (1987) *Economic Development Policies: An Evaluative Study of the Newcastle Metropolitan Region*, Oxford, Clarendon Press.

Room, G. (1986) *Cross-National Innovation in Social Policy: European Perspectives on the Evaluation of Action-Research*, London, Macmillan.

Self, P. (1975) *Econocrats and the Policy Process*, London, Macmillan.

Stern, E. (1987) *Evaluation Strategies for Local Economic and Employment Development*, Paper prepared as part of EEC Action Research Programme for Local Economic and Employment Development, Tavistock Institute.

Storey, D.J. and Johnson, S. (1987) *Are Small Firms the Answer to Unemployment?*, London, Employment Institute.

Townroe, P. and Brenton, P. (1987) 'Local authority aid to small firms in neighbouring areas', *Local Economy*, Vol. 2, No. 3, pp. 169–80.

Tricker, M.J. *et al.* (1983) *An Evaluation of the Development Commission's Activities in Selected Areas of England*, Birmingham, The Development Commission and JURUE (now ECOTEC).

Tricker, M.J., Bovaird, A.J. and Hems, L.C. (1987) *An Evaluation of the Peak District Integrated Rural Development Programme*, Interim Report, Public Sector Management Research Unit, Aston University.

Turok, I. (1988) 'The limits of financial assistance: an evaluation of local authority aid to industry', *Local Economy*, Vol. 2, No. 3, pp. 286–97.

Turok, I. (1989) 'Explanation and evaluation in local economic policy', *Urban Studies*, forthcoming.

Whitting, G., Burton, P., Means, R. and Stewart, M. (1986) *Urban Programme and the Young Unemployed*, Department of the Environment, London, HMSO.

Willis, K.G. (1985) 'Estimating the benefits of job creation from local investment subsidies', *Urban Studies*, Vol. 22, pp. 163–77.

·PART 4·

Prospects

The Future of Local Economic Policy: A Public and Private Sector
Function

CHAPTER 10

The Future of Local Economic Policy: A Public and Private Sector Function

David Miller

INTRODUCTION

At the beginning of 1989, the Government introduced legislation which will for the first time provide a statutory basis for local authorities' economic development activities. The legislation establishes new powers for local authorities to 'take such steps' that they consider 'appropriate' for promoting economic development in their area. These steps are defined as including financial and other assistance for the setting up or expansion of any commercial, industrial and public undertaking, and for the creation or protection of opportunities for employment with these bodies.[1]

This could be seen as a welcome, though belated, stamp of approval for the wide range of economic initiatives undertaken by local authorities, as well as other locally based non-statutory organizations, over the last decade. However, the recent direction of central government thinking, articulated in a wide range of White Papers, consultation documents, ministerial statements and research reports, points to two divergent conclusions. First, it now seems to have been accepted by central government, based on experience in Europe and North America as well as in Britain, that locally initiated, implemented and managed initiatives can play a significant role in the response to economic and employment problems. Second, local authorities are seen by central government as only minor actors, rather than central agents, in the regeneration of local economies.

The emphasis is increasingly being placed on the role of the private sector – in the person of local 'entrepreneurs' and 'managers' – not only as the supporters and nurturers of local enterprise but also as the Government's agents in the management of various schemes and initiatives, particularly for training but increasingly in the wider economic development field. This chapter charts the pattern of change in the development of local economic policies: the growing significance of locally initiated measures; the impact of the Government's locally implemented, but centrally controlled measures; and the more recent initiatives of Government which will result in the marginalization of local authorities and the creation of a much wider private sector role. Some attempt is then made to assess the implications of these trends for the future of local economic development.

LOCAL AUTHORITIES AND ECONOMIC DEVELOPMENT

Local authorities in Britain have been involved in economic development policies of various forms for over 50 years, the nature and intensity of these activities tending to vary with economic cycles and geographical location. The local authority role until the recession of the late 1970s was largely seen as complementing national economic measures, particularly regional policy, and facilitating the operation of national policies aimed at influencing the distribution of industrial development. To achieve this local authorities relied on: development powers, available under planning legislation, to provide industrial infrastructure; promotional campaigns to attract new, 'mobile' industry; and the judicious use of financial incentives or subsidies. At the same time, successive governments provided subsidies for large manufacturing firms to move to declining areas, or attempted to manipulate the national economy in the expectation that the benefits would eventually 'trickle down' to those areas most in need. Whilst this combination of national and local measures seemed to be appropriate for much of the post-war period, during the 1980s it became clear that such ineffective and imprecise tools of economic management were not capable of meeting the challenge of economic change, particularly in the declining urban and industrial areas (Miller, 1989).

The recession of the late 1970s and early 1980s resulted in fundamental changes in economic circumstances. Faltering national economic performance was exacerbated by local structural weaknesses. In many parts of the country, major sectors of manufacturing industry collapsed and it was recognized that many of the jobs lost would be unlikely to reappear again in the same form and in the same place. High unemployment spread throughout the country, with the traditional, urban, manufacturing areas being particularly affected and some groups – young people, older people, black people and women – being marginalized in the labour market.

From the beginning of the 1980s, 'intervention' in the local economy became an accepted role for local authorities. This was a response to the form and scale of problems experienced at the time, stimulated in part by the urban politics of the period (Mawson and Miller, 1986), as well as a reaction to the apparent policy void left by central government in the form of direct measures to combat persisting unemployment. The emphasis of local economic policies had moved from the earlier attempts to influence the *distribution* of employment to policies aimed at the *generation* of employment.

Concern that central government seemed unwilling to recognize or respond to the mounting social and economic problems endemic in the major industrial areas of the country resulted in the increasingly widespread adoption by local authorities of indigenous industry-based strategies which aimed to build on the skills, knowledge and expertise of the local workforce and local industry. A wide range of policies were developed which recognized that the economic domain concerns quality of work, access to opportunities, industrial democracy, distribution of incomes and, ultimately, living standards (Mawson and Miller, 1986). A variety of measures were devised and implemented: to raise investment levels in, and provide long-term support for, local industries; to improve the quality of training programmes, particularly for the disadvantaged in the labour market; to introduce new forms of economic enterprise; and to provide for the needs of the unemployed and low-paid. In some cases new agencies were created by the local authorities to undertake these measures. Enterprise Boards were set up in Greater London, the West Midlands, Merseyside, West Yorkshire and Lancashire to provide the vehicle for investing in local firms, to help in the development of co-operatives and to provide training in new and traditional skills.

This wider approach was exemplified in the 'interventionist' strategies adopted by the Greater London Council, West Midlands County Council, Sheffield City Council and a number of other local authorities. In part, these strategies reflect the realization that in most areas the local authority is the largest employer and wields significant power and resources which can be used as effective levers in the local economy.

The strategies developed by these authorities represented a complete break with the earlier passive compliance with the Government's economic policy and the development of an alternative source of policy measures, analysis and resources. For the first time, local economic policy was seen not just as an adjunct to the wider planning responsibilities of the authority but as an important area of policy and implementation in its own right. In spite of the fact that there was no statutory requirement for local authorities to involve themselves in economic policy, nor any provision in the legislation which sanctioned the use of financial resources in the implementation of policy, during the 1980s economic development became the most rapidly expanding area of local authority activity. In a period when local authority finances were being generally constrained by central government, both the personnel and funds allocated to economic development functions were increasing.

The freedom, given by Section 137 of the Local Government Act 1972, to spend up to the product of a 2p rate to meet the needs of the local area provided some of the bigger authorities, particularly the former metropolitan county councils, with sufficient resources to make a significant impact on their local economies. While most authorities have fewer funds available, this has not stopped the widespread adoption of the approach initiated at the beginning of the 1980s, with the preparation of an economic development strategy now being an almost standard function for most large local authorities.

Since the middle of the 1980s, some degree of recovery has been apparent in the national economy, with a number of sectors and areas expanding. But the recovery has been uneven: the 'turning point' has not been reached in every area. There still remain major unemployment problems in many localities, and significant disparities in economic prospects between different parts of the country and within some of the major urban areas. It is clear, however, that the response to current local economic problems cannot now be argued simply in terms of 'countering accelerating redundancies' or responding to the 'restructuring of manufacturing industry'. Both changing economic circumstances and a major reorientation of central government policies have signalled basic changes in the approach of local authorities to economic development.

CENTRAL GOVERNMENT'S 'LOCAL' ECONOMIC POLICIES

Whilst local authorities, and other regional and locally based agencies, have made significant strides in the formulation of economic development policies during the 1980s, this has to a large extent represented only a small encroachment on the sub-national economic policy making which has historically been the preserve of central government. In the same period, the Thatcher Government has become more centralized in its economic decision making and yet, paradoxically, has intervened more heavily at the local level than any other government in modern British history.

The proliferation of economic development activities and agencies during the 1980s, both within central government and at the local level, has posed questions about the duplication and overlap of activities and demonstrated a lack of co-ordination and overall direction in public policy. The response of central government has been a series of direct and indirect attempts to review certain aspects of policy in this area. The reviews of regional policy in 1983/4 and at the beginning of 1988, the examination of inner city policy by the Department of the Environment in 1983, the Burns Committee's inquiry into local economic initiatives in 1983, the Widdicombe Committee's inquiry into the conduct of local authority business in 1986, the consultation paper on local authorities' interests in companies in 1988, the relaunch of inner city policies in the 'Action for Cities' initiative in 1988, two employment White Papers during 1988, and the various proposals for the reform of local government and its financing all reflect attempts made, but demonstrate a failure to come to grips with this complex problem. Local authorities and their economic development activities have been a constant focus of attention for central government.

A feature of the change in economic policy making has been the increasing withdrawal of central government from the regional – sub-national and strategic – level of operation. The post-war consensus around the need for some form of regional economic policy has collapsed. The function of traditional regional policy has changed from being a tool of economic management to become an arm of social policy. Spending on regional policy is now at its lowest level since 1972 (Armstrong and Taylor, 1987). The restructuring of the regional aid system proposed in the White Paper issued at the beginning of 1988 (HMSO, 1988b) and subsequently pursued in legislation introduces: more selectivity in the allocation of aid and the associated termination of Regional Development

Grants; more nationally applicable schemes of assistance; and, undoubtedly in the long run, a further reduction in investment in those parts of the country where it is most needed. The implication of these changes is that there will need to be a significant change in the complementary economic role that local authorities have played in relation to regional policy.

The present Government has also all but withdrawn from economic and physical planning at the regional or strategic level. For all practical purposes, only the vestiges of an effective regional planning system now remain. The argument that regional planning had become a mechanism for regulating both local intraregional and central–local conflicts (Martins, 1986) has clearly been overtaken by the view that many of the issues involved can, and should, be settled centrally. More significantly, it reflects an ideological rejection of 'regional planning' as a process too closely associated with 'public planning'.

A related manifestation of this process of institutional change was the abolition, in March 1986, of the Greater London Council and the metropolitan county councils – a strategic level of local government policy making. These changes were part of the trend towards the centralization of government functions. This has led to an erosion of the autonomy of local government and, in some areas, has resulted in the removal from local accountability of significant elements of decision-making power. Economic development decision-making power has been increasingly concentrated in Whitehall and Westminster, with the implementation process being retained in the hands of central government or its agents down to a very localized level. Attempts are being made to bypass the local authority in the operation of economic measures and the local and regional dimensions of economic policy are being peripheralized in favour of more central manipulation of local economies.

The local economic measures being pursued by central government are a manifestation of the view that local problems can best be resolved by action from the national level (Coulson, 1986). There is now a complex web of inner city programmes, special employment measures, enterprise initiatives, European projects and regional incentives which in some cases involve central government or central-government-backed agencies operating within the geographical and functional areas of local authority responsibilities, and in certain cases assuming the powers of the local authority.

The series of measures devised by central government which are defined on a very localized geographical basis – for example, Urban

Development Corporations, Enterprise Zones and Freeports – have all been superimposed on, and in some cases within, local authority areas irrespective of the policies already being developed or implemented within the locality and sometimes in direct contradiction to local aspirations. These measures, taken together with the formation of City Action Teams and Task Forces and the variety of other institutional innovations – 'Action for Cities' and 'The Enterprise Initiative' – are designed to involve civil servants and the private sector directly in the application of local economic measures. This approach is consistent with central government's philosophy of 'encouraging enterprise' and removing obstacles to industrial development. However, the impact of many of these measures is questionable not only in terms of the economic efficiency of 'area-based' measures but also in relation to cost and effectiveness. Some of these initiatives have been shown to be both expensive and doubtful in the form and level of employment provided. A brief assessment of the achievements of some of these measures will help to illustrate this point.

Enterprise Zones were introduced as one of a series of economic initiatives in the 1980 Budget. A total of 23 sites have been designated since then; it is unlikely that any more Enterprise Zones will be created. The purpose of the Zones was 'to see how far economic activity could be encouraged by the removal of tax burdens and by relaxing or speeding up the application of certain statutory or administrative controls' (National Audit Office, 1986). It is estimated that the Government spent £400 million on the Enterprise Zones between 1981 and 1986. This included compensating local authorities for rate relief, tax relief from capital allowances, and public spending on infrastructure. In spite of the fact that Exchequer costs of £100 million would have been incurred on infrastructure investment in the Zones, the net cost was still £300 million (D.o.E., 1987).

While Enterprise Zones can be argued to have been successful in generating economic activity, drawing in investment and providing jobs, there is a 'deadweight effect' in the form of property development, especially in the retailing sector, which would probably have occurred without the designation of the Zones. Whilst rate relief has been identified as an important incentive by Enterprise Zone tenants, this is probably illusory as the financial benefits have usually been internalized into rents. In terms of employment, 35,000 jobs have been provided in the Enterprise Zones, but the majority of these are in firms which have transferred into the Zones. About

13,000 are probably directly attributable to Enterprise Zone policy. The cost of each new job was £23,000, or £30,000 if construction costs are included (D.o.E., 1987). The cost per job is, therefore, not unfavourable in comparison with other measures such as regional policy. With overall expenditure in the Zones reaching levels comparable with regional policy as a whole, there has been some questioning of the viability of Enterprise Zones as an arm of policy (Tyler, 1987). This is confirmed by the finding that the simplified planning regime, which was originally identified as a significant part of the policy, actually plays a relatively minor role in facilitating economic change (Lloyd, 1986).

At the same time as the Enterprise Zones were being designated, a similar experiment in the form of Freeports was initiated. The first Freeport was opened in 1984 at Southampton; five more have followed in Belfast, Liverpool, Birmingham and Cardiff and at Prestwick Airport in Scotland. The original concept of the Freeport was that a reduction in regulation and taxation would entice new manufacturing into these areas. In practice, the availability of development assistance and grants within some of the Freeports has been just as important in attracting new industrial development (Davies and Butler, 1986). In the words of two of the original protagonists of Freeports, 'the general concept has achieved considerable success, however, the efforts to translate it into policies that would guarantee the emergence of a series of vibrant, working UK Freeports was an almost unrelieved failure' (Davies and Butler, 1986). Thus, this policy measure, constructed around the idea of reduced public involvement and control, has demonstrated not only its reliance on financial assistance from government but also its lack of success in the cost-effective generation of new employment.

The designation of an Urban Development Corporation (UDC) represents a more specific displacement of some of the functional responsibilities of local authorities. The experience of the first two UDCs – in the London docklands and Merseyside – resulted in five more being set up in 1987, in Tyneside, Teesside, the Black Country in the West Midlands, Trafford Park in Greater Manchester, and Cardiff Bay. In 1988 four 'mini-UDCs' were designated in central Manchester, Leeds, Bristol and Sheffield. Between 1981 and 1989, £793 million of public money was directly given in grant aid to UDCs, with about a further £500 million from other central government programmes. The UDCs are also seen as vehicles for bringing the private investor back into the inner city areas. The London Docklands Development Corporation claims a private:public investment ratio of 9:1, while the equivalent figure for Merseyside is less than 2:1. The difference reflects the buoyant London property market. However, the Merseyside experience is likely to be much closer to what will happen to the UDCs established outside London. It has also been found on Merseyside that, while blighted sites in the docks area have been successfully regenerated, there has been little impact on the wider social and economic problems of the inner city or Liverpool as a whole (Liverpool City Planning Department, 1987). The implication is that UDCs through the public and private funds they attract can achieve significant redevelopment within their designated areas but not generate major 'spill-over' effects which would benefit the wider urban economies.

Assessments of the UDC programme undertaken to date have been critical of the terms of reference of UDCs and their lack of local accountability. The National Audit Office (1988) have recommended that proper monitoring of UDCs should take place, and the House of Commons Employment Committee in 1988 urged the Government to provide a more precise definition of 'regeneration' and said that UDCs should work to specific employment targets. These are significant comments in view of the fact that, in terms of both finance and public profile, the UDCs have become the main plank of central government's policy for inner city regeneration. One of the primary benefits claimed for the UDC is the additional public funds it attracts to an area. This is seen as more than adequate compensation for the loss of planning and other statutory powers to an agency directed by central government. While some local authorities have been persuaded of this view, and have either passively or actively accepted the imposition of UDCs, other authorities, such as Birmingham, Leeds, Sheffield and Manchester have attempted to propose alternative, locally controlled structures or to negotiate some degree of direct involvement or co-operation with the UDC. While some minor concessions have been made to the involvement of local authorities, in the form of the appointment of local councillors as directors of the Development Corporations, no significant changes have been achieved in the application of UDC policy. Local authorities such as Sheffield have had to accept 'a removal of some of [their] general economic planning powers (including for instance, land disposal and the administration of the Urban Programme) which have passed to an Urban Development Corporation' (Sheffield City Council, 1988).

Central government, acting through intermediary agencies or by direct application of policy, now controls a complex set of economic measures which operate at a very localized level. Central government also has control over the allocation of a major part of the public sector resources which are essential for 'pump-priming' private sector investment. The use of local authority resources for economic development is increasingly restricted to specific purposes, while finance made available through the local government finance system is becoming more constrained. Local authorities, which have been at least as innovative as central government in the formulation and implementation of local economic initiatives, have been effectively marginalized. Central government is now relying on the private sector to take up the challenge of regenerating local economies.

THE PRIVATE SECTOR: FROM PARTNER TO PRIME MOVER

The recovery of the national economy through the later part of the 1980s, and the redirection of some local authority and central government economic development measures, has resulted in the greater acceptance, and pursuit, of public–private sector financial partnerships in the realization of economic development policies. Whilst such partnerships have been nothing new to local authorities, the context within which these arrangements have been encouraged is different. First, financial pressures brought about by the constraints imposed on local government finances made the search for alternative sources of funding from the private sector the only means through which many projects were likely to be implemented. Second, in a period of growth, the private sector was increasingly willing to become involved in ventures where a high degree of success was probable and the risks were shared with a public body.

With the Government's blessing, agencies such as Business in the Community have been positively promoting the involvement of the private sector in many different types of regeneration project. Local authorities have entered into these arrangements recognizing that they are not wholly to their detriment (Mackintosh, 1988), and that they offer an effective means of achieving some development objectives. Indeed, many partnerships provide a way of complementing the local authorities' other activities. The model for this approach has to a large extent been the experience of effective public–private sector co-operation in the United States. the 'Massachusetts miracle' (Graves, 1987) is but one of the achievements of effectively harnessing private sector finance, 'concern' and interest in the well-being of the local community to meet wider public regeneration objectives. Much of this approach relies on the commitment of local entrepreneurs and businesspeople to their localities and their recognition that a healthy local economy is in their business interests. In Britain, the same local 'infrastructure' of entrepreneurs and especially local banks does not exist, and it is therefore more difficult to establish the relationship between a strong local economy and the fortunes of local industries.

The process of 'partnership' has been taken a step further with the apparent adoption of another North American model in recent central government policy statements. The Training and Enterprise Councils (TECs) proposed in the Department of Employment White Paper 'Employment for the 1990s' (HMSO, 1988b) clearly owe their antecedents to the Private Industry Councils (PICs) established throughout the United States under the 1982 Job Partnership Training Act (JPTA). This legislation re-emphasized the need to provide training for economically disadvantaged individuals and others facing serious barriers to employment, and provides funds for comprehensive, employer-supported education and training systems. The PICs are established by State Governors with 60 per cent of their membership drawn from the private sector and the rest from trade unions, education, economic development agencies and the voluntary sector. The role of PICs is to determine procedures for the development of a local job training plan, to approve the job training plan and submit it to the State Governor, and to establish skill level guidelines for occupational training. The Boston PIC jointly administers the funds available under the JPTA with the city's Neighbourhood Development and Employment Agency, and offers a full range of programmes including adult literacy, youth career development, vocational skills training, and job placement. The PIC has also been a prime force in shaping a successful relationship between the business community and the Boston public schools, the centrepiece of which is the Boston Compact – a concept which is now beginning to be adopted in Britain.

The form and organization of the proposed TECs is strikingly similar to the PICs. The TECs will:

contract with Government to plan and deliver training and to promote and support the development of small businesses and self-employment within their area . . .

examine the local labour market, assessing key skill needs, prospects for expanded job growth and the adequacy of existing training opportunities . . .

draw up a plan . . . for securing quality training and enterprise development . . .

manage training programmes for young people, unemployed people, and for adults requiring new knowledge and technical retraining . . .

not run programmes themselves . . . they will sub-contract training and enterprise activities to local providers . . .

seek to represent the interests of both large and small employ- ers in their area and a wide range of community interests. At least two-thirds of TEC members should be employers drawn at top management level from the private sector. Others on the Councils will include senior figures from local education, training and economic development activities and from volun- tary bodies and trades unions who support the aims of the Councils. (HMSO, 1988b)

A national network of about 100 TECs is planned, each responsible for between £15 million and £50 million of public funds. The TEC members will be accountable to the Employment Department's Training Agency for the use of these public resources.

Whilst the emphasis of the TECs' work will be on training, the process is being taken a step further in Scotland. The White Paper on 'Scottish Enterprise' proposed a restructuring of the Scottish Development Agency and the Training Agency in Scotland, using a market-based approach led by private sector employers. The aim is to integrate the work already being done on economic development and training in Scotland into a coherent strategy under the lead- ership of private sector employers. The local delivery and planning of 'Scottish Enterprise' functions would be carried out by local agencies. The White Paper accepts that the local agencies should have a considerable degree of independence, even recognizing that 'freedom to succeed is also a freedom to fail' (Scottish Office, 1988).

In establishing the new TECs and 'Scottish Enterprise' the Gov- ernment is moving the private sector from the position of partner to prime mover in the local economic development process. At the same time, local authorities are not even acknowledged as appropriate agencies to be represented on these bodies or, indeed, as agencies with which these bodies should actively co-operate. Even in the United States, the PICs are required to agree their plans with local elected officials. This is consistent with the advice given to the Department of the Environment suggesting that:

> The next step must be to find new and appropriate ways of more fully involving the private sector in the broader process of economic development. This may involve public/private sector partnerships which provide an opportunity for the private sector to experience economic development in areas where it has not previously been very active, and which ultimately may enable private sector institutions to engage in economic development activities which have so far been the province of the public sector. (CURDS, 1988)

All of this is pointing to the achievement of central government's stated aim that 'local authorities should be discouraged from becoming involved in activities that can more appropriately be undertaken by the private sector or other public sector agency' (HMSO, 1988b).

CONCLUSIONS

It is ironic that at a time when legislation which legitimizes local authority economic development activity is being introduced, when there are a growing number of local authorities formulating economic development strategies, and when the introduction of the new nationally uniform rating system for businesses will break the link between rates and the attraction of industry in favour of more indigenous strategies, that local authorities should be denied a significant role in local economic development initiatives. Whilst the new legislation is long overdue, there is still the possibility that, with so much left to the discretion of the Secretary of State through the application of regulations, a fairly restricted local authority function may eventually emerge. However, even legislation which offered wider freedom of action would be unlikely to divert the general trend in policy. Local authorities will need to carve out a role for themselves in a situation where new, private-sector-dominated agencies will be expected to take the lead in economic development.

In practice, local authorities must establish that they have a continuing and significant role to play in the training field, something which relates to both their education and economic development functions. In addition, it is not clear that the private sector in all areas is either able or willing to take on all of the responsibilities being thrust upon it. Community spirit or charitable endeavour has in the past spurred local entrepreneurs and managers to play their part in encouraging and supporting 'new enterprise'. However, significant new responsibilities are involved in the measures now being introduced. The management of public funds, where an element of 'failure' may exist, will not be attractive to those with their own business responsibilities. There are also other problems inherent in attempts to transplant North American concepts to Britain. In the USA, the voluntary sector is much more highly developed and undertakes many of the functions expected of the public sector in Britain. Conversely, less is expected of the relatively weak American local authority sector, which is not assumed to be able to undertake the range of services expected in Britain. The traditions and institutions of North America are much more attuned to altruism on the part of local entrepreneurs who also probably recognize the importance of a strong local economy to their own business activities. The strong individuals who have been recognized as essential in the regeneration of city areas in the USA are less common in Britain due to the management structures of many industries (Davie, 1988). Experience has also shown that, while there have been very creditable successes in some areas, in others Private Industry Councils have failed to generate any development momentum.

It is these factors that indicate where the local authorities' future role might lie. Not all areas will find that they have successful private-sector-led initiatives and the compensating activities of local authorities will be necessary in these areas. In other areas, the involvement of local authorities as significant land owners and development agencies in their own right will be needed to achieve regeneration objectives. Other functions of the local authority, such as education, will remain significant in the achievement of economic and training objectives. The economic strategies that local authorities will need to develop in the future must recognize the scope for action defined by the legislation and the opportunities that exist for engaging with the private sector agencies in the economic development process. Of course, should economic conditions or the political complexion of central government change in the early 1990s then the nature and weight of the respective roles of central government, local government and the private sector may undergo further changes, but rather different ones from those of the 1980s.

NOTE

1. The views expressed here are those of the author and not of any organization that he represents.

REFERENCES

Armstrong, H. and Taylor, J. (1987) *Regional Policy: The Way Forward*, London, Employment Institute.

Coulson, A. (1986) 'Economic development', The Future Role and Organization of Local Government, Functional Study No. 6, Institute for Local Government Studies, University of Birmingham.

CURDS (1988) *Area Economic Development Studies*, Report for the Department of the Environment, Newcastle upon Tyne, Centre for Urban and Regional Development Studies.

Davie, M. (1988) 'Dukes Dream City', *Observer*.

Davies, W. and Butler, E. (1986) *The Freeport Experiment*, Edinburgh, Adam Smith Institute.

D.o.E. (1987) *An Evaluation of the Enterprise Zone Experiment*, London, HMSO.

Graves, I. (1987) 'The Massachusetts miracle', Paper to a Town and Country Planning Association Conference, Sheffield.

HMSO (1988a) *DTI: The Department for Enterprise*, London, Department of Trade and Industry.

HMSO (1988b) *Employment for the 1990s*, London, Department of Employment.

Liverpool City Planning Department (1987) 'Merseyside Development Corporation: The Liverpool Experience', Liverpool City Council, Liverpool.

Lloyd, M.G. (1986) 'The continuing progress of the Enterprise Zone experiment: a note as to recent evidence', *Planning Outlook*, Vol. 29, No. 1, pp. 9–12.

Mackintosh, M. (1988) 'Planning the public sector', Paper presented to the Centre for Local Economic Strategies National Conference, Newcastle upon Tyne.

Martins, M.R. (1986) *An Organisational Approach to Regional Planning*, Aldershot, Gower.

Mawson, J. and Miller, D. (1986) 'Interventionist approaches in local employment and economic development: the experience of Labour local authorities', in Hausner V. (ed.) *Critical Issues in Urban Economic Development*, Vol. I, Oxford, Clarendon Press.

Miller, D. (1989) 'Local economic development initiatives' in Oc, T. and Trench, S. (eds) *Current Issues in Planning*, Aldershot, Gower.

National Audit Office (1986) *Department of the Environment, Scottish Office and Welsh Office: Enterprise Zones*, Report by the Comptroller and Auditor General, London, HMSO.

National Audit Office (1988) *Department of the Environment: Urban Development Corporations*, Report by the Comptroller and Auditor General, London, HMSO.

Scottish Office (1988) *Scottish Enterprise*, London, HMSO.

Sheffield City Council (1988) 'The politics of partnership', typescript.

Tyler, P. (1987) 'An evaluation of the Enterprise Zone experiment', Paper to an ESRC Urban and Regional Economics Seminar Group Conference, University of Lancaster.

Index